The Praeger Handbook
of Learning and the Brain

Advisors

Marilee Sprenger Ph.D
Pat Wolfe Ed.D

The Praeger Handbook
of Learning and the Brain

Volume 2: M–Z

Edited by Sheryl Feinstein

Westport, Connecticut
London

Library of Congress Cataloging-in-Publication Data

The Praeger handbook of learning and the brain/edited by Sheryl Feinstein—1st ed.
    p. cm.
    Includes bibliographical references and index.
    ISBN 0-313-33265-7 (set: alk. paper)—ISBN 0-313-33979-1 (vol. 1: alk. paper)—ISBN
    0-313-33980-5 (vol. 2: alk. paper) 1. Learning–Encyclopedias. 2. Brain–Encyclopedias.
    I. Feinstein, Sheryl.
    LB1060.P683 2006
    371.15'2303–dc22   2006015087

British Library Cataloguing in Publication Data is available.

Library of Congress Catalog Card Number: 2006015087
ISBN: 0–313–33265–7 (set)
          0–313–33979–1 (vol. 1)
          0–313–33980–5 (vol. 2)

First published in 2006

Praeger Publishers, 88 Post Road West, Westport, CT 06881
An imprint of Greenwood Publishing Group, Inc.
www.praeger.com

Printed in the United States of America

The paper used in this book complies with the
Permanent Paper Standard issued by the National
Information Standards Organization (Z39.48-1984).

10 9 8 7 6 5 4 3 2 1

Dedicated to
Mom, Dad and my sister Susan

Contents

List of A–Z Entries

Guide to Related Topics

Adolescent
Adolescent Addiction
Adolescent Cognitive Development
Adolescent Social and Emotional Development
Anorexia
At-Risk Behavior
Legal Culpability and Correctional Facilities
Sexual Learning
Sleep

At-Risk
Addiction
Adolescent Addiction
Anorexia
At-Risk Behavior
Legal Culpability and Correctional Facilities
Obesity
Poverty

Brain Development
Adolescent Cognitive Development
Adolescent Social and Emotional Development
Adult Brain
Aging Brain
Critical Periods (Sensitive Periods)
Early Childhood Brain
Infant Brain
Prenatal Brain

Classroom Management
Classroom Management
Handling Specific Classroom Management Problems
Motivation
Proactive Classroom Management Strategies
Visual Strategies for Classroom Management

Complex Cognitive Processes
Creativity
Critical Thinking
Mastery
Transfer

Culture
Gender Differences
Poverty
At-Risk Behavior

Curriculm and Instruction
Art
Bilingualism
Drama
Math
Mozart Effect
Multimedia Technology
Music
Reading and Comprehension
Reading and Fluency
Reading in the Content Areas
Reading Vocabulary and Word Recognition
Writing

Emotion
Aggression
Anger
Animal Studies
Depression
Emotion
Emotional Intelligence
Pleasure
Stress

Emotional or Behehavioral Issues
ADD and ADHD
Emotionally and Behaviorally Challenged
Emotionally and Behaviorally Disturbed

Foods
Aroma and Learning
Beverages
Nutrition

Learning and Instruction
Assessment
Attention
Challenge and Enrichment
Communication
Feedback
Forgetting
Motivation
Nature of Knowledge
Patterns and Programs
Pedagogy
Processing Time
Social Context of Learning
Teaching Model for the Brain

Learning Challenges
ADD and ADHD
Autism Spectrum Disorders
Blindness
Cognitive Disabilities
Deaf and Hard of Hearing
Emotionally and Behaviorally Challenged
Emotionally Behaviorally Disturbed
Fetal Alcohol Syndrome
Gifted
Language Acquisition and Disorders
Learning Disabilities
Schizophrenia
Trauma

Learning Environments
Classroom Environment
Classroom Management
Motivation
Physical Environment
Social Context of Learning
Visual Strategies for Classroom Management

Learning Styles
Auditory Development and Learning
Learning Cycles
Learning Styles
Multiple Intelligences
Suggestopedia and Accelerated Learning
Visual Images and Learning

Learning Theories
Behaviorism
Constructivism
Distributed Intelligence
Episodic Memory
Information-Processing Model
Procedural Memory
Semantic Memory

Physical Movement
Early Childhood Brain and Physical Movement
Physical Movement
Play

Reading
Reading and Comprehension
Reading and Fluency
Reading in the Content Areas
Reading Vocabulary and Word Recognition

Senses
Auditory Development and Learning
Blindness
Deaf and Hard of Hearing
Language Acquisition and Disorders
Visual Images and Learning

Social, Emotional and Moral Development
Self-Efficacy
Self Esteem
Moral Development
Spirituality

Preface

Study of the brain holds promise and fascination for almost every educator and parent. Recent strides in the field of neuroscience are impacting and changing the quality and quantity of information on the brain. Modern medical technology and brain scans enable us to view the brain while it's alive and functioning. We can literally see which areas of the brain are involved in various thought processes. Observing the brain while in action provides rich information on attention, making meaning, memory, and social/emotional development; confirming many things we're already doing in education and giving insight into meaningful changes. The field of cognitive neuroscience opens the doors to understanding the brain, adding to medical findings, pedagogy and child rearing.

The purpose of this handbook is to provide practical and informative explanations of the most important issues and Best Practice in education. Best practice refers to exemplary instructional strategies and curricula for students. This book provides through coverage of each topic. The themes for the entries are wide-ranging, offering a comprehensive look at teaching and learning. I began by tapping into my own long-term memory storage and from there expanded to journal articles, textbooks, the Internet, classroom teachers, and leading authorities in education, psychology and cognitive neuroscience. The entry topics fall under three main areas: student characteristics, classroom instructional topics, and learning challenges. It would be difficult to imagine more fertile soil than the brain for understanding the development and learning processes of students.

Selecting authors was done in a purposeful manner. Cognitive neuroscience is an interdisciplinary field involving neuroscientists, psychologists and educationists. Their joint purpose is to understand the mind, brain, and behavior. Authors came from all three disciplines. After reading their books, journal articles, and/or research endeavors authors with an expertise in a subject area were invited to participate. I contacted them and invited them to be part of this project. Most authors were leaders in their field; others were junior faculty at universities, graduate students, and classroom teachers. This book gave them an opportunity to grow and contribute to the body of knowledge in their chosen profession. I believe it is a testament to the field that almost everyone contacted chose to participate in the book. I found their generosity and commitment to education personally inspiring.

Educational topics are covered systematically and comprehensively. Each entry provides enough information to enable the serious reader to grasp the fundamental concepts and instructional strategies to take directly into their classroom. The entries are organized with an extensive connection to the latest discoveries in cognitive neuroscience, an overview of the educational topic, and then classroom instructional strategies. The book combines a justification of how the brain works, why a strategy is brain-compatible, followed by practical applications.

Three unusual features of this encyclopedia deserve mention. First, is the "See Also" listing and in-text items in BOLD included with each entry. They refer to cross-references in the book; entries are extensively cross-referenced in the book. For example, the entry on Adolescent Social & Emotional Development is cross referenced with Adolescent Cognitive Development and At-Risk. The purpose of the cross-references is to enable a reader who has looked up a topic to obtain additional information that is either directly or indirectly relevant to it. This aids the reader in serious scholarship. Secondly, a Further Readings section is included with each entry. Further Readings are suggested books, journals, and Internet sites that the individual authors recommended in order to learn more about their specific topic. They are current and practical in nature. In Addition, a glossary of terms exclusively dedicated to brain structure and function is provided.

Acknowledgements

A special thank you to the following individuals: Susan Jordan for her unwavering capacity to listen and offer valuable advice; my children, Jennifer, Scott, Rachel, and James Feinstein for their patience and encouragement; Belinda Kaffar for her perspective and assistance; Jyl Baartman, Michelle Buboltz, Laura S. Anderson, Cory Sweet, Sarah Hanna, and Annmarie Kowalczyk for their help and initiative; Bob Wood for being my first mentor; Bob Kiner for his support and vision; and to the Augustana College community, and in particular the library staff for their expertise and support of scholarship.

I would also like to thank my acquisition and copy editors, Marie Ellen Larcada, who conceived and shepherd the project, Sarah Colwell who supported and saw the book to completion and Bharath Parthasarathy who's attention to detail was a necessary pleasure.

Introduction

How does emotion impact learning? What is plasticity's role in fostering lifelong learners? Are there sensitive periods in brain development? What is the importance of the first five years in future learning? Are there differences between the male and female brain? These are intriguing questions facing educators and they are all questions this book will answer.

Educators are becoming increasingly aware of the advances in neuroscience and what it can offer to improve educational Best Practice. Developments within neuroscience have provided new ways of examining the mind and brain. In the past, an autopsy or an examination of brain-damaged individuals was the only way to gather information. Studying an inactive brain was a severe limitation to educators whose purpose was to actively engage the brain. The invention of functional neuroimaging such as functional magnetic resonance imaging (fMRI) and positron emission tomography (PET) changed the landscape. With these new technological advances, the U.S. scientific community declared the 1990's the Decade of the Brain. This has resulted in study focused on areas such as perception, memory, and emotion and added support to a new discipline called cognitive neuroscience.

Cognitive neuroscience integrates scholarship from neuroscientists, psychologists and educationists. The structure and function of the brain plays an integral role in their research. The purpose is to better understand how the brain processes, stores, and retrieves information and how this then impacts behavior. Universities across the country are endorsing this area of study. Many programs include a combination of understanding content areas of learning (language, science, reading, and math) and the cognitive neuroscience of learning (transfer, lateralization, social aspects, and brain development) in their global objectives.

There's no magic bullet to solve all of education and society's challenges. Some over zealous educators have stepped over the line connecting neuroscience to education, creating a prickly feud between educators and neuroscientists. In some instances this may be true, box it is equally irresponsible to ignore what is being learned about the brain. A synthesis of what neuroscience, psychology and education have to offer is important in offering a quality educational experience. Knowledge helps us make better decisions. While we must be cautious when interpreting research, it holds the potential to inform our teaching and increase students' academic achievement.

Classroom teachers will find this book helpful because it not only validates much of their teaching through research-based instructional strategies, but also adds to their stockpile of strategies. It provides a rich rationale for why we structure educational experiences the way we do. Teachers, principals, and parents (children's first teachers) will find substantial options to select and deliver instruction. As we understand more how the brain is structured and functions the greater is our ability to unleash brain power.

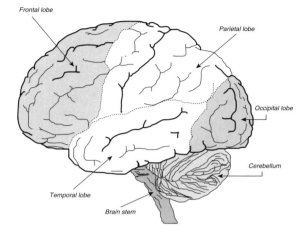

The structure of the brain.

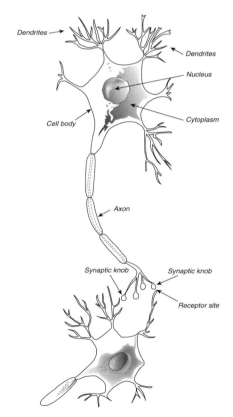

The structure of a neuron.

M

Mastery

Learning is the result of physiological changes in the brain and these changes take time and involvement of the body–brain learning partnership. Previous definitions of learning/mastery learning were not based in brain research; in hindsight, they made little impact on the everyday practice of classroom teachers. Now, however, brain research gives us a powerful definition of learning that provides practical guidance beginning with curriculum development through lesson design, selection of instructional strategies, and assessment.

Although we have only scratched the surface in our exploration of the brain, there is now sufficient information to provide a basis for defining learning and guiding school improvement efforts. Two concepts from brain research are especially important to a new working definition of mastery learning:

(1) Learning is the result of real physiological change in the brain.

Such changes occur as the result of sensory input that causes the brain to create new dendritic connections that become hardwired over time and thus readily available for future use. If physiological change in the brain does not occur, there is no long-term memory storage or mastery learning.

Unfortunately, the possible range of sensory input needed to create physiological change is far more extensive than that elicited by textbooks, worksheets, and lecture. Human beings have at least nineteen senses, not five, most of which cannot be activated inside the traditional classroom. Consequently, students need *being there* experiences, opportunities to experience what they are learning in real-world contexts; for example, walking a key section of a local watershed to track water flow, or going behind the scenes in a grocery store, aquarium, or mall to see a business in action. The greater the sensory input, the greater the physiological change in the brain. The greater the physiological change in the brain, the greater the likelihood that long-term memory/mastery learning will occur.

(2) Learning is a two-step process:

Step 1: Detecting and then understanding patterns—a process through which our brain creates meaning. This is the sensory input stage.

Step 2: Developing meaningful mental programs to use what is understood and to store it in long-term memory. This is the output stage—the capacity to use what is understood, first with assistance and then, when learning is complete, almost automatically. The importance of such near-automaticity is that old information and skills can then be used to help create new mental programs in response to new situations with new information and skills.

Toward a New, Brain-Based Definition of Learning

This two-step definition of learning contrasts sharply with definitions of learning inherent in current assessment practices. For example, in our multi-billion dollar standardized testing programs, responses to true/false and multiple choice are interpreted to mean learning has occurred. However, the typical multiple choice and true/false questions can be answered based on a faint ring of familiarity of one answer over another: "Choice B rings a bell." "Hmm, that statement doesn't sound familiar, so it must be false." The student does not even have to understand the content. And step two of this new definition of learning—being able to use what is understood and store it in long-term memory—is not even considered by test makers. Likewise in the classroom, 90 percent on a pop quiz does not necessarily mean that students understand and can use the knowledge or skills.

Step one of learning, the brain's ability to detect patterns—large or small, subtle or gross—is finely tuned. For example, the brain easily recognizes a capital H in size 3 font as well as on the hills of Hollywood. Subtle degrees of sadness can be detected, for example, melancholy, pensive, despondent, depressed. These similarities and differences are not academic; they are important because they tell us how to interact with someone in these emotional states. A pattern is any object (teapot, toothbrush), action (walking, running), procedure (getting dressed, driving a car), system (transportation, government), relationship (family, cause/effect), or situation (first day of school, meeting a stranger at a party) that we are capable of noticing and naming.

Pattern seeking is an innate capability of the brain. It is how we identify something and how we make connections between that new thing and previous understandings so that we emerge with larger understandings about our world, how it works, and our place in it. We do not need to teach students how to detect pattern, they are born with this capacity; it is quite simply how the brain works. It is our job as teachers to state curriculum in ways that enhance this pattern seeking and to select instructional strategies that invite students to explore these patterns until they are fully understood. As no two brains are alike, due to genetic predisposition and prior experiences, each brain goes about pattern seeking differently. Thus, the input one person perceives may not be what another picks up, yet both brains, given enough input, can come to a core understanding of our curriculum's concepts, significant knowledge, and skills through each person's unique pattern-seeking processes.

Recommendations: (1) State curriculum as conceptually as possible; eliminate factoids. Concepts are rich in patterns; factoids provide little for the brain to hang on to. (2) Give them a learning environment that is rich enough to provide multi-sensory input (different strokes for different folks). The fullest sensory experiences come through *being there* visits to locations that give real-world context to the concepts and skills students are studying. (3) Use low sensory-input tools, such as textbooks and lecture, to expand what students understand and can use; to introduce or re-teach, use high-sensory input.

Step two of this new definition of learning requires that students develop a mental program(s) for using the patterns they understand in real-world situations, not just the artificial environment of the classroom. The first phase of this process requires guided practice, with all its fits and starts, errors and approximations. The final step is the use of these programs with expert ease, almost automatically, which occurs as the brain hardwires the necessary connections into long-term memory.

Learning to drive a car is a good example of this two-step learning process. The patterns to be identified and understood include finding the right remote button to unlock the car door, fastening your seat belt, finding where the key goes and what the different positions are for, checking that the transmission is in park or neutral, turning the key the right number of clicks, pressing the brake pedal before shifting, and so forth, through a long list of steps that become a single program, selected and used daily as we drive our car.

Student drivers can understand all of this and pass the written driving test but can they drive the car to the grocery store? Learning to apply these patterns requires conscious attention to each step and lots of guided practice. Sometimes steps may be forgotten, sometimes done out of order. But a safe trip to the grocery store requires that these steps become virtually automatic so that the driver's attention can be given to the traffic ahead—cars, pedestrians, and the unexpected.

In the final phase of building a program for driving a car, the mechanics of driving become one large mental program, not a check list of individual tasks. To test this, ask yourself if you have ever driven somewhere and upon arrival realized that you do not recall a single thing about large portions of the journey. This expert level, near automaticity, is important because it frees our brain to attend to other things—how to use what we know and new learnings. It also indicates that the necessary connections in the brain have become hardwired into our long-term memory and available for use in the years to come, for example, the order of the alphabet when using a dictionary, typing, interdependence in a habitat, the algorithm for long division, punctuation rules for periods and commas, adding fractions in a recipe, and so forth.

What role does rote learning play in building programs? While rote learning has its place, it should be relegated primarily to those things that are necessary to remember but are not understandable (the things simply are what they are), for example, the order of the alphabet, state capitals, the multiplication tables (not the concept of multiplication), the location of keys on a keyboard, and so forth.

Recommendations: (1) Give students many and varying opportunities to use what they are learning in real-world situations. (2) Allow them time to practice using the concept or skill using all the multiple intelligences. (3) Ensure they get immediate feedback through the pattern-seeking and program-building stages of learning to ensure their understandings and applications are correct. (4) Require that students take action and use their bodies (the movement centers of the brain also sequence thought).

See also: **Patterns and Programs.**

Further Readings

Goldberg, E. (2001). *The Executive Brain: Frontal Lobes and the Civilized Mind.* Oxford: University Press.

Hart, L.A. (1999). *Human Brain and Human Learning.* Covington, WA: Books For Educators.

Kovalik, S.J., Olsen, K.D. (2002). *Exceeding Expectations: A User's Guide to Implementing Brain Research in the Classroom* (2nd ed.). Kent, WA: Susan Kovalik & Associates, Inc.

Ratey, J.J. (2001). *A User's Guide to the Brain: Perception, Attention, and the Four Theaters of the Brain.* New York: Pantheon Books.

KAREN D. OLSEN, ED.D.

Math

Mathematics is often viewed as a complex subject to teach and to learn. Historically, mathematics is a subject at which only a relatively select few people are able to excel and appreciate. As more is learned about how the human brain intakes, processes, stores, and recalls information, the accessibility of mathematics grows to encompass even those who tend to avoid the subject. The practical applications of this brain research have implications in many areas of mathematics instruction. These findings typically paint a starkly different picture of an effective mathematics classroom than a traditional one in which students simply view examples followed by time spent practicing in class and at home. Research strongly supports the mathematics classroom that is involved, movement oriented, filled with rich discussion, focused on complex problem-solving, low in threat, and geared for deep understanding as opposed to the memorizing of facts and figures. These positive characteristics are closely related and come together to form a classroom that is more congruent with how we understand the brain learns mathematics.

Involvement

Getting students involved and engaged, physically, socially, and mentally, in the acquisition of mathematical knowledge can take many forms and has many benefits. During a traditional mathematics lecture in which students watch the teacher solve several problems, only a small percentage of the brain is highly active. To maximize attention and retention, it is critical that the mathematics educator involve as many parts of the brain as possible. Involvement in the broadest sense may encompass simply activating the motor cortex as an additional active sector.

The concept of involvement includes the learners' level of engagement with the material, each other, and the teacher throughout the acquisition and processing of the material. Each of these areas will engage a larger percentage of the brain than is stimulated through lecture. Effective mathematics learning is social. A classroom, then, should involve communication between peers about the content as well as teacher–student communication. Through this communication, students will be able to make personal sense of the content and develop meaningful mathematical knowledge. This communication will also bridge into the students interacting with the content itself. This can begin to be accomplished by the teacher allowing the students to discuss with each other what the content *means* to them. In a more traditional classroom, the *teacher* assigns the meaning of the content. This shift in focus requires the teacher to become skilled at facilitating discussion to ensure the students are guided to a proper perspective with respect to the content.

Movement Oriented

Although movement is a helpful key to learning any content, it is especially helpful in the mathematics classroom. Much mathematical content can be viewed as quite abstract. In any classroom, the ability for the learners to process and retain abstract concepts varies greatly from one student to another. Research shows some learners will never be as good at this skill as others. To make mathematics accessible to a wider range of learners, then, procedures must be in place throughout the lesson to help make mathematics more concrete. Movement is a way to help this conversion take place.

Besides increasing the amount of blood, and therefore oxygen, in the brain, movement does several other things to increase the effectiveness of instruction. Kinesthetically involving students in a mathematics lesson can help to bring holistic, right brain, random thinkers into the world of understanding and appreciating the subject. If the teacher would like the students to practice twenty problems on a certain topic, those problems could be written, in pairs, on ten sheets of paper. The sheets of paper can then be hung around the room. In small groups, the students can take their papers from sheet to sheet solving the problems. In the experience of many educators, students, because they are active, complete the problems more quickly than if they were given a worksheet with twenty similar problems. This is because the students are active, involved, and more awake. This can be done with practice problems, an assessment, as well as many other problem sets. A great benefit of this strategy is that it can be used with any level of mathematics.

Another powerful way to use movement to great effect in the mathematics classroom is to use what we know about **episodic** and **semantic memory.** These two memory pathways contrast and interact with each other. This is useful because it is common in mathematics to present a series of steps that the learners are asked to remember to recall them for future use and application. Focusing on the semantic memory pathway (used for memorizing facts and concepts) alone will not maximize the retention of such material. To engage the episodic memory in mathematics, try the following.

Consider a mathematical process that involves four steps. Begin by writing the four steps on large, separate sheets of paper and hang them in four distinct, physically separate areas of the room. When it comes time to present the steps to the learners ask them to stand and gather by the sheet that contains step number one. As the class gathers around sheet number one, the teacher can take time to explain the importance of the step, its pitfalls, its strengths, etc... When it is time to move on to step number two, simply ask the class to join you in another corner of the room. This process is repeated until the steps have all been described, the learners are creating memories of the movement and the event, not just the content. Later, when the students are asked to recall step number two, the teacher may even find students turning to look at the corner of the room in which it was previously placed. Rechecking their environment will likely give them clues to the content that was experienced there. This is a significant tool that can also be used to classify equations, organize equations, and many other common mathematical tasks. Again, this is a powerful strategy at any level.

Rich Discussion

Learners create meaning mainly through the process of social interaction and processing. This interaction involves the process of the construction and discovery of mathematical concepts, communicating mathematical ideas both written and verbally, supporting and defending mathematical ideas, scrutinizing approaches with supporting evidence of such scrutiny, and building formal and informal complex mathematical arguments. It is the rich discussion about mathematical concepts that leads to true understanding of the material. The antithesis of this point is to encourage the students to simply recall facts and figures. In the modern age of the internet and readily available information, the acquisition of facts is not difficult. The analysis and discussion of those facts often proves to hold the difficulty.

Fostering discussion about the above details gives the students the ability to acquire new mathematical knowledge more quickly because they are building a larger base of experience with the content. This *experience* with the content utilizes a different memory pathway in the brain than the recall of rote memorization. Utilizing these additional memory pathways has shown to increase the retention of material.

Complex Problem-Solving

The ability to solve problems on a worksheet is becoming less useful as society turns to rapidly changing technology, newly researched ideas, and ever changing job roles. Recalling the rules and procedures required to complete many worksheets do not serve a great purpose in terms of applying knowledge to a novel situation. In other words, focusing on obtaining the solution to problems is not as helpful as focusing the process involved to arrive at a solution. Mathematics educators must go beyond rote memorization of facts, figures, and equations to facilitate the learning of *mathematical thinking*. It is the rehearsal of logical thinking and problem-solving that makes mathematics useful in an ever changing world.

Including complex problem-solving can take different forms. An easy strategy is to solicit student ideas *how* to solve a particular real world problem that invites a specific approach. This can be utilized even before the desired problem-solving strategy is presented. With the right guidance, students will often be able to, through discussion and experimentation, formulate a plan similar to the strategy intended for the lesson.

Another form of complex problem-solving takes place in a prescribed environment, set up by the teacher, meant to solve a specific problem. These problems may not require a specific strategy to obtain a solution. It may be the discussion about the problem itself that accounts for complex problem-solving. In essence, including *complex problem-solving* is a gateway to foster many other mathematical skills. It is closely tied to the topics of rich discussion, deep understanding and requires a lower threat environment. Problem-solving is the best way to build a better brain, and it's the process not the product, that is the influential factor.

Lower Threat

Appropriate levels of challenge can certainly help provide an enriched environment capable of fostering mathematical understanding. High levels of threat, however, can quickly contribute to the large amount of anxiety toward the potentially daunting subject of mathematics. Threat comes in many forms and current research suggests that a threatened brain has trouble absorbing and retaining complex subjects such as mathematics. Anything an educator can do to reduce the threat in the math classroom will help increase participation, maximize attention, and increase retention.

If learners come into the mathematics classroom feeling threat, which is quite common, the teacher's first job is to reduce the stress and then teach the content. To tackle this we must first look at some of the causes of math anxiety. One source of anxiety comes from mathematics being presented as a process through which you must find the one answers. The answer, then, becomes the focal point of the energy spent. Students may get to a point where, if they believe they cannot reach the correct answer, they refuse to even attempt the first step of a problem. Another source of anxiety stems from the reality that learners at any given level vary greatly in mathematical ability. Students not proficient in a piece of the content may feel inferior to students with a higher proficiency, thus potentially stunting their future performance. A third source of high threat comes from the presentation of mathematics. If mathematics is only presented as a strict set of rules and procedures, less skilled learners can view mathematics as a nearly impossible task consisting of confusing, unrelated webs of steps and processes.

If these three sources of threat work as a beginning point for discussion, educators can attempt to tackle each source in turn. Many learners, either naturally or through conditioning, tend to get "obsessed" with the answers to a problem. This can happen to such a degree that the actual process involved in obtaining that answer can begin to seem irrelevant. This rears its ugly head in many classrooms in the following manner: A student takes an assessment and only puts the answers on the paper contrary to the directions to include supporting work and evidence of the answer. When the teacher does not give the student full credit, it may be met with a confused look and a response of, "why didn't I get full credit, I got the write answer?" This type of response is a clue that the student places heavy weight on the answer as opposed to the process itself. A strategy to help "rewire" this thinking is to write the problem, leave some white space, and provide the answer. The instruction then becomes, "please show me how to get from the start to the finish." This technique often can be used even when the topic is new. For instance, when teaching the order of operations [The "order of operations" is the prescribed order in which mathematical operations (addition, division, etc…) must be computed to obtain the correct answer. For instance, in the problem, "ten plus eight divided by two," the correct answer is fourteen. The division must be computed prior to the addition. If the addition is computed first, the answer would be nine, which is incorrect.], the students need not be told the prescribed order in advance. If provided several example problems with their answers included, groups of students can, relatively easily, create the rule themselves. This social activity of working in groups in conjunction of the reduction in the level of threat (because the answers are provided) will help the students construct the knowledge and, therefore, have a greater attachment to the content. Surprising to some, many students are able to create knowledge in this complex nature well into advanced mathematics.

The second source of high levels of anxiety toward mathematics, differing levels among peers, can vary greatly from class to class. Many experts spend time studying differences in "innate" mathematical ability among people. Both through nature and nurture, mathematical ability (or apparent inability) is developed early in life. The disparity of mathematical ability among peer groups is obvious even in the first grade and earlier. One way to reduce the threat in the teaching of mathematics is to keep learning social. The human brain is more likely to create meaning from mathematical content if there are social times to process, discuss, and evaluate. Varying the mode of presentation will also help in reaching learners who do not predominantly think "mathematically." For instance, an effective mathematics classroom has occasional hands-on manipulatives and, at other times, quiet practice time. This practice time is balanced by small and large group discussions and problem-solving.

The third source of anxiety toward math comes with some irony. In general, mathematics educators are people who are quite knowledgeable about their subject. This type of thinker tends to be a linear, logical, mathematical, left-brain thinker. If mathematics is presented predominantly in that manner, however, students who do not naturally process in that manner are at a disadvantage. The days of thinking that students should just, "try harder" are long past. We know now that different brains have different strengths. This is not to say that random, holistic, right-brain thinkers cannot excel at mathematics, quite the contrary. The secret lies in the presentation of the material to this type of learner. Mathematics can be presented as a language to explain the world around us. Setting students up to discover principles and rules allows them to create meaning instead of viewing mathematics as a prescribed set of rules. The strict hierarchical presentation of mathematics can greatly increase threat in students who do not have a dominant **learning style** that is congruent with such a presentation. To present mathematics in a manner congruent with the wide variety of learning styles, educators should actively include tasks, problems, activities, and assessments that also include the creative and artistic side of mathematics, thus reducing the level of threat in many students. At the same time, this causes the concepts to seem integrated and purposeful.

Deep Understanding

Many people who succeed at finding correct answers to math problems have trouble when asked for further explanation as to *why* that answer is correct. Any push to go beyond merely quoting a rule, principle, or algorithm (a given set of step-by-step procedures to find an answer to a problem…the pre-defined steps taken in long division, for example) as the supporting explanation causes many to pause and respond with, "because that is just how you do it." An individual who has a true understanding of the material would be able to explain the reason the particular rule exists and, therefore, be more likely to be able to apply that rule to a new and different situation.

For instance, consider the problem "4 1/3 divided by 1/3." Most people who have recently been involved in a mathematics course would be able to work out the answer of thirteen. Many students, however, would also be unable to give a description of *why* the answer is thirteen. If a student cannot explain the purpose of their chosen process, they are less likely to be able to adapt to novel mathematical situations that arise throughout their life. If a student focuses on the answers, those answers are paired with specific problems instead of growing the knowledge base in regards to the content in general. If a student spends their time learning the process, the answers will naturally follow and the specific numbers or organization of the problem in question do not have a crippling effect on the student's ability to obtain a solution.

If an educator, then, simply increases the number of "why?" questions the students are asked, they are moving toward a teaching model more compatible with what is known about retention. Once students get comfortable communicating with each other about the "why?" they will begin to develop the skills to begin answering questions such as, "what next?" Since we know mathematics is hierarchical, being able to connect new information to previous information as well as predict future occurrences is critical to deep understanding. Teaching for deep understanding lies in contrast to solely teaching for the rote memorization of facts, tables, and equations. Teaching for deep understanding is credited by the National Council of Teachers of Mathematics as a reason for increased math scores, according to the National Center for Education Statistics, in the United States.

See also: **Classroom Environment; Constructivism; Social Context of Learning Physical Movement; Processing Time.**

Further Readings

Allen, R.H. (2002). *Impact Teaching: Ideas and Strategies for Teachers to Maximize Student Learning.* Boston, MA: Allyn & Bacon.

Burke, M.J., Curcio, F.R. (Yearbook; 2000). *Learning Mathematics for a New Century.* Reston, VA: National Council of Teachers of Mathematics.

Cuoco, A.A., Curico, F.R. (Yearbook, 2001). *The Roles of Representation in School Mathematics.* Reston, VA: National Council of Teachers of Mathematics.

National Council of Teachers of Mathematics http://nctm.org

DUKE R. KELLY

Moral Development

Character education, values clarification, and moral education are terms that have all been used to describe the process of actively defining and teaching students about right and wrong as they make socially significant decisions. Even within our pluralistic society that draws its standards from a variety of sources, there is a broad spectrum of common values that help us to get along without harming self or others, treating each other with dignity and respect.

Moral behavior is dependent on the ability to predict potential outcomes of our own actions, take the perspective of another, and delay gratification. Some researchers believe that empathy is required to make moral decisions, while others have discovered that the ability to experience empathy does not guarantee that someone will use his or her understanding of another's feelings ethically. These abilities grow over time and with experience. Morality and moral identity are constructed through reflective interaction with others inside a particular social and cultural context. There are both spoken and unspoken rules that come to govern our relationships and there are consequences we experience when we violate them. We are able to use memory, emotion, reasoning, language, social feedback and finally choice to act with moral consistency.

Solving moral dilemmas involves multiple areas of the brain. The prefrontal cortex, sometimes called the executive brain, is actively involved in moral reasoning. Studies of people with early damage to this area indicate that these individuals do not develop effective connections between cause and effect, have trouble with impulse control and may not benefit from social correction. Damage to the prefrontal cortex at or before birth, however, when separated from intellectual functioning deficits, may not be as significant as damage done to the brain between one and two years of age.

A National Institute of Mental Health study that tracked healthy brain development with MRI technology concluded that the prefrontal cortex is not fully developed at age twenty-one, and may not be until the age of thirty. This has important implications for moral reasoning and behavior. Even young children can think with regard to others—babies in the nursery respond to the distress of other infants, and toddlers can act with compassion. Still, the human brain may not have the cognitive skills until well into adulthood to fully think through the impact of one's actions upon others and to control one's impulses accordingly.

Emotions associated with morally laden images or circumstances involve not only the frontal lobes, but the amygdala, the thalamus, and the upper midbrain. Malfunction in these areas may interfere with a person's ability to accurately "read" either the situation or the feedback he or she receives in response to the situation. For example, perceived threat may cause someone to misinterpret or ignore facial expressions or body positions that are usually interpreted and responded to without conscious thought. So moral reasoning develops within a process that involves both thinking and feeling what is right based on feedback and introspection.

The ability to make moral decisions and the development of conscience as an internal guide has been linked to early bonding and nurturing experiences, as well as inborn temperamental differences. **Trauma** and lack of predictable care can interfere with the establishment of the relational background necessary for connecting doing good with feeling good. Healthy children develop the ability to respect others and care about their needs as they themselves are respected and cared for. From a brain perspective, the complex neural networking that occurs in early childhood literally forms the moral fiber we draw on throughout life.

Moral instruction needs to be seamlessly integrated within the educational process and must be based in an understanding of developmental characteristics. In infancy and toddlerhood, the focus is on differentiation of the self and others and helping children to find commonalities between their experience and the experiences of others. The preschool years include an emphasis on learning self-control, interpreting the perspectives of others, and learning social behaviors that promote peace and fairness such as sharing and using appropriate language to express one's own needs. Elementary level moral instruction includes helping children to recognize their ability to influence others through their actions, and adolescent instruction might focus on helping students to self-identify their moral convictions and explore the history and implications of ethical philosophy. These developmentally based instructional goals should not be taught in "morals time," but should be entrenched within the curricular framework, as they are entrenched in life. Challenges that refine these basic skills are encountered throughout the life cycle, so in a sense our moral development is never complete.

Most researchers agree that foundational moral development requires experience with externally imposed rules that contribute to the development of personal habits and acculturation. These external rules are developed independent of the child, and help to insure justice. A child needs to see these rules as firm and consistently applied to come to view them as fair. At early stages of cognitive development, when children have limited capacity to reason for themselves, these rules—delivered by trustworthy, loving, caregivers—establish safe boundaries of behavior toward the self, others, and the environment. Limits and stated reasons for the limits from parents, teachers, and others granted authority in a child's life help to define what will eventually become self-imposed limits established by internal convictions.

Teachers can help to develop these internal convictions by having only a few memorable and unchanging rules that invite reflection and make the classroom a lab for moral reasoning experimentation. These rules must be based on the teacher's own core values because children seem to absorb more of the hidden agenda of authority figures than what is expressed. This may reflect back to the amygdala's unconscious voice in the moral reasoning process. Morally stimulating rules must be developed intentionally to be broad enough to generate dialog based upon moral values, and firm enough to be inviolable. For instance, the classroom rule, "safety first" can form the basis for discussions that inspire morally based reasoning about domains of safety (physical, emotional, environmental), prediction of outcomes, expression of feelings, elaboration of details in internal rule-making and risk-taking choices, and discussing mitigating circumstances within the rule (such as sacrificing the safety of one to secure the safety of others). The process of working out the rule with individuals, both teachers and students, who have different moral backgrounds and who are at different moral developmental levels thus becomes the tool for moral training, while the ethical absolute of safety within the community is reinforced.

One time-honored way to discuss moral issues is through literature. Students learn to pick out words that cue moral issues, behavior, and reasoning. As students are emotionally engaged with fictional or historical characters that are making moral decisions, they are personally invested in the decisions that are made. As there is emotional engagement, the brain work that is happening is more than just objective analysis. Students are actually practicing moral reasoning along with the character and they get to vicariously experience the consequences of the behavior that the characters choose. Students might be encouraged to imagine different choices that might be made by the character and what the outcomes might be, to imagine how another character in the story might have responded, or be asked how they would respond if they were faced with the same choices the character had. This helps to build a sense of moral consistency and identity. Stories can also be told from alternative points of view, such as is done in "The True Story of The Three Little Pigs" (told by A. Wolf) by Jon Scieszka to encourage an understanding of perspective-taking.

Also in the realm of literacy, students can be encouraged to discuss and discover the relevance of sayings, maxims, or significant quotes in small groups or to create their own wisdom sayings that synthesize their ideas about good living. These activities reinforce literacy skills with embedded moral content.

Service learning has been found to be effective when students engage in a learning project by choice and follow the experience with purposeful debriefing questions that help students to connect the what and why of the event. To plant trees for community service credit is nothing more than acting in self-interest to earn a reward, but to have the opportunity to reflect on the significance of those trees both now and in the future can help students to see the moral value of giving of themselves for the benefit of the community.

Similarly, problem-based learning that involves students in brainstorming and implementing solutions to real life conflicts or issues offers them the opportunity to experience the benefits of good actions.

Simulations and orchestrated experiences such as "If the world were a village," mock election debates, or model United Nations councils that help students to have a concrete experience of real-world social structures can provide rich material for perspective-taking. Establishing a classroom bank or corporation and introducing moral conflicts as part of the experience gives students the chance to explore the consequences of operating with or without an ethical system in place.

Teachers can help linear-thinking students design flow charts for decision making and self-assessment processes that include moral considerations and can include such tools in classroom use, encouraging the use of multiple cognitive domains in the moral reasoning process.

Moral development is nurtured through daily interactions in home, school, and society. Values are integrated as they are modeled indirectly and as they are taught intentionally. Sound moral reasoning involves critical thinking, choice making, and attention to the needs of both the self and others. To neglect teaching morals does not mean that moral development will not occur; only that it will occur with greater attention to the self than to others. Intentional integration of moral reasoning opportunities within the curriculum helps insure that kids grow up sensitive to the needs of others and able to make moral choices in the real world.

See also: **Emotional Intelligence; Self-Esteem; Spirituality.**

Further Readings

Borba, M. (2002). *Building Moral Intelligence: The Seven Essential Virtues that Teach Kids to Do the Right Thing.* San Francisco: Jossey-Bass.

Damasio, A. (2003). *Looking for Spinoza: Joy, Sorrow, and the Feeling Brain.* New York: Harcourt.

Sapolsky, R. (2003). "A Bozo of a Baboon: A Talk with Robert Sapolsky" http://www.edge.org/3rd_culture/saplsky03/sapolsky_print.html. Viewed online, 29 October, 2004.

Stilwell, B., Galvin, M., Kopta, S.M., Kopta, S. *Right Vs. Wrong: Raising a Child with Conscience.* Bloomington, IN: Indiana University Press.

New Horizons for Learning, Character Education http://www.newhorizons.org/strategies/character/front_character.htm

Studies in Moral Development and Education, http://tigger.uic.edu/~lnucci/MoralEd/

LORI NILES, M.A.

Motivation

Motivation is defined simply as the "why" of behavior. Psychologists refer to motivation as an organism's internal state that directs and instigates their behavior in persistence and energy. Understanding the factors that determine what makes some students engage in tasks or persuades other to avoid similar task is important to predicting academic outcomes. Motivation has been characterized by the intensity, direction, and duration of behavior, and studies have shown that heightened motivation increases effort, persistence, and responsiveness.

Motivation constructs include self-worth, attributions, self-regulation, and achievement goals. Especially important to educators are students' reasons for learning and the reinforcement of their locus of control. Intrinsic reward is associated with activities that are their own reward in contrast to an extrinsic reward that is created by external factors like rewards and punishments. Psychological studies with children and adults show that intrinsic motivation directs behavior more effectively than does externally administered rewards. Although educators know the benefits of intrinsic motivation, most school policies and methods use extrinsic rewards.

Educators often make judgments about which students appear to be "motivated" and those who are "unmotivated." These judgments may not always be supported by evidence, for example, a student in a math class may be considered to be unmotivated during class instruction but otherwise may eagerly count the money in her pocket. Effective teachers develop attitudes in students that contribute to a long-term commitment to learning. One example used is how homework affects motivation. One teacher grades all daily homework with letter grades counting 30 percent toward the final grade. Another teacher grades homework as satisfactory or unsatisfactory, lets students correct their work, and counts the homework for only 10 percent of the total grade. While the casual observer may think more stringent evaluation would increase student performance, research shows that the teacher who lets the students correct homework improves motivation.

Brain-based research broadens our understanding of motivation by analyzing the neurogenic causes of external and internal motivation, and causes of temporary and chronic demotivation. Neuroscience reveals that the brain rewards the cerebral cortex with natural opiates called endorphins through the hypothalamic reward system. This pleasure system rewards the cerebrum on a daily basis, although each person responds differently based on genetics, brain chemistry, and life experiences. Research has found that external rewards do not stimulate the brain's internal reward system in the same way. Learning is not dependent on promises of good grades and future employment; studies show that animals and humans will seek new experiences and behaviors without perceivable immediate gratification.

Using rewards as a teaching strategy is complicated. Behaviorism's stimulus–response approaches have only been effective with simple physical responses. Rewarding students for creative, critical, and higher level thinking actually impairs internal motivation. When teachers offer strategies to "motivate" students typically they rely upon external rewards by offering choice, time, food, and other privileges. These methods work for some students, but not others, especially for students who exhibit temporary apathetic states or characteristics of chronic demotivation or learned helplessness. Teachers must distinguish between these states to accurately diagnose and refocus students.

Students who come to class with an "apathetic glaze" may be temporarily unmotivated. Eric Jensen reports three reasons for temporary apathy. First, memory associations from a poor educational experience create a negative response. These associations are reported to be stored in the brain's amygdala, and when triggered, adrenaline, vasopressin, and adrenocorticotropic hormone (ACTH) are released by the adrenal glands into the bloodstream. Students who suffered a past embarrassment or failure with math can be retriggered by present sounds, smells, and visual cues. Sensory signals journey to the thalamus that serves as a relay station to the neocortex, the cognitive part of the brain, and the amygdala, which stores our emotions; the emotional brain reacts ahead of the thinking brain. This is why we often feel anger before understanding where it originates.

The second source of a temporary lack of motivation stems from the environmental factors that are formed from the patterns arising from those negative educational experiences. These factors include adverse learning styles, poor classroom environments, social problems such as prejudice, and **self-esteem** factors such as fear of exclusion and failure. Teachers routinely adapt their teaching methods according to students needs by using visual displays and reinforcing content with auditory supplements; however, solutions to social problems often lie outside the scope of a school's context. The third source for a temporary lack of motivation is the student's relationship with the future such as the ability of the student to define their goals. This source includes efficacy expectations where students believe that they can achieve tasks and perceive that the task has interest, attainment, and utility value. Positive beliefs trigger the release of chemicals such as dopamine and endorphins that are natural self-rewards that reinforce positive behaviors. Efficacy itself is situation specific; however, efficacy affects self-worth that is threatened when the task is important and when one's ability is questioned. In classrooms, all student effort can be made important through the use of external rewards and evaluation, and self-worth can be potentially threatened.

Teachers extensively use external motivators including telling students what to do, punishing them if they do not comply, and rewarding obedience. The problem with this reward–punishment approach is that it becomes more objectionable as the child matures. Jean Piaget and Lawrence Kohlberg believed that moral responsibility depends on cognitive growth. Piaget further believed that external rewards can lead to conformity, deceit, or revolt. Incentives in elementary and middle schools set students up to be dependent on reward rather than appropriate behavior. As these students become adolescents, the need for approval changes from teacher-based to peer-based as the students' reference group changes. Adolescents are motivated by social goals as much if not more than academic goals so that the adolescent culture creates their cognition. Adolescents' need for inclusion and avoidance of exclusion motivates their behavior toward school, activities, and learning. These principles dramatically alter how teachers motivate adolescents versus motivating younger students.

Unfortunately, grades and achievements are only incentives for students interested in those rewards. When a student asks, "Will this be graded?" The focus is not learning, but the external incentive, thus grades change motivation. In some situations, competition for grades can produce deceit and cheating which in reality is a systems problem, not a student problem. This paradox of external incentives creates an environment where the student cannot learn at the same time as being perfect. This competitive environment diminishes a student's tolerance for risk, and research shows that creativity declines with competition but not with collaboration.

Rewards and punishments teach students to make decisions based on other's reactions and are a short-term answer to disruptive behavior. Teachers use rewards because they create obedience through manipulation with M&Ms, games, free time, but after the rewards are gone, the students' attitudes are unchanged. After years of a stimulus–response psychology, students and teachers believe that rewards are necessary for learning. Teachers often believe that rewards such as flattery and grades build self-esteem; however, praise give transient good feelings that do not significantly change our self-perceptions. Even young students easily detect insincerity and manipulation, and a teacher's good intentions can be counterproductive; thus, coercion creates compliance, but not commitment. Thus, rewards actually punish when one student is praised and the other is not. The "good" student is embarrassed or disliked by their classmates, and the "bad" student senses rejection and manipulation—a no-win situation. Achievement itself brings self-acceptance and satisfaction.

Characteristics of chronic demotivation or learned helplessness are emotional responses such as anxiety, depression, a liking for hostile humor such as sarcasm. Learned helplessness is a belief that a student's outcomes are independent of a student's actions. Learned helplessness stems from a trauma of an uncontrollable event where the student does not have the skills to effectively deal with the circumstance. Bullying, household abuse, and humiliation in front of peers all qualify as trauma while pulling a student aside with a quiet reminder does not. The amygdala, the center of our fear response, sends neural impulses throughout the entire sympathetic system stimulating the release of adrenaline, vasopressin, and cortisol. These chemicals have an immediate effect on feelings and behaviors. Children who have had frequent exposure to threat have receptor sites adapted to survival-oriented behavior. These students fight for "rank" and territory and have difficulty maintaining attention because of fear of or preying upon others. While moderate amounts of stress enhance learning performance, a survival mode diminishes higher order learning and complex problem-solving. These threats initiate defense mechanisms and behaviors that work well for survival but are deficient for learning.

While conjecture might lead us to think that providing successful outcomes might alleviate learned helplessness, literature shows that success for these children is not sufficient to help them construct a belief that they can reverse failure. Training students to attribute their failures to effort rather than ability, and crediting success to ability rather than chance leads to persistence. These students need practice in using strategies to achieve short-term goals instead of focusing on outcomes. Students who suffer from chronic demotivation may need fifty (or more) positive reinforces before they can become mobilized again. Teachers who become frustrated with these students after a few positive attempts do not understand the nature of learned helplessness. A teacher's frustration may even result in reprimands or threats that further impede a student's progress. Research on intrinsic motivation recommends that these students need to have control in decision-making and personal choice to alleviate the symptoms of learned helplessness.

Human beings have three needs: relatedness, competence, and especially autonomy. Social psychology research suggests that intrinsic motivation is based on experiencing autonomy. If there is no experience with self-determination, the student only feels pressure and tension. They also suggest that activities that enhance perceived competence and are optimally challenging will enhance intrinsic motivation. Mastery goals develop competence and self-regulation and low avoidance behaviors. Teachers who communicate with failure statements imply incompetence and undermine intrinsic motivation. Deadlines, surveillance, and threats convey external control thus decreasing autonomy and inhibiting intrinsic motivation. Reward and control orient people toward wanting success, but not toward challenging tasks or risking failure. Thus, students who are more extrinsically motivated have more difficulty solving problems. Students who learned to teach others had greater conceptual learning and were more intrinsically motivated; the shift toward competition, toward cooperation, produced greater self-esteem and autonomy.

Jensen recommends several practical strategies for reducing **stress** in these students that include eliminating threats from outside the class, threats from other students, and internal threats within the students themselves. Although teachers cannot eliminate all environmental stress, they can create a safe classroom by setting clear expectations of behavior, setting realistic deadlines, and managing transitions within the class and in hallways. Allowing students physical activity is important because exercise releases brain-derived neurotropic factor (BDNF) that improves neural connectivity, elevates mood, and aids in long-term memory formation. Teachers need to allow students to stretch, dance, or walk during classroom transitions. Teaching students alternative ways to reframe failure can help them minimize negative self-talk; teaching them that they have choices and to see that there are connections between their actions and outcomes. For a chronically demotivated brain to rewire itself, teachers need to provide frequent, consistent, and positive replenishment into the student's environment.

Most students are intrinsically motivated for certain things. Students who will not read may spend hours learning a sophisticated video game. Modern society has a multiplicity of literacy that includes not only reading and writing, but multimodal texts that mix words and images through multimedia. Challenge, complexity, and uniqueness stimulate both hemispheres and result in more learning. Any discussion of intrinsic motivation must include the learners' construction of meaning that corresponds to their semiotic drives and beliefs. Natural neurotransmitters mediate intrinsic motivation. With mild cognitive motivation, increased levels of norepinephrine or dopamine manifest while more vigorous motivation escalates levels of peptide vasopressin or adrenaline.

Jensen suggested five strategies to aid students to uncover their own intrinsic motivation. The first and most important strategy is to eliminate threat that only inhibits intrinsic motivation for learning. Asking small groups of students to identify barriers that inhibit learning can facilitate their search for solutions as well as benefit classroom management. A second strategy is to allow students to participate and choose their goals for learning. This includes priming a student's interest and connection when introducing a topic. Allowing for construction of connections makes the material relevant and meaningful for students. A third strategy involves activating and engaging positive feelings and emotions. Effort at community building creates belongingness that instills cooperation. Building students' self-efficacy includes using affirmations, celebrations, win-win games, and creative activity through music, art, and theater. The fourth strategy is similar to the third in teaching students to manage their emotions through constructive means. Creating a positive environment through celebrations, rituals, optimizes relationship building. Increased feedback may enhance intrinsic motivation.

John Goodlad believed that learning was enhanced when students understand expectations, are recognized for their efforts, learn from their mistakes, and are guided to improve their performance. Today computers can create endless, self-managed **feedback**, although well-organized projects, cooperative learning, and other activities can do the same. Peer feedback is more motivating than teacher feedback and obtains greater long-term results. Using peers for feedback also has potential to create a cooperative classroom community and to assist teachers with classroom management.

Thus, using rewards to motivate students impairs their internal motivation. Teachers typically try solutions to "motivate" students who are disengaged. While these strategies may aid some students they may be unnecessary because the brain has natural opiates to daily reward the cerebrum that are not sustained by external rewards. Some students exhibit temporary apathetic states, others may display characteristics of chronic demotivation or learned helplessness. Teachers must distinguish between these states to accurately diagnose and to help students refocus. Learned helplessness stems from a trauma of an uncontrollable event where the student does not have the skills to effectively deal with the circumstance. Students who are not intrinsically motivated need to feel like they have control in decision-making to alleviate the symptoms of learned helplessness. Eric Jensen suggested five strategies for teachers to increase students' intrinsic motivation: (1) eliminate threat, (2) set goals involving students, (3) activate and engage positive emotions, (4) create a strong positive climate, and (5) increase feedback. Although some of these strategies have been known for a long time, researchers are gaining greater understanding of what motivates the brain. Teachers need this information to use the brain's internal mechanisms to naturally motivate students and create long-term results.

See also: **Behaviorism; Classroom Management; Social Context of Learning.**

Further Readings

Ames, C. (1999). Motivation: What teachers need to know. In A.C. Ornstein & L.S. Behar-Horenstein (Eds.), *Contemporary Issues in Curriculum* (pp. 135–144. (2nd ed.). Needham Heights, MA: Allyn & Bacon.

Dahl, R. (2003). *Emotional Learning: The Crucial Role of the Adolescent Brain in Developing Lifelong Motivation, Passion, and Drive.* Columbus, OH: McGraw-Hill.

Jensen, E. (1998). *Teaching with the Brain in Mind.* Alexandria, VA: Association for Supervision and Curriculum Development.

Marshall, M.L. (2001). *Discipline Without Stress.* Los Alamitos, CA: Piper Press.

Rogers, S. (2003). *Hot Topics: Key Connections: The Brain, Motivation, and Achievement.* San Diego, CA: The Brain Store, Inc.

CAROL A. ISAAC AND
LINDA S. BEHAR-HORENSTEIN, PH.D.

Mozart Effect

The Mozart Effect is popular terminology identifying the positive effects of music in health and education. French physician Alfred Tomatis in his book *Pourquoi Mozart* (1991) highlighted Mozart's music in his work to improve children's speech and communication disorders through auditory stimulation. Beginning in the 1950s, he used Mozart's music extensively because of its musical clarity, elements of form, and abundance of high frequency overtones.

In the 1990s, University of California-Irvine researchers Frances H. Rauscher, Gordon L. Shaw, and Katherine N. Ky explored music listening effects upon spatial-temporal reasoning using Mozart's music. The researchers suspected that Mozart, who began composing at age four, might have had extraordinary access to inherent spatial-temporal firing patterns. The research found that mental image rotation improved temporarily following brief listening exposure to Mozart's music. Controversy arose when the media inappropriately claimed that "Mozart Makes You Smarter" associating music listening with increased general intelligence. Ensuing studies to replicate the music listening results have been inconsistent perhaps due to methods and purpose variability.

Further research by Rauscher, Shaw, and others detected significant, long-term improvements in mental object rotation through music learning and practice. The theoretical explanation proposes that early exposure to music may support development of built-in cortical firing patterns and enhance the ability for spatial-temporal reasoning.

See also: **Music.**

Further Readings

Campbell, D. (1997). *The Mozart Effect.* New York, NY: Avon Press.

Rauscher, F.H., Shaw, G., Levine, L., Wright, E., Dennis, W., Newcomb, R. (1999). Music training causes long-term development of preschool children's spatial temporal reasoning. *Neurological Research* 19:2–8.

The Mozart Effect Resource Center http://www.mozarteffect.com/learn/read.html

Musica: The Music and Science Information Computer Archives http://www.musica.uci.edu

CHRIS BREWER-BOYD, M.A., FAMI

Multimedia Technology

Children and teenagers spend more time with media than with their parents. In fact, they spend more time with media than on any other activity except sleeping. Media technology is becoming more portable all the time, and it is delivering multimedia, the integration of text, graphics, audio, and animation. Concerned by the increasing availability of media at home and school, some parents and educators worry that media overload is incompatible with the brain's optimal learning conditions. There is no doubt, however, that multimedia technology, if used wisely, presents unparalleled opportunities to engage students' creativity and stimulate higher order thinking skills.

The manner in which information is communicated to students has become increasingly complex. Long ago, listening attentively was essential to learning, with teachers lecturing and students listening. Texts became available, pictures were added to lessons, then music or a recorded voice, radio, films, educational television, and video. As schools have added computers and connected them to the internet, multimedia technology has become more common in classrooms.

Computers are used for word processing, research, games, programming, social interactions, and artistic activities. The Internet provides access to increasingly complex combinations of text with graphics, sound, music, animation, and streaming video, and enables students to make connections across time and space with text messages or videoconferencing.

Although writing is still essential, students often do presentations incorporating pictures, animation, video, audio, objects, and graphs. Educators are aware of the need to reach as many learners as possible by teaching to the way they learn, and technology to do so is available. No longer do students have to choose whether to listen to an audio presentation, look at a visual, or read a text for information. They can do all three at once.

A landmark study by the Kaiser Family Foundation in 1999, called "Kids and Media @ The New Millenium," teaches us that the students of today are indeed "The Media Generation," with extended, mostly unsupervised, access to televisions, audio systems, print materials, and game systems in their own rooms, and increasing access to computers.

Researchers have questioned whether the characteristics of multimedia technology can be reconciled with what educators know of brain compatible environments. Some believe that before age twelve students should spend their time "doing" rather than "viewing," while others say total immersion in multimedia is the future of education. David Sousa and others contend that student brains of today are different from the brains of the past, as they have been exposed from an early age to multimedia and have adjusted their learning styles to this technology. We know much about how the brain learns, and what it needs to learn best, and we continue to learn more.

Many recent studies by neuroscientists, physicians, and educators, tell us important things about how the human brain works, how it learns, and what disrupts learning. We know that the brain naturally searches for meaning, creating patterns and solving problems, and that it is influenced both positively and negatively by **emotions**. If students are to be receptive to new information, intellectually engaged in the classroom, and able to retain and build on what they learn, they must be taught in ways that are brain compatible.

Many authors have applied the latest scientific findings about the brain to learning environments, and established elements needed to create the optical learning environment. Multimedia technology may be evaluated in relation to these elements necessary for a brain compatible classroom.

Absence of Threat

The brain notices first, and remembers longer, information that has a strong emotional component. Text, music, and pictures that evoke emotional responses will be remembered longer than others, but if **emotions** are too intense, such as anxiety or fear, learning is impeded. Mass media often bombards users with sound, rapid action, and color, and uses emotions to attract and keep the audience. Multimedia technology, including virtual reality, attempts to make the viewer feel the complete experience, and if that virtual reality is one of danger or anxiety, it may also impede learning. While an emotional "hook" works to get the immediate interest of a student, an ideal learning situation requires a feeling of trust and the absence of threat. Learners will take more intellectual risks in an environment that feels safe and non-threatening. The optimal condition for complex learning combines low threat and high challenge.

Choices

A brain-compatible environment offers choices, whenever possible, about how to learn, how to demonstrate learning has occurred, and how to receive **feedback**. Research has shown that each learner has a preferred method of learning, or a "learning style." According to Howard Gardner, of the Harvard School of Education, there are 8 1/2 different **learning styles**. An individual usually prefers one learning style, but often employs other styles too. Multimedia technology is available to create opportunities for all different types of minds to access knowledge, gain a fuller understanding, and demonstrate that understanding.

For example, the Verbal/Linguistic learner will enjoy e-books, interactive books, multimedia authoring, story creation software, and desktop publishing. The Logical/Mathematical learner will use the Internet to research, record, and analyze data, and will enjoy problem-solving software and Computer Assisted Design programs. Visual/Spatial learners like pictures, and can employ video and digital cameras, photo software, and graphic arts programs. Bodily/Kinesthetic learners will prefer robotics, dancing and filming the movement, claymation creation and recording. Musical/Rhythmic learners will favor using CDs and DVDs, video and audio recorders, music composition software, and music files. Intrapersonal learners like to use technology that helps them explore feelings and record their ideas, such as mind maps, multimedia portfolios, and problem-solving software. Interpersonal learners enjoy working with others. They will be enthusiastic about technology such as collaborative webquests, group Power Point presentations, and teleconferencing. The Naturalist learns through contact with nature. This student will be happy with a digital camera or videocamera recording outdoors, in a virtual nature setting, and with microscopes and projections of their views. The Existentialist (1/2 intelligence) asks philosophical questions about the world, and wonders about everything. Listservs, e-mail, and teleconferencing would enable this learner to contact other people.

Time

The brain learns by attaching new information to known information. To make connections and process new information, the brain requires adequate time to integrate, experiment, and reflect. Multimedia programs usually offer students a comfortable beginning level before the challenge of something more difficult. If the gap between the known and the new is too wide, the learner will be frustrated. Multimedia designed to be compatible with this element will run in real time, allowing opportunities to pause or change the pace, providing time for reflection. Students must also learn to use the technology in ways that are brain compatible, and not speed from one webpage to another without time for reflection. Individual differences among students dictate different lengths of time needed for learning, whether the learner is reading a book or using multimedia.

Regardless of the medium, learning requires repetition. Different types of rehearsal are necessary for different types of learning. Rote rehearsal is most effective for learning a skill or habit, and repetition will form the strong neural connections needed to insure that the skill is automatic. Elaborative rehearsal strategies help the learner bring additional meaning to the information. Elaborative rehearsals may include mnemonics, creating associations, and role playing or simulations.

Multimedia technology can include repetition of audio and visual components as well as requiring repeated responses from the users. Some programs elicit a certain number of correct repetitions before allowing students to progress to the next level. Gaming systems teach players that rote repetitions are necessary; and the faster the better. Rewind and replay buttons on many forms of technology assure the possibility of repetition, and allow additional time if needed, to master the learning. Virtual museums, CD-ROMs, and music videos, to name a few, all employ elaborative rehearsals.

Movement

Physical movement accompanying a song or rhyme increases the likelihood that the song will be remembered because another aspect of learning has been added. Physical movement aids memory, language acquisition, and learning. Multimedia technologies that include physical movement in any aspect, rather than prolonged periods of sitting still, are more brain compatible.

Enrichment

The brain is built to respond to novelty, complexity, and enrichment. Neurons and dendrites grow when surrounded by sensory stimuli, 3D resources, and real life applications. Multimedia allows the student to make new connections, changing presentations to add sound, color, light or motion to create an original project.

When using multimedia technology, as with all teaching, planning the assignment is important. The brain pays attention to one thing at a time. Without structure, it is easy for students to ignore content and focus on adding images, animation or music, endlessly reconsidering the font for the title page, or the right sound for one page of the Power Point presentation.

Another aspect of enrichment important in a brain compatible environment is optimizing the sensory input. Multimedia technologies regularly stimulate the senses of sight, hearing, and touch, and continue to experiment with smell, taste, balance, and the touch-related senses of heat and pressure to provide a richer experience.

Music is part of an enriched environment, and may also be used to help establish an atmosphere of calm and safety. Music can reduce stress, yet help the mind stay alert and ready to learn. Music affects the levels of several brain chemicals and triggers various **emotions**. Musical experiences can activate the motor, visual, cognitive, auditory, or affective system depending upon whether you are writing, reading, listening to or performing music.

Multimedia technologies use music as the main attraction and also to enhance programs. Most people have musical preferences, so technologies often have musical style choices available, whether you are designing a game, sending an e-card, or creating a presentation. Music must be used with caution in the classroom, because some students can relax with it in the background while others become distracted.

Collaboration

Working with others allows students to increase understanding by examining what is known and comparing it with new knowledge. Collaboration is effective when it allows students to experiment and compare or contrast information. Video- and computer-based learning programs, interactive computer programs, and videoconferencing all enable remote collaboration. Through multimedia, students can be connected with other students and with experts such as artists and scientists who enrich learning experiences and make deeper understanding possible.

Feedback

Effective feedback or assessment, a necessary component to learning must be timely, specific, and part of the learning process. Most educational software programs and computer games provide feedback for the user that is immediate, such as a flashing score, a sound, or advancement to the next level. Multimedia technology used incorrectly also provides immediate feedback. A Power Point presentation that does not buzz or change pages gives the student feedback. Immediate feedback can be incorporated in multimedia use through student projects with a peer-feedback component, employing instant messaging, teleconferencing, webcam, or e-mail feedback for distance collaboration.

Mastery

Mastery involves putting knowledge into long-term memory. The student should understand the concepts, be able to apply them to real life situations, and retrieve them when necessary. Many types of multimedia technology are available that enable students to demonstrate understanding and mastery. Multimedia is often best when used creatively to demonstrate knowledge.

Multimedia technology can, if used correctly, enhance the educational experience for any style of learner. When an assignment is meaningful and challenging, multimedia technology can be employed to help students make connections between the known and the new, create associations and make meaning, enhance communication, and foster collaboration. Multimedia technology offers a myriad of possibilities for learners to demonstrate mastery of information, and share what they know. Multimedia technology offers an opportunity for creativity and open-ended exploration. It helps students use **multiple intelligences**.

Multimedia technology is growing more conspicuous in every aspect of our lives, but it is still just one component of the big picture that is education. Having multimedia technology in the classroom or at home does not guarantee that learning will occur in greater depth or last longer. It does not guarantee that the learning will occur at all. Many parents and educators worry that students are spending too much time with electronic media and are missing other important experiences. Parents and teachers should establish clear and reasonable guidelines for usage, and students should have time for other activities and time to relate with friends and family members. Good teaching and learning occur, regardless of what technology is used, when meaningful activities are planned that require higher order thinking skills.

See also: Challenge and Enrichment; Information Processing Model.

Further Readings

Erlauer, L. (2003). *The Brain Compatible Classroom: Using What We Know about Learning to Improve Teaching.* Alexandria, VA: Association for Supervision and Curriculum Development.

Kaiser Family Foundation. (November, 1999). *Kids and Media @ The New Millenium.* Retrieved August 12, 2004 from http://www.kff.org/entmedia/1535-index.cfm

Lamb, A. (January, 2004). *Technology and multiple intelligences.* Retrieved August 18, 2004 from http://www.eduscapes.com/tap/topic68.htm

Veenema, S., Gardner, H. (November 1, 1996). *Multimedia and multiple intelligences/ The American Prospect.* Retrieved August 6, 2004 from http://www.prospect.org/print/V7/29/veenema-s.html

Wilson, D.K. (February 2, 2004). *Understanding how human brain works essential to good teaching and learning/Bridgewater State College News.* Retrieved August 3, 2004 from http://www.bridgew.edu/bridtoday/2004/feb/davidsousa.cfm

CHARLENE K. DOUGLASS, D.A.S.L.

Multiple Intelligences

The theory of multiple intelligences (also known as "MI theory"), was created by Dr. Howard Gardner, currently the John H. and Elizabeth H. Hobbs Professor of Cognition and Education at the Harvard Graduate School of Education in Cambridge, Massachusetts, in the course of his broad investigations in cognitive psychology, neuropsychology, developmental psychology, anthropology, and a number of other fields. The inauguration of the theory can probably best be marked by the publication in 1983 of his book *Frames of Mind: The Theory of Multiple Intelligences.* In this book, Dr. Gardner argued that the psychometric construct of "Intelligence Quotient" or "IQ" as originally developed in 1905 by Alfred Binet, and modified by a number of European and American psychologists (as evidenced by the subsequent development of other standardized IQ tests), was seriously flawed, and needed to be replaced by a new theory based upon the idea that there are many or "multiple" intelligences that constitute the core of human cognition.

In *Frames of Mind,* Gardner proposed seven candidates for these multiple intelligences. They are as follows: linguistic intelligence: the intelligence of the spoken and written word; logical-mathematical intelligence: the intelligence of numbers and reasoning; spatial intelligence: the intelligence of pictures and images; bodily-kinesthetic intelligence: the intelligence of the whole body and of the use of the hands; musical intelligence: the intelligence of rhythm, melody, and timbre; interpersonal intelligence: the intelligence of being able to make distinctions in the mood and intentions of other people; and intrapersonal intelligence: the intelligence of being able to access one's inner feelings, purposes, skills, and goals. In 1995, Gardner began writing about an eighth intelligence, the naturalist, which he describes as the intelligence of being able to discriminate among different plants or animals, or the ability to differentiate other features of the natural world such as clouds or mountains.

More recently, Gardner has considered the possibility of a ninth intelligence, which he calls the existential, and describes as the intelligence of concern with ultimate life issues (such as "what happens after we die?" "why do bad things happen to good people" and "what is the purpose of life?"). Thus far, he has declined to add it definitively to his list of intelligences because it does not meet all the criteria for an intelligence. Currently, Gardner speaks of there being "8 1/2 intelligences"—the 1/2 referring to the existential intelligences.

Perhaps the key feature of the theory of multiple intelligences, and one too often neglected by practitioners of MI theory, is the set of eight criteria used by Gardner to generate his list of intelligences. Gardner originally described these criteria in a chapter entitled "What Is An Intelligence?" in his book *Frames of Mind*; a chapter which should be required reading for anyone who wishes to go further in investigating MI theory. The first criterion that must be met for an intelligence to be included in his theory is that it must be able to be isolated by brain damage. In the course of Gardner's work at the Boston VA Hospital as a neuropsychologist, he noted how certain cognitive abilities could be wiped out by lesions in a specific area of the brain due to an illness or an accident, while leaving other cognitive abilities intact. Gardner suggests that a key prerequisite for the candidacy of "intelligence" in MI theory, is that one should be able to find evidence in the neuropsychological literature of a given intelligence being severely compromised as a result of specific brain damage, while leaving the other intelligences relatively unimpaired. For example, an individual with damage to linguistic areas of the brain might still be able to sing, relate to others non-verbally, dance, do logical problem-solving, and have insight into his or her own inner emotional life, because the areas of the brain required for these activities were unimpaired. Brain injury provides indisputable evidence of the existence of multiple intelligences.

A tentative, partial, and generalized list of areas of the brain specialized for the eight intelligences include: linguistic (left temporal and frontal lobes), logical-mathematical (left frontal and right parietal lobes), spatial (posterior regions of the right hemisphere), bodily-kinesthetic (cerebellum, basal ganglia, motor cortex), musical (right temporal lobe), interpersonal (frontal lobes, temporal lobes—especially right temporal lobe—and limbic system), intrapersonal (frontal lobes, parietal lobes, limbic system), and naturalist (areas of left parietal lobe important for discriminating "living" from "nonliving" things). It should be noted here that one of the reasons that Gardner has not included the existential intelligence as a definitive part of his theory is that he feels it does not fully meet this particular criterion.

A second, related, criterion, is that one should find instances of an intelligence working at a high level of competence in individuals that have come to be called "savants." This criterion, like the first one, is based on neuropsychology and an understanding of how brain dysfunction can create instances of individuals who, while possessing low levels of functioning in other intelligences, have gifts in one or more specific intelligence areas. Examples include individuals with low IQ scores who can sing opera in twenty-six different languages, or compute numbers and calendars rapidly in their minds, or paint with astonishing accuracy, or read encyclopedias at the age of three without understanding, or show a spectacular ability to mime or dramatize, or relate exceptionally well to others. In these cases, one sees a specific intelligence (or a component of a specific intelligence) working in isolation, demonstrating its relative autonomy from the other intelligences. In this sense, the second criterion is an instantiation of the first.

The third criterion is that each intelligence should have an identifiable core operation or set of operations. In other words, for example, one could conceivably break down or analyze the ability to perform a dance into a set of specific motor operations. It should be noted here that Gardner has held back on adding the existential intelligence fully to his model because he feels that it fails to fulfill this particular criterion as well as the first criterion. The fourth criterion is that each intelligence must have a distinctive developmental history and set of "end-state" performances. In other words, one should be able to chart the history of an individual proficient in an intelligence, say a musician, from her first infant experiences banging on a xylophone, to her "end-state" performance as a percussionist at Carnegie Hall. The fifth criterion is that each of the eight intelligences should have an evolutionary history and an evolutionary plausibility. That is, one should be able to see instances of each intelligence in earlier stages of human prehistory—as for example, in primitive musical instruments found at archeological sites—as well as in other species—as for example, in bird song.

The sixth criterion is that the existence of each intelligence should receive support from experimental psychological tasks. In particular, studies that show, for example, how the ability to dance does not make one a better mathematician, or that demonstrate how reading better does not necessarily make one a better salesman, may indicate the relative independence of each intelligence from one another. It should be noted that Gardner has acknowledged recent studies that suggest that early music training may facilitate mathematical or spatial ability, and has left room for a reevaluation of the validity of these intelligences in the light of future confirming studies along these lines. The seventh criterion is that the relative autonomy of each intelligence should receive support from psychometric findings. An examination of the subtests of an IQ test, for example, should reveal in at least certain individuals, an uneven profile among those subtests that assess different intelligences (picture completion, which requires spatial intelligence being much higher or lower, for example, than vocabulary, which draws upon linguistic intelligence).

The eighth criterion is that each intelligence must be capable of being encoded in a symbol system. This is seen in the different symbol systems used by practitioners highly skilled in working with a specific intelligence (writers using linguistic symbol systems like English, French or Russian, musicians using different musical notational systems, computer programmers using different computer languages and so on). Finally, it should be noted that while not included as a specific criterion, Gardner has written that each intelligence should represent the ability to solve problems and/or fashion products that are culturally valued. In other words, a person demonstrating an intelligence should show the ability to solve a real problem, such as fixing a broken machine, or fashion a culturally valued product such as a painting, a novel, or an invention. In this regard, one has to question whether the tasks required on typical standardized IQ tests really represent authentic culturally valued activities, or are instead artificial skills contrived for the purposes of furthering relatively obscure academic research.

In the two decades that have passed since its inception, the theory of multiple intelligences has grown from a relatively obscure concept embraced mainly by private schools for gifted children, to a mainstream concept in contemporary education. Hundreds of schools based upon multiple intelligences have developed in the United States and in scores of other countries around the world (e.g., the August 16–18, 2002 conference in Beijing, entitled the "International Conference on Pushing Forward the National Education and Improving Student's Quality: Research on the Development and Assessment of Multiple Intelligences," included nearly two hundred papers on multiple intelligences). Multiple intelligences have been woven into the staff development goals and instructional frameworks of many school districts worldwide. Hundreds of books and thousands of articles have been written about the theory of multiple intelligences and its educational applications in English and at least thirty other languages. The theory of multiple intelligences has been applied to virtually all levels of education, from infancy to adulthood, and to a wide variety of settings including vocational and career education, literacy, technology, special education, gifted education, substance abuse prevention programs, parochial education, outdoor education, arts education, bilingual and english for speakers of other languages (ESOL) education, and higher education, among other areas.

The variety of applications of multiple intelligences to educational settings has likewise been quite diverse. One criticism of traditional academic schooling, according to Gardner, is that only two intelligences are primarily emphasized: linguistic intelligence and logical-mathematical intelligence. On the broadest level, then, MI theory has helped educators see the value of content areas typically deemed of less value in the overall curriculum by traditional educators, including music programs, arts education, physical education, and the development of personal and social skills in students. MI theory has served as a major conceptual support to these programs in arguing for more funding and greater presence in school programs. In addition, many magnet schools specializing in one or more of these areas have received validation for their raison d'etre, and have used MI theory as a foundation for their goals.

On a more strategic level, the theory of multiple intelligences has been used in staff development programs to help teachers at all grade levels and in all content areas develop curricula, lesson plans, and instructional approaches that incorporate the eight intelligences over time into their teaching repertoire. Thus, for example, instead of simply giving a lecture on the Battle of Gettysburg in U.S. History, a teacher might show a movie or a slide show, involve the students in a re-enactment of the battle, engage the students in writing songs detailing the events of the battle, create time-lines or other cognitive organizers to help students master the material, or lead discussion groups, debates, or cooperative learning groups seeking to investigate the impact of the battle on the course of the

Civil War. This broader approach to instruction has had the effect of reaching students who had previously been unreachable in the classroom, due to their relative weaknesses in the academic intelligences (linguistic and logical-mathematical), and their relative strengths in intelligences typically not addressed in traditional lecture-based, textbook-based classrooms. In one study of forty schools using multiple intelligences conducted by researchers at Harvard Project Zero, a number of positive outcomes related to decreased dropout rates, improvement in students labeled "learning disabled," and standardized test scores were noted.

A related application of multiple intelligences to education consists in educating students about their own multiple intelligences profile. A variety of informal checklists and formal diagnostic activities exist for assessing multiple intelligences in students. Teaching students about their own multiple intelligences may be particularly helpful for those students who have had school difficulties, or received labels such as "learning disabled" or "attention deficit hyperactivity disorder." These students may discover that they possess gifts that when recognized and developed can serve to raise their self-esteem and that can provide a means of acquiring skills in areas of difficulty through strategies based on their most highly developed intelligences. These checklists or diagnostic approaches can also be helpful in counseling students as to their own career proclivities.

Another major application of MI theory to educational settings consists in its impact upon how students are tested concerning their mastery of material taught in the schools. Again, the typical academic approach has relied heavily upon linguistic and logical-mathematical intelligences, usually through paper-and-pencil tests. MI theory has supported the development of assessments in all content areas that include the eight intelligences, so that students might be assessed in their understanding of fractions, for example, not simply by taking a traditional test, but by solving hands-on problems using math manipulatives, or relating fractions to the musical scale, or writing an imaginative story based upon their understanding of fractions.

The theory of multiple intelligences, while popular among educators at all levels, is not without its critics. MI theory has found disfavor particularly in the field of psychology where academicians still hold tightly to the idea of IQ, or some other equivalent single generalized intelligence factor. Critics claim that MI theory is based primarily on intuition, and not quantitative measures. Some educators, likewise, have claimed that MI theory lacks good empirical evidence to back up its claims that using all eight intelligences in instruction boosts academic achievement. Such criticisms often come from those with a positivist orientation, that is, from those with a belief that knowledge, in order to be true, must be quantifiable. Such critics have difficulty with the qualitative aspects of MI theory and that it bases many of its knowledge claims upon findings from anthropology, autobiography, clinical psychology, and other non-quantitative sources.

Despite its critics, the theory of multiple intelligences has made a major impact upon the face of American education over the past twenty-one years. It has caused educators to think differently about how children learn and significantly contribute to a wave of school reform that has made academic institutions more interesting and lively places for students. In a sense, Gardner's work has initiated a kind of paradigm shift in contemporary education, by taking educators out of their myopic focus on splinter skills and narrow instructional objectives, and causing them to see a broader view of learning that encompasses not simply the 8 1/2 intelligences of his model, but that opens new questions about what is truly valued in schools and in culture at large, and what are the limits to human knowing and achievement. In this respect, the theory of multiple intelligences deserves credit for opening many people's eyes to a new vision of learning and teaching.

See also: **IQ.**

Further Readings

Armstrong, T. (1999). *7 Kinds of Smart: Identifying and Developing Your Multiple Intelli- gences.* New York: Plume.

Gardner, H. (1993). *Frames of Mind: The Theory of Multiple Intelligences.* New York: Basic Books.

Gardner, H. (2000). *Intelligence Reframed: Multiple Intelligences for the 21st Century.* New York: Basic Books.

Multiple Intelligences, www.thomasarmstrong.com

THOMAS ARMSTRONG, PH.D.

Music

We all have firsthand examples of the mental, emotional, and physical effects of music. Music triggers memories of images and feelings. We intuitively listen to music that helps us energize or relax. Science has verified these experiences and established that music alters multiple physiological and psychological parameters that impact cognition and emotions. Music affects the chemistry and rhythms of the brain and body, patterns and frequency of neural firing in the brain, and creates changes in emotional and physical states.

Music Instruction and Academics

Harvard psychologist Howard Gardner endorses music as a form of human intelligence speculating that it is the earliest of the **multiple intelligences** to emerge. The recognition of music as an innate human intelligence and the prominence of music as a universal mode of expression justify unconditional inclusion of music education in schools. Beyond the intrinsic value of music, there is evidence that music instruction strengthens skills necessary in academic endeavors. A 1980 survey of thirty six published and unpublished studies by James Hanshumaker established that learning and practicing music significantly enhance reading readiness, language acquisition, verbal skills, motor development, creativity, and personal and social growth. The survey noted greater student motivation and lower middle school truancy rates.

Norman M. Weinberger, professor of neurology and biology at the University of California-Irvine, identified skills acquired through music instruction that are basic to various academic domains. These include development of the sensory and perceptual systems (visual, auditory, kinesthetic and tactile); the symbolic and linguistic arenas of cognition; the movement planning, muscle action and physical coordination networks; feedback and evaluation systems; and motivation skills. Weinberger points out that music involves repeated practice, resulting in continual strengthening of synaptic connections between the networking brain cells that support these skills. When students learn and practice music they are reinforcing brain connections useful in many academic areas.

Neuroscience has discovered that synchronous neural firing in multiple areas of the brain is characteristic of higher thinking skills and is stimulated in music listening and performance. The fundamental music elements, such as pitch or rhythm, are processed by networked groups of neurons in different areas of the brain including the cerebellum and regions of the frontal, parietal, and temporal lobes. Both left and right hemispheres are involved. Music listening and performance activates these associated neural groups simultaneously. This neural firing across multiple brain sites is called *neural synchrony* and is believed to assist the brain with pattern recognition necessary in cognition and memory.

Prominent research has specifically correlated music instruction with language development and increased abilities in certain spatial-temporal reasoning tasks. The College Board reported in 1999 that students with one half-year of music instruction demonstrated an average 7- to 10-point increase in verbal and mathematics test scores, respectively, over students not exposed to music. The report shows these benefits improve over time. Four years of music instruction resulted in average gains of 58 points in verbal test scores and 39 points in math scores. Music lessons in early childhood that include keyboard instruction and singing have demonstrated significant increases in test scores, specifically mathematics and language comprehension. Improvements have been noted in mathematics even when music lessons reduced the amount of time spent on direct math instruction.

Music and Spatial Reasoning

Scientists have detected similarities in neural firing patterns between spatial-temporal reasoning skills and high-level brain functions including music, math, and chess. Physicist Gordon L. Shaw and mathematician Xiaodan Leng theorize the presence of cortical structures pre-disposed for development of specific firing patterns. They believe early music instruction accesses and reinforces the inherent firing patterns related to spatial-temporal reasoning. This strengthens pattern development within the specialized cortical building blocks designated for spatial skills and makes it easier to accomplish spatial tasks. In studies with preschool children Shaw and cognitive psychologist Frances H. Rauscher concluded that learning music keyboards in early childhood stimulates greater capability in the spatial task of mental object rotation, particularly important in understanding proportional math. Providing early music instruction may be a natural way of building the necessary cortical hardware for working with fractions, ratios, and other spatial math operations.

Music Instruction and Language

Scientists generally agree that music is an intrinsic human function that supports verbal communication. Hearing is the first sense to develop in the womb, establishing brain structures for processing sound. The idea that we are pre-wired for musical development is further suggested by the fact that even six-month-old infants recognize tunes and detect small changes in melody. Some researchers theorize that music is a pre-language communication.

Brain imaging has affirmed the link between music and language by confirming certain jointly shared processing structures. The part of the right hemisphere sensitive to musical pitch also reacts to pitch in speech. The left hemisphere section of Broca's area recognizing verbal incongruity responds to inappropriate sounds and chords in music. The same left brain region designated for split-second discrimination between sounds like "pa," "ba," or "da" is activated during music listening. When musicians read music the area in the right hemisphere responsible for reading text is stimulated.

Language text-reading and reading music notation involve very similar processes. Many of the skills developed for music are required for language and reading. Symbol decoding, phonemic awareness, sight identification, orthographic awareness, and cueing systems awareness are among the language abilities learned in music instruction. Pitch discrimination, a primary component in music education, stands out as an important common element between music and reading. The second stage in the reading acquisition model developed by cognitive psychologist Uta Frith requires readers to associate a letter with the corresponding sound or phoneme. Readers must be able to distinguish between pitches in this step. Beginning readers with strong ability to identify pitch differences have higher reading scores than readers who experience difficulty.

Educators can use the relationship between music and language to students' advantage. Pre-K children and beginning readers benefit from music education that builds rhythm, pitch, and melody skills. Rhymes, chants, songs, and rhythmic movement are highly effective music activities that can be integrated directly into language and reading programs. Academic benefits from these activities have also been noted in secondary language classes.

General classroom teachers can use content-oriented songs to help students remember important facts while strengthening language abilities. Student- or teacher-written songs using academic content for lyrics and set to familiar tunes help with recall. Chunking information into short, memorable verses with a repeated chorus of essential content assists with semantic memory. The melody acts as a carrier of the information and triggers recall. Student involvement in writing the lyrics motivates participation and further enhances memory.

Raps engage semantic memory and can also stimulate students' procedural knowledge. The rhythmic emphasis can trigger movement-oriented neural pathways. Raps have special appeal to secondary students. Student-written raps are often quite complex and include a great deal of content information.

Simple rhythmic raps using key terms can be chanted in basic musical meters. An example for a lesson on atomic particles is:

e-lec-tron-**-**neg**-a-tive-**

pro-**-tons-are—**pos**-i-tive-**

neu-**-trons-**-**neu**-**-tral-**

In this 4/4 meter example (four beats to a measure), the asterisks represent a half-beat rest. Bold syllables are accented to help hold the rhythm. This rap could be chanted in unison, as a round, or with groups of students chanting each line at the same time.

Music Education in Schools

Administrators are encouraged to prioritize music instruction as an academic essential. Maintaining or expanding existing programs with music education specialists can facilitate academic improvements in proportional math, reading, and higher thinking skills. Music education methods, like the Kodaly and Kindermusik systems, that emphasize singing and include concrete body involvement when teaching pitch, rhythm, and rhythmic patterning are most effective in building language skills. Music therapists have developed techniques to assist with specific populations and classroom challenges that offer unique strategies for facilitating reading and special education programs.

Programs demonstrating improved academic abilities through music study have incorporated music from two to five days per week. One year of instruction has not proven to offer substantial long-term results. While research has not provided definitive specifics on optimal years of music study or at what age music instruction should begin, results from SAT test scores correlated with instruction show the greatest advances occur after four years. Pre-school music instruction will provide special benefits in neural pattern development but music instruction at all age levels demonstrate benefits.

Music Listening and the Brain

Neuroscience has documented physiologic changes in the brain and body during music listening that impact **attention**, energy, and attitude. Music can be used as an effective teaching and classroom management tool for gaining and holding student attention, motivating student participation, increasing attention span, stimulating **creativity**, assisting in memory and recall, and building classroom community. All teachers, even those with no musical training, can play appropriate recorded music to enhance students' ability to learn, remember, and create.

Music listening has been attributed with enhancement of learning in a variety of ways. Brain imaging shows that certain music helps students attain a coherent brain and body state that increases focus on learning tasks. French physician Alfred A. Tomatis discovered that the higher frequencies in music overtones provide electrical stimulation to the brain that heightens attention and has effects throughout the body. Some music, including certain Mozart selections, activates a brain area used when working with short-term memory and is theorized to result in enhanced recall. It is also hypothesized that music stimulates firing in the 4 Hertz low frequency theta wave range essential for memory encoding by the hippocampus. Research does not support that listening to recorded music has the same degree of effect on cortical pattern development for spatial reasoning that is attributed to active music participation, but it is hypothesized that there is some strengthening of neural networks and firing patterns derived from music listening.

The use of recorded music for classroom management requires that teachers understand the effects of music, techniques for implementing music in the learning environment, and how to select music appropriate for desired results. Recorded music becomes less than effective if played indiscriminately or if inappropriately selected.

Basic physics laws are used in music therapy to understand how listening to live or recorded music affects the mind, body, and **emotions**. The principle of musical entrainment explains changes in physical and mental states. Derived from Latin, entrainment means *to bring along with* and accurately defines how the rhythm, tempo, and feel of music can bring us to different moods or energy levels.

Upbeat music prompts changes in body rhythms by engaging rhythmic entrainment to help students re-energize or maintain focus. The effect can alter neurochemistry through the release of adrenaline and cortisol. These hormones heighten attention levels in the brain and body and, in appropriate amounts, enhance learning tasks. Conversely, slow, calming music increases parasympathetic system activity and entrains listeners to a relaxed state. This music can also induce the release of the neurotransmitter acetylcholine, important in long-term memory formation and found in higher levels in the afternoon and during **sleep**.

Under stressful situations cortisol and adrenaline levels rise and can inhibit memory and learning and cause damage to physical systems. Chronic **stress** destroys brain cells in the hippocampus causing deterioration of declarative memory and hampering explicit memory. High adrenaline levels can inhibit activity in the left pre-frontal cortex, an area responsible for maintaining positive feelings. This shut-down results in development of negative expectations that discourage learning. Listening to music can lower cortisol and adrenaline levels, reducing stress effects. It can shift negative mood states to more positive moods that promote learning. College students ranked music third of twenty-one anxiety mood regulators indicating that students intuitively seek to reduce stress with music.

Gaining and holding student attention requires lesson-planning that considers daily mind and body rhythms. Playing music as students enter the classroom, during breaks, to cue transitions, or for project work, sets the mood for a positive, low-stress environment and reduces the negative effects of stress. During low-energy times of day or following long periods of academic focus, play upbeat music to re-energize mind and body for more effective learning. Novelty and change are recognized as important elements of attention regulation. Music is a fun classroom management tool for gaining student attention. Short snippets of music used for classroom transitions will cue students when it is time to leave, begin class, take a break, return to work, or for other tasks. For example, playing the theme from the Pink Panther movie can cue students to quietly line up for lunch while "Rock Around the Clock" lets students know when it is time to begin the next classroom activity. Background music played as students read, write, or study can extend attention span if not overused.

The principle of habituation is important to effective classroom music use. The brain determines if a stimulus is critical to survival and whether or not it deserves attention. When music is over-used and played continually for long periods of time habituation can occur as the brain decrees the sound insignificant and filters it out. Purposeful use of music at periodic intervals is more effective than constant sound.

Generally, music quickly shifts attention and mood but sometimes change does not occur immediately. The *iso principle*, referring to "equal" in Greek, explains why at times teachers may need to play music that matches an existing mood or attention level and gradually shift to music matching the desired state. For example, a first grade teacher wanting to calm students after recess can use the iso principle if students have difficulty slowing down. The teacher matches the high student energy with a short selection of upbeat music, sung or played as students enter the classroom. This is followed with somewhat slower music and concludes with a slow, relaxing selection. This gradual calming process helps students entrain to a focused attention state and need only take three or four minutes.

A successful technique using music to assist in teaching course information originates from the Accelerated Learning model, developed by Bulgarian doctor Georgi Lozanov as Suggestopedia in the 1970s. His lesson-planning design includes the use of content "concerts" of essential lesson information read over background instrumental music. The content may be formatted as vocabulary words and definitions, metaphorical stories, important text, short plays, quotes, or facts. These concerts generally involve only the basic information in concise presentation. Ensuing activities elaborate further.

The Accelerated Learning model uses two distinct concerts to access different information processing modes through brainwave state and attention level. An Active Concert initiates an active beta brainwave mode while the Passive establishes a calm alpha-theta brainwave state referred to as relaxed alertness. The concerts are presented during a lesson or unit when the learner will benefit most by accessing the information in the associated state. The Active Concert introduces content information at the beginning of a lesson to stimulate attention levels as a way of helping students establish neural connections for the new information. The Passive Concert is most often presented at the end of a lesson and serves as a review. Passive Concert music assists students by encouraging a relaxed state of internal focus that provides an opportunity for reinforcement of neural connections and networks established during previous learning experiences.

When selecting recorded music, consider the energy level needed for classroom activities, matching music to the desired level. Tempo, rhythm, and dynamics are key elements but mood is equally important. Is the music bright and happy, calm and reflective, energized and dynamic? Does the music make you want to move or be quiet? Generally, the way music makes you feel is how it will affect your student although individual mental associations can impact music experiences. Emotion provides a strong memory hook that can be beneficial in learning. Music with strong emotional context can be highly effective in helping students remember content, but if you do not want to initiate emotional reactions, use music with a more neutral emotional tone.

The majority of recorded music for classroom use is instrumental. Many musical styles are effective. Classical music is recommended for encouraging focus. Concerto and symphonic works of the Baroque era by composers like Bach and Handel and Classical-era music of Mozart is commonly used. These styles have predictable harmonies and consistent rhythms effective for regulating and holding attention. This music works well for setting a positive learning environment, welcoming students to class or playing during breaks, and as students are leaving. If energy levels are low use the faster movements from 100 to 150 beats per minute. During reflective activities, or when a quiet but attentive state is optimal, the slower movements are best, around 50 to 75 beats per minute. Slow movements are often named by tempo markings like largo, adagio, or lento. Moderato is a medium tempo while allegro and allegretto are fast. Romantic, Impressionistic and contemporary classical music varies greatly and may be especially useful in setting specific moods related to course content. For example, Gustav Holst's *The Planets* provides interest when studying astronomy.

New Age music offers a wide range of options for setting moods and facilitating relaxation. Solo piano is often reflective. Big Band and 50's music can be fun and upbeat. Incorporating music from different cultures is a positive way of incorporating diversity but cultural music has an array of effects. Celtic music is widely appreciated. Some selections are invigorating while others are reflective. Much of African music is energizing. Native American flute music is frequently calming. Using a mixture of music styles provides interest and options for energy and mood shifts. Music specialists can be invaluable in helping make appropriate selections. Recordings designed especially for classroom use are available.

Early childhood teachers have long used recorded songs to teach topics like counting, letters, and behavior. Teachers of secondary grades can use popular music, selecting songs that connect with content. For example, "The Wind Cries Mary" by Jimi Hendrix can be used to teach personification. Marvin Gaye's "Mercy, Mercy Me" relates to ecology. Contemporary music with uplifting, motivating words can be played for all grades during transitions or breaks for a change of pace and to build student rapport. Music can set an appropriate theme for a day or unit. "I Can See Clearly Now" emphasizes accomplishments while the "Mission Impossible" theme motivates when beginning a challenging lesson. Music with lyrics is generally not recommended as background to focused classroom tasks as it can be distracting. Students may be taught how to select music for learning as a way of helping them use music to assist in homework and independent learning.

See also: **Classroom Management; Mozart Effect.**

Further Readings

Blakeman, S.J. and Frith, U. (2005). *The Learning Brain: Lessons for Education.* Malden, MA:Blackwell Publications.

de l'Etoile, S.K. (2002). The effect of a musical mood induction procedure on mood state-dependent word retrieval. *Journal of Music Therapy* 39(2):145–160.

Hansen, D., Bernstorf, E. (2002). Linking music learning to reading instruction. *Music Educators Journal* 88(5):17–21.

Hanshumaker, J. (1992). *Music for every child.* Woodridge, CT: Schirmer Books.

Jensen, E. (2000). *Music with the Brain in Mind.* San Diego: The Brainstore, Inc.

Leng X, and Shaw, G.L. (1991). Toward a neural theory of higher brain function using music as a window. *Concepts in Neuroscience,* 2, 229.

Rauscher, F.H. (2002). Mozart and the mind: Factual and fictional effects of musical enrichment. In J. Aronson (Ed.), *Improving academic achievement: Impact of psychological factors on education* (pp. 269–278). New York : Academic Press.

Register, D. (2001). The effects of an early intervention music curriculum on prereading/writing. *Journal of Music Therapy* 38(3):239–248.

Shaw, G.L. (2000). *Keeping Mozart in Mind.* San Diego: Academic Press. http://www.mindinstitute.net

Tomatis, A. (2004). *The ear and the voice*. Lenham, MD: Rowman and Littlefield Publications, Inc.

Weinberger, N.M. (1998). Brain, behavior, biology, and music: Some research findings and their implications for educational policy. *Arts Education Policy Review*, 99, 28–36.

CHRIS BREWER-BOYD, M.A., FAMI

N

Nature of Knowledge

"What should students know and what do students really know?" These questions drive much of the debate, and expenditure, on education. They impact such issues as standards, instruction, and assessment. Yet, although frequently discussed by philosophers, psychologists and others, the nature of knowledge remains unsettled and a vexing question for educators. Nor is it always dealt with directly in the context of education because it is bound up or implied in questions about information, meaning, understanding, skill, curriculum, and more. In recent times neuroscience has been added to the mix of resources available to educators but even that has been a mixed blessing because neuroscience can be invoked and applied in many different ways and can be used to support opposing positions and points of view.

The approach taken here is based on a synthesis of ideas and research from psychology, the neurosciences, and other domains. There are three points of departure. First, the learner is not a blank slate. Every human being enters life with a repertoire of basic capacities and predispositions that are then influenced and expanded through a combination of nature and nurture. Second (and more controversial) is that although the brain "makes inner representations of reality" it is not simply a device that stores objectively true facts and categories. Rather, the brain is a patterning device so that, even if most people subscribe to a set of ideas or believe that some ways of looking at the world are "right," each individual brain must come to see the patterns and make sense of things itself. This approach is popularly called **constructivism**, though constructivism does have many faces. Third, no person is an island. Although each of us comes to know individually, it is also true that we are social creatures and that people have much in common and construct understandings and knowledge together, both directly and indirectly.

Thus there is a dance between what is sometimes called formal knowledge and the knowledge developed by individuals—what could be called personal knowledge. When educators and policy makers prescribe standards and spell out levels of accomplishment in different subject areas, they are working with formal knowledge. Yet, formal knowledge needs to be worked on and digested by learners if it is to become personal.

From Inert Knowledge to Dynamical or Performance Knowledge

Not everything that people learn is useful. In the term used by the philosopher A.N. Whitehead, much personal knowledge is "inert." It sits in the mind and is rarely called into play. Many students, for instance, can recite a math formula or describe some of the basic features of a democracy. Yet, many of those students who "learn" facts, concepts, and procedures are lost when faced with real world situations that call for the use of that knowledge. There is a wealth of evidence, for instance, that even college graduates well versed in physics fail to apply basic principles of physics to ordinary, everyday situations such as explaining what happens as a coin is tossed or in explaining the seasons. On the other hand, much that is learned is personalized in such a way that it can be used naturally and appropriately to solve problems and deal with unplanned situations in the everyday world. Geoffrey Caine and Renata Caine call this latter, useful type of knowledge dynamical or performance knowledge.

A valuable platform for discussing the limits of inert knowledge and the differences between inert knowledge and dynamical or performance knowledge can be found in the work of Howard Gardner, originator of the theory of Multiple Intelligences. He describes three types of learners:

- *The intuitive learner (or unschooled mind)* is superb at mastering a great deal of information and understanding. So, although the child's knowledge is immature or "naïve," it is used in the real world and hence is dynamical.

- *The traditional student* is one from whom educators expect memorization but no genuine understanding is guaranteed. Schooled knowledge is largely inert, surface knowledge. Surface knowledge consists of both rote remembered but relatively meaningless facts and procedures, and of concepts and procedures that are intellectually understood but which cannot be used naturally, another term for which is technical/scholastic knowledge.

- *The disciplinary expert or skilled person* is the person that understands information in a content area and can apply it. The expert's knowledge is dynamical, but within the domain of expertise it is more mature and more appropriate than the knowledge of a novice.

Note that memory researchers have long made a distinction between declarative and procedural memory. Declarative memory has to do with what can subsequently be expressed or articulated by the learner. **Procedural memory** has to do with skills and procedures that show up in performance. Educational psychologists translate this distinction into declarative and procedural knowledge. And educators, including those who refer to the neurosciences, often rely on these differences in making suggestions for instruction. In addition, several other memory systems have been identified.

The point is that none of these memory systems individually account for dynamical or performance knowledge. All memory systems work interactively in the real world of experience, even when rote memory is involved. When a math problem is being solved, for instance, a formula must be recalled—declarative knowledge, and applied—procedural knowledge. Performance knowledge is formed as a result of the interactive engagement of multiple memory systems. It is, therefore, not the same thing as procedural knowledge.

What, then, is the difference between inert knowledge and dynamical knowledge, other than the fact that one is useful in the real world and the other is not?

Dynamical Knowledge is Perceptual

Caine and Caine developed an approach to knowledge that corresponds to the distinction that Gardner and others have made. They suggest that the crucial similarity between the unschooled or naïve mind and the mind of the expert is that dynamical or performance knowledge is *perceptual* as much as *conceptual*. Appropriate action in new situations become possible because the learner has acquired new ways of seeing and perceiving the world. As performance knowledge is perceptual, it both reflects and guides the ways in which knowers internally structure and organize their worlds.

Even though young children may not grasp situations in the ways that adults do, their knowledge is being applied to whatever they experience. A cow may be called "doggie," for instance, because doggie is what the child thinks it sees. The child is developing categories and perceiving patterns, a process first described by Jean Piaget. The categories are still immature, which is why the child seems to "get it wrong" sometimes, but a child's naïve knowledge is still used for the purpose of navigating through the world.

Experts have also developed new categories and perceive additional patterns within their domain of expertise. Knowledge that is thoroughly processed and reorganized in the brain becomes perceptual, and so becomes the foundation for a way of seeing and doing. Rather than simply knowing some math, a person begins to think like a mathematician; rather than just taking photographs, a person begins to see like a photographer.

The need to grasp the inner essence of knowledge that is used in the world has prompted the examination of mental models. Mental models are the way we interpret the world, they are our assumptions and generalizations. According to organizational theorist Chris Argyris, people frequently do not behave congruently with what they say (their espoused theories) but they always behave congruently with their mental models (their theories-in-use). In short, espoused theories are part of a person's technical/scholastic knowledge because they do not actually guide or shape behavior. Mental models, on the other hand, are aspects of a person's dynamical or performance knowledge. They are perceptual in nature and guide the way that a person reads and responds to a situation.

The Feeling of Knowing

The word "knowledge" tends to be associated with the cognitive domain, as though knowing is a purely intellectual process. Nothing could be further from the truth. At the heart of expertise and skill and dynamical knowledge is what psychologist Eugene Gendlin called a felt sense or felt meaning. It is an appropriate feeling of knowing.

Everyday usage takes the feeling of knowing for granted. In story after story, in sports as diverse as baseball and billiards, there is talk of a "feel" for the game. But the term reaches into every discipline. For example, Nobel Laureate and biologist Barabara McClintock advocated getting a "feeling for the organism" that was being researched. And noted management consultant Peter Vail specifically invites people who wish to understand something in depth to get a felt meaning for it.

Caine and Caine have therefore suggested that one of the characteristics that marks a shift from inert knowledge to dynamical knowledge is whether or not a person has gained a feel for what is being learned. It is as though we come to know something with our whole body and mind. We get it "in our belly." In effect, really high intellectual standards, expertise, mastery and great skill always rely on the blending and integration of thought with a feel for what needs to be known. That integration is at the heart of the perceptual shift that must occur for performance knowledge to develop.

The notion of felt meaning helps to address the vexing question of why it has been so difficult to convert formal knowledge into dynamical knowledge, and why so much of what students learn in school remains inert. The way to gain a feel for concepts and processes, and to grasp the patterns of a domain of knowledge as they play out in reality, is through experience. Young children and experts are typically immersed in a great deal of experience in which the "stuff" to be learned is embedded and, often, examined and processed. Schools, typically, rely on the transmission of information with almost no relevant experience for learners. That is why most schools are what Marion Diamond calls "impoverished environments."

Finally, a word of caution is needed here. The feeling of knowing is complex, and by itself is never enough for the development of dynamical knowledge. First, the feeling of knowing occurs through the engagement of the entire system of body, brain, and mind, and is not simply an emotion. Second, a feeling can also be inappropriate because novices often feel that they know when it is clear that they don't. Third, an adequate felt sense develops in partnership with rigorous analysis and appropriate action. And fourth, even experts sometimes get it wrong.

Practical Implications

The distinction between inert and dynamical knowledge has significant implications for learning outcomes, approaches to instruction, assessment, and more.

Outcomes

The public needs to be clear about the type of knowledge that it wants students to have if the goal is to be dynamical or performance knowledge. As a minimum, standards need to be framed in terms of what students can do in authentic situations, and not just in terms of what they "know" and "understand." For example, rather than learning about or understanding democracy, students need to be able to function naturally and appropriately in a democracy; rather than mastering some rules of grammar, they need to be able to read and write and deal with text in both simple and complex ways in the real world.

Instruction

Technical/scholastic knowledge is an important step on the way to developing performance knowledge. So there are times when memorizing information and practicing skills and routines are essential building blocks along the way to genuine competence. However, if the desired outcome is performance knowledge, then students must also have multiple opportunities to learn from experience. Caine and Caine, therefore suggest that good instruction involves at least three interacting elements:

Relaxed alertness, a combination of low threat and high challenge as the optimal state of mind in the leaner;

The orchestrated immersion of the learner in complex experience in which the curriculum is embedded, with direct instruction being regarded as one element in the larger immersion; and

The active processing of experience so that the learning is deep enough.

Assessment

Genuine understanding and performance knowledge cannot adequately reveal themselves on multiple choice tests or tests that call for written explanations. The key to knowing what students really know, therefore, is authentic assessment, a process that involves several different modes of performance to complement examinations and tests.

The nature of knowledge is a complex one, and has only been partially addressed here. Many additional questions can be asked ranging from the role of consciousness to the nature of other types of knowledge such as tacit knowledge. The essential point for educators is that a person's knowledge is not all of the same general quality. Some types of knowledge are more useful than other types of knowledge. Insofar as educators want students to be able to use what they learn in the real world, the objective needs to be the development, in the learner, of dynamical or performance knowledge—in all grades and in all subject areas.

See also: **Teaching Model for the Brain; Patterns and Programs.**

Further Readings

Caine, R., Caine, G., McClinitic, C., Klimek, K. (2005) *The 12 Brain Mind Learning Principles in Action: The Field Book to "Making Connections: Teaching and the Human Brain."* Thousand Oaks, CA: Corwin Press.

Fuster, J.M. (2003) *Cortex and Mind: Unifying Cognition.* New York: Oxford University Press.

Root-Bernstein, R., Root-Bernstein, M. (1999). *Sparks of Genius.* New York: Houghton Mifflin.

GEOFFREY CAINE, LL.M.

Nutrition

As you eat, so shall you think. Every day people make decisions about what to eat, and these foods have a direct impact on the quality of their lives. The brain needs certain amounts and specific types of nutrients daily to function properly. Too much or too little (deficiency) of any nutrient can affect the nervous system negatively.

For example, if a new mother is lacking the vitamin folic acid at conception, then spinal bifida, a nervous system disease, could occur and affect that child's entire life. Foods greatly impact which chemicals and how many chemicals are being manufactured in the brain. These chemicals control daily behaviors or states of mind.

Neurons or brain cells need the following two main fuels to function—oxygen and glucose. Neurons cannot store these fuels, rather they use them up readily. A constant supply of these fuels is required for the brain to function. This indicates that in addition to eating three balanced meals a day, the brain benefits from several small snacks so that there is a supply of glucose when needed.

The second fuel needed for brain cell functioning is glucose. Foods are broken down though the digestive process into various nutrients. Glucose is one of the key nutrients, and most foods can be converted into glucose. Scientists are learning how nutrients such as glucose alter the neural networks within the brain, and ultimately affect daily behaviors or states of mind. A person's behavior, learning, mood, intelligence, stress, sleep, disease/sickness, aging process, and energy levels have been proven to be impacted by diet.

How it Works: Nutrients to Neurotransmitters to States

After a food is eaten, it goes through a process that allows the nutrients to be used by the brain. After food is broken down within the stomach, it

Table 1. Nutrient-Neurotransmitter-State cycle how foods affect behavior

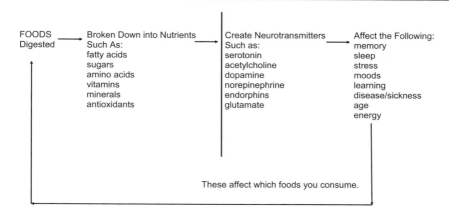

FOODS ⟶ Broken Down into Nutrients ⟶ Create Neurotransmitters ⟶ Affect the Following:
Digested   Such As: Such as: memory
                    fatty acids   serotonin   sleep
                    sugars   acetylcholine   stress
                    amino acids   dopamine   moods
                    vitamins   norepinephrine   learning
                    minerals   endorphins   disease/sickness
                    antioxidants   glutamate   age
                                            energy

These affect which foods you consume.

travels along the digestive tract where it is absorbed by the intestinal cells and then transported through blood vessels into the bloodstream. These foods are broken down into the following nutrients: fatty acids, sugars, amino acids, vitamins, minerals, and antioxidants. Now the nutrients need to reach the neurons within the nervous system by crossing over a semi-permeable membrane called the blood–brain barrier (BBB).

The BBB protects the brain by blocking harmful, toxic substances from entering the brain. The BBB allows for nutrients to pass through so neurons can utilize them, but not all nutrients make it through. This is another reason why it is so important to eat foods high in the needed nutrients so enough is available for the neurons. Once the nutrients pass through the BBB, they are available for the neurons to soak them in so that neurotransmitters, or brain chemicals, can be created within the nucleus of the neuron. There are over two hundred neurotransmitters, and at least seventy of those regulate nerve function. Some examples are: dopamine, serotonin, acetylcholine, and epinephrine. Neurotransmitters are stored in tiny sacs, called vesicles, within the axon terminal, just waiting to be released to transport a message throughout the brain and eventually throughout the body.

Neurotransmitter manufacturing can be disrupted when there is an insufficient nutrient supply. When this occurs with even just one neurotransmitter a host of cascading effects follow. The electrical message coming down the axon will not have sufficient amounts of the correct neurotransmitter at the terminal. Communication to the next neuron is disrupted and the flow of information stops. For example, if there is a deficiency of calcium then receptor sites (site on a cell membrane where neurotransmitter can bind) can be blocked so that neurotransmitters cannot make it to the next neuron. Calcium cleans out these receptor sites so strong messages can be sent.

Vitamins, minerals, proteins, and fatty acids all aid in or protect the manufacturing of the neurotransmitters. If a person's diet does not have the sufficient amounts of these helpers or protectors, then the certain neurotransmitters are not made or stored in the right amounts, decreasing optimal moods, thinking, learning, and other life functions.

In summary of the nutrient–neurotransmitter–states cycle, foods are broken down into nutrients such as fatty acids, sugars, amino acids, vitamins, minerals and antioxidants which in turn pass through the BBB to be transformed into neurotransmitters that greatly affect our everyday life functions or states of mind such as sleep, learning, thinking, aging, energy release, stress, moods, and disease/sickness.

Nutrient–Neurotransmitter–States Connections

Certain foods contain precursors or starting materials for some neurotransmitters. When a person's diet is deficient in certain precursors, the brain is not able to produce necessary neurotransmitters. All kinds of problems exist with the brain because of the imbalance of certain neurotransmitters. The manufacture of most neurotransmitters is controlled by the brain, but some are influenced by what a person eats. The manufacturing of the following neurotransmitters can be directly linked to diet: serotonin, dopamine, norepinephrine, and acetylcholine. Table 2 below shows how the foods we eat are digested into certain nutrients which are precursors for the manufacturing of neurotransmitters within the neurons. These neurotransmitters in turn create certain states of behavior.

Carbohydrates for Quick Energy

According to the current food pyramid, carbohydrates should be about 60 percent of a person's diet. Carbohydrates are not created equally. Carbohydrates are rated with glycemic index levels based on how quickly the food is broken down. Depending on the glycemic index, two categories of carbohydrates are created: simple carbohydrates or complex carbohydrates. The larger the grains in the carbohydrate, the longer it takes to break down, and therefore, the smaller is the glycemic index. Complex carbohydrates (low glycemic index foods) are better for the brain than the simple carbohydrates (high glycemic index foods).

Complex carbohydrates such as any whole grain food (100 percent whole wheat bread, brown rice, oats, whole wheat pasta, etc.) should be the "carbs of choice." A complex carbohydrate is broken down gradually giving a person a gradual rise in blood sugar and gradual lowering of blood sugar. A person feels full and can concentrate for a long period of time.

Foods that break down quickly, simple carbohydrates (such as white bread, cookies, and cakes) leave you feeling hungry, weak, sluggish, and irritable about thirty to forty-five minutes later. These foods give a person high energy because of the high blood sugar rush at first, then the

Table 2. Nutrient – Neurotransmitter – State

Foods Eaten	Nutrient (Precursor)	Neurotransmitter	States It May Bring About (The below states/conditions have many other causal factors)
Milk, turkey, complex carbohydrates	Tryptophan	Serotonin	*Just Right Balance:* calm, concentrate, relaxed
(whole wheat breads and cereal, brown rice and pasta), bananas, foods high in Omega-3s (salmon, walnuts, tuna, flaxseed)			*Unbalance of the Chemical:* Depression, insomnia, increase sensitivity to pain, drowsiness, low motivation
Protein foods (meats, tuna, cheese, eggs chicken, yogurt), almonds, beets, soybeans,	Phenylalanine Tyrosine	Dopamine which manufactures norepinephrine (also called noradrenaline)	*Just Right Balance:* Attentive, focused, decreased appetite, energized, joyful, anticipation, quick thinking
dairy products			*Unbalance of the Chemical:* Low motivation, depression, irritability, moodiness
Egg yolk, soybeans, nuts, whole wheat bread, lean pork, spinach, foods high in vitamin B,	Choline (member of B family)	Acetylcholine	*Just Right Balance:* Healthy brain functioning, alert, short-term memory enhanced
wheat germ, cauliflower, liver			*Unbalance of the Chemical:* Alzheimer's Disease, memory loss, dementia, reduced thinking ability

blood sugar drops rapidly leaving a person with less energy than when eating started. This is detrimental for learning and for the body. A small candy bar will increase energy levels for about thirty minutes, but a decrease in energy levels will follow for the next hour or two. If the person does not make an effort to eat more food to raise this blood sugar level, then the hypothalamus might signal the release of cortisol, a stress hormone, to raise energy. Cortisol in large amounts for long periods of time can kill neurons.

Proteins for an Optimally Functioning Brain

Proteins are needed to manufacture brain tissue, enzymes, and neurotransmitters that boost alertness. Carbohydrates provide quick energy, but proteins provide stamina. It is important to know how protein affects the body.

When the brain is rapidly using up its supply of dopamine and norepinephrine, it will use tyrosine supplied by the protein food to manufacture more of these two neurotransmitters. When that happens, the brain will help a person respond more quickly and with greater accuracy to mental challenges. A person will feel more alert, more motivated, more joyful, and more mentally energetic. When dopamine and norepinephrine levels drop, a person is more likely to feel depressed, irritable, and moody.

Proteins are ideal for all meals, but especially for breakfast and lunch when the brain needs extended energy to get through the rest of the day. Breakfast is the most important meal of the day. The body's glucose reserves have been relinquished because of the eight-hour fast from sleeping. To rev up those neurons, a good breakfast with several energy reserves is needed. The optimal breakfast for brain energy is to have the following: two servings of fruit or vegetable; one to two servings of high complex carbohydrate with high fiber, one serving of protein and a little bit of fat. Each one of these types of foods release energy at different times providing sustained energy release throughout the morning. To make sure that there is enough energy in the afternoon, make sure to include a protein at lunch time.

Antioxidants for Protecting the Brain

Throughout a person's life, all of the cells in the human body are bombarded by attacks from unstable chemicals called free radicals that are the result of breathing chemicals in the air around us, eating foods (notably fatty foods), and drinking water. These free radicals are formed when the mitochondria within each cell burn oxygen to make energy for the cells. Free radicals are the by-products. They accumulate over time and lead to accelerated aging and several chronic diseases.

The brain generates more free radicals than any other organ because it is comprised of 50 percent fat, and free radicals thrive on fat. The brain uses more oxygen because it is a constant hotbed of activity. The brain also contains the least amount of antioxidants, a chemical that neutralizes and kills free radicals. Free radical damage within neurons causes dendrites to retract, synapses to vanish, and can even kill neurons.

As a person ages, free radicals proliferate. Free radicals are more successful after the age of twenty-five as the antioxidants slow down their production. They can get out of control and corrupt the cell's genetic DNA causing a host of diseases like Parkinson's Disease, ALS (Lou Gehrig's disease), Alzheimer's, arthritis, cancer, heart disease, and other degenerative brain diseases. The strength of antioxidant defenses—or free radical fighters—will affect the amount of cumulative damage and potential intellectual decline.

The more antioxidants that are in the brain, the more they neutralize the destructive free radicals. Increasing intake of foods high in antioxidants has been shown to prevent and reverse memory loss in aged animals, and even retard the progression of Alzheimer's in humans. Antioxidants attack free radicals and slow the aging process of the entire body, save a body from susceptibility to genetic diseases, and save cells at all ages and in all circumstances. In fact, antioxidants repair at least 99 percent of the free radical damage to cells.

Antioxidants vary in their ability to combat free radicals. When one of them gets exhausted from destroying the free radicals, one of the other antioxidants will go in and donate an electron to help the other regain strength to finish the job. The strongest antioxidants are: Vitamin E, Vitamin C, glutathione, coenzyme Q10, and Lipoic Acid.

Antioxidants are highest in the most colorful fruits and vegetables, but most prevalent in fruits. Those people who consume a high amount of fruits and vegetables slash the risk of developing cancer in half. In the past several years, researchers have dissected fruits and vegetables to find the types and levels of antioxidants. Some of the more common antioxidants are: carotenoids, lycopene, lutein, and flavonoids. Foods highest in antioxidants include prunes, raisins, blueberries, blackberries, garlic, kale, cranberries, strawberries, spinach, raspberries, tea (black and green), red wine, and chocolate. People should strive to eat five to seven fruits and vegetables a day.

Foods not Created Equally

Not all foods are created equally. Each food has unique nutritional values. There are foods that have been proven to help prevent cardiovascular disease, type II diabetes, cancers, dementia, and hypertension. Because of the high levels of nutrients, fourteen foods were labeled as being powerful foods. They are: beans, blueberries, broccoli, oats, oranges, pumpkin, salmon, soy, spinach, tea, tomatoes, turkey, walnuts, and yogurt. Because of the BBB, we need to make sure the right amounts of nutrients are reaching the neurons. Eat foods that are highest in the essential nutrients to ensure that the nutrients make it to the brain.

Some foods are processed, changed in original form with several steps involved, and have very little nutritional value. Food additives or preservatives are added to foods to aid in appearance, taste, and shelf life. Monosodium glutamate (MSG) and tyramine (in aged cheese) were shown in research studies to greatly affect brain activity. Additives can do the following: block neurotransmitters so that the receiving neuron is unable to comprehend the message; can increase your cells' deliverance of neurotransmitters, or can affect the enzymes that normally regulate how many neurotransmitters remain in the gap between nerve cells. Eat whole, natural foods as much as possible, and little, if any processed foods.

Fats for Structuring the Brain

Dietary fats are broken down into fatty acids that the body uses for many purposes such as body metabolism and forming the outer membrane of every cell in the body, including those in the brain. In fact, the myelin sheath around the axon of the neuron is made from a waxy, fatty substance (See Table 1). It coats the axon just like a chord covers an electrical wire. This is formed from the fat that we ingest. The myelin sheath allows faster electrical transmissions throughout the brain and prevents cross communication among other neurons. It is very important that good fats are a part of every person's diet, especially younger children.

Of the many fatty acids the body uses, two are called "essential" because the body cannot manufacture them—they must be supplied by diet. Essential fatty acids (EFAs) are also called Vitamin F or polyunsaturated fats. They are found in high concentrations in the brain and a deficiency of EFAs can lead to an impaired ability to learn and recall information.

Not all fats are created equally either. There are good fats and bad fats. Unfortunately, people tend to ingest too much of the bad fat and not enough of the good fat. There are three main types of fats: saturated fats, unsaturated fats, and partially hydrogenated fats (type of saturated fat).

Saturated fats are solid fats and are found primarily in animal products. A high diet of these can impair student's ability to learn rules of a task and to remember how to apply them. Too many could raise chances of heart disease and raise blood cholesterol levels. Some examples are: steaks, butter, cheese, and the like.

Unsaturated fats are liquid fats that get thicker when chilled or stay liquid when chilled. These fats are considered "good" fats. There are two different categories of these fats: mono-unsaturated and poly-unsaturated. Mono-unsaturated fats are found mostly in vegetable and nut oils such as olive, peanut, and canola oil. These fats reduce the bad cholesterol (LDLs). These fats cannot be made by the body. Research indicates that high mono-unsaturated fat diets lower the risk of cardiovascular disease even more effectively than do the standard low-fat diets. Poly-unsaturated fat are called essential fatty acids and examples are corn oil, safflower oil, soybean oil, and omega-3 oil.

Research has come out about how little omega-3 fats people are consuming and how this deficiency affects people. Omega-3s increase the amount of acetylcholine. A Purdue University study found that hyperactive and attention deficit students had lower levels of omega-3. Omega-3 deficiencies have been tied to the following problems: violence, depression, memory problems, cancer, eczema, allergies, and more. Researchers believe that about 60 percent of Americans are deficient in omega-3.

There are two ways to ingest omega-3 fats. Plant-derived foods that are high in omega-3s are: flaxseeds, nuts (walnuts are highest), canola oil, flax oil, and olive oil. Marine-derived foods that are high in omega-3s are: salmon, mackerel, sardines, tuna, grouper, and herring.

The third and worst kind of fat is called partially hydrogenated fat or trans fatty acids. They are man-made and solid. These fats are found commonly in margarine, shortening, doughnuts, French fries, fried chicken, potato cheese, and imitation cheese. Excess amounts of this type of fat can impair neuron function and learning.

Vitamins are Vital

When the brain is not given enough vitamins and minerals, it can get the same damage caused by radiation. Brain cells lacking vitamins and minerals suffer DNA and mitochondrial damage. Multivitamins are highly recommended to ensure that the brain receives the proper nutrients. The following is some research that explains why taking multivitamins is vital.

1. Ten out of thirteen studies show that giving children multivitamins/ mineral pills raises their non-verbal IQ scores as much as 30 percent, reports psychologist David Benton from Britain's University of Wales Swansea.

2. Taking multivitamins for a year boosted immune functioning and cut infections, such as the flu, 40 percent in diabetics and 50 percent in the elderly, compared with taking a placebo.

3. In a new Swedish study, men who took multivitamins had a 20 percent lower risk of heart attacks, and women had a 35 percent lower risk, than those not taking supplements.

4. Harvard studies show that taking multivitamins containing folic acid cut the risk of colon cancer by 50 percent in women with a family history of the disease.

5. Taking a multivitamin pill for more than ten years slashed the risk of clouded vision by 60 percent.

British psychologist David Benton did research that showed that a multivitamin could improve IQ scores. He gave thirty children (12 years old) a special vitamin-mineral supplement and thirty others a placebo pill for eight months. The students then took a standard intelligence test before and after these eight months. Scores on the "verbal" part of the test did not change, but scores of the vitamin-taker's "nonverbal" part soared an average of nine points compared with one point in non-supplemented kids. Vitamins did not raise verbal IQ scores because they measure achievement and reflect cultural, educational, and environmental factors. Nonverbal intelligence reflects brain potential. Benton contends the vitamins work because they correct substandard intellectual functioning due to marginal deficiencies caused by a poor diet. Brain cells starving for nutrients cannot function optimally. The conclusion drawn was that taking vitamin supplements does not push a kid's brain beyond normal capacity, but instead, the lack of the vitamins cause a youngster to perform below capacity. Since this study, there have been many other studies that support his findings.

See also: **Aroma and Learning; Beverages.**

Further Readings

Carper, J. (2000). *Your Miracle Brain.* New York, NY: HarperCollins Publishers.

Jensen, E. (2003). *Tools for Engagement: Managing Emotional States for Learner Success.* San Diego, CA: The Brain Store, Inc.

Somer, E. (1999). *Food & Mood.* New York, NY: Henry Holt and Co.

Wolfe, P. (2002). Healthy Brains for Healthy Educators. *The Health Educator.*

United States Department of Agriculture Food and Nutrition Services www.fns. usda.gov/nn/

LEANN NICKELSEN, M.ED.
WITH CONSULTATION OF RDLD DIETITIAN,
TERRI ANDERSON

O

Obesity

Today's children may be the first generation to live shorter lives than their parents, and much of this is due to physical problems associated with obesity. Obesity issues are pandemic and are affecting our children's mental and physical health. Diabetes, hypertension, and other obesity-related chronic diseases once only prevalent among adults, have now become more common in children. Today's youth are considered the most inactive generation in history caused in part by reductions in school physical education programs and unavailable or unsafe community recreational facilities. Metabolism, eating habits, exercise have all been chronicled as having a role in obesity; now with new technology we are able to examine the brain's role.

Overweight and Obesity Defined

- Overweight and obesity for children and adolescents are defined respectively in this fact sheet as being at or above the 85th and 95th percentile of body mass index (BMI).

- Some researchers refer to the 95th percentile as obesity. The centers for disease control and prevention (CDC), which provides national statistical data for weight status of American youth, avoids using the word "obesity," and identifies every child and adolescent above the 85th percentile as "overweight."

- The American obesity association (AOA) uses the 95th percentile as criteria for obesity because it corresponds to a BMI of thirty which is obesity in adults. The 85th percentile corresponds to a BMI of twenty-five, adult overweight.

Bad News for Brains

While studies have linked obesity to serious cardiovascular diseases including strokes and heart attacks, University of Toronto researchers have found that overindulging can damage overall health—from slower thinking to experiencing more pain. Figures from Statistics Canada's National Population Health Survey were used to analyze the overall welfare of Canadians from 1996 to 1997. Overweight and obese people reported slower cognitive abilities, increased pain, and limited mobility among other ailments.

Leptin is a hormone released from fat cells that signals the brain when the stomach is full. Normally it takes about ten minutes for the brain to receive the message and for the individual to stop eating. This is a strong argument for eating slowly. Regrettably obese people's brains have a difficult time interpreting leptin's message. It is unclear if this is due to the brain not receiving leptin or if it is unable to properly interpret the message. The reality is that obese people don't get the signal to stop eating, which leads to overeating. The problem then becomes cyclical. It is speculated that people go into an eating frenzy trying to get leptin to the brain. They eat more and more in an effort to get the signal that they are satiated.

The more obese a person becomes, the more they eat to get significant amounts of leptin into their brain. Research on rats and humans indicate that individuals are not born with this blockage, but instead the communication problem develops over time.

Preliminary studies show that individuals who have received leptin treatment not only had dramatic weight loss, but also experienced vivid changes in their brain. These changes occurred in the inferior parietal lobes and the cerebellum on the left side of the brain, and the anterior cingulate gyrus; all areas related to self-regulation behaviors. There was an increase in gray matter, overproduction of dendrites and synapses, in these areas. Of particular interest is the anterior cingulate gyrus, an area of the brain associated with cravings and **addiction**. The anterior cingulate gyrus and leptin may hold the key to understanding the craving for food, and drug addiction.

Dopamine and Obesity

Dopamine, a neurotransmitter that modulates motivation and reward circuits, is also likely to be involved in obesity. Dopamine receptor availability was significantly lower in obese individuals than in average weight people. Normally, eating causes the body to release dopamine. This causes the pleasurable feeling a person gets after eating a satisfying meal. The availability of dopamine receptors is decreased in obese individuals in proportion to their BMI. Dopamine and hence dopamine deficiency in obese individuals may perpetuate pathological eating as a means to compensate for decreased activation of these circuits. Strategies aimed at improving dopamine function may be beneficial in the treatment of obese individuals.

Obesity and Dementia in the Aging Brain

A study by the researchers from Kaiser Permanente and the University of California has revealed the links of obesity with risks of dementia in old age. The study found that fat people with a body mass index (BMI) of at least thirty have a 74 percent increased risk of developing degenerative brain diseases including Alzheimer's later in life. Among the overweight with a body-mass index over twenty-five the risk of dementia was increased by 35 percent. It may be possible to enhance the cognitive performance of even healthy elderly people through changes in diet and lifestyle. Recent data indicate that improved prenatal and perinatal care along with greater access to educational opportunities may result in a decreased incidence of dementia in future generations of older adults.

Impact in the Classroom

Exercise has a profound effect on weight and mood control. Studies have found that exercise influenced the activational state of synapses as well as serving as an anti-depressant. Exercise increases the release of endorphins and in turn leads to an increase in positive emotions. Studies have also shown that exercise increases a student's ability to concentrate on academic material and reduce stress. Increase exercise in the following ways:

- Use energizers in the classroom.
- Encourage students to walk to school.
- Provide physical education every day.
- Use physical activity as a reward.
- Role model good physical activity.
- Require recess at the elementary level at least once a day.

What we eat also impacts the brain. A diet high in total fat reduces hippocampal levels of brain-derived neurotrophic factor, a crucial modulator of synaptic plasticity and a predictor of learning efficacy. Eating healthy is the other important component to reducing obesity; the following are ways to facilitate this:

- Adopt a health curriculum.
- Establish healthy eating policies in the lunchroom and classroom.
- Start a school health team consisting of students, teachers, administrators, and parents.
- Eliminate vending machines with unhealthy food options and replace them with healthy choices.

See also: Anorexia; Beverages; Nutrition; Physical Movement; Pleasure and Love.

Further Readings

Gill, T. (2005). A matter of fat: Understanding and overcoming obesity in kids. *Nutrition & Dietetics: The Journal of the Dieticians Association of Australia.* 62(1):54.

Summerford, C. (2005). *Action-Packed Classrooms: Strategies to Motivate and Invigorate the Learning Process.* San Diego, CA: The Brain Store Inc.

Adding an Hour a Day May Fight Childhood Obesity. http://www.azcentral.com/health/kids/articles/0907GirlsExercise07-ON.html

National Heart, Lung, and Blood Institute Obesity Education Initiative http://www.nhlbi.nih.gov/guidelines/obesity/practgde.html

Unsafe Areas and Kid's Obesity. http://www.azcentral.com/health/kids/articles/0914teenobesity0914.html

World Health Organization http://www.who.int/nut/obs.htm

CATHIE SUMMERFORD, M.S.

P

Patterns and Programs

Brain compatible learning came to the interest of the education world with the publication of several books by the late Leslie A. Hart. For educators, brain compatible learning simply means learning activities that are in sync with how the brain processes information. We know much more today about the brain's internal working through new imaging processes developed through neuroscience and the work of cognitive researchers.

The complexity of the brain challenges our imagination. The brain has hundred billion neurons and many million times more connections among the neurons, a network more complex than the entire telephone system of the world. We are still in the early stages of unraveling the mysteries of the brain. The brain appears to have two basic structures for organizing learning. It forms patterns and creates programs.

Patterns

Patterns can be described with the words: recognition, identification, and understandings. Patterns are structures in the brain for organizing information. We see this most clearly watching an infant learn. Given a stable, loving home an amazing amount of learning or understanding develops in the child's brain before school starts. By the age of five a child can distinguish between mother, sister, aunt, grandmother, woman, and friend. Interestingly, none of these concepts was taught in any formal sense. Through exposure, repetition, and endlessly varied circumstances, the **infant's brain** sorts this information into patterns readily available for use.

The brain continues on its unrelenting path of developing patterns for everything it encounters, even incidentally. If we see a table set with plates and silverware, our brains recognize it as a mealtime pattern. We have highly sophisticated patterns for faces, sounds, smells, tastes, and touches. We may recognize a face we haven't seen for five years in a crowded room because the brain connected the face to a pattern in its memory. One can only speculate how many billions of patterns or elements of patterns the brain holds.

The brain thrives on input. Amazingly, the input does not need to be highly organized and sequenced. The brain has an enormously powerful pattern detecting device. It sorts even random input into patterns if provided large quantities of details, variations of situations and ample opportunities to "play" with or manipulate material.

Patterns develop from experience. The more rich and stimulating the environment the more efficiently patterns are developed. They develop through large amounts of input to the brain. Schools must increase variety, experiences, activities, and stimulation enormously, even tenfold, for healthy brain development. Most parents know this instinctively and try to provide a great variety of experiences for their child. It also appears that the brain works most efficiently from complexity; it works better from a holistic view. Increasing age, meaningfulness and reality impact what we, that is, our brains attend to. These findings on the brain have major implications for schools.

Certainly not by design, but unfortunately, many traditional classroom practices might be described as brain antagonistic. The brain starves without massive amounts of varied, complex and meaningful input. Providing the brain with huge amounts of input is done by immersing students in issues that have meaning and emotional content for students, using real world projects, taking many field trips, hearing enlightening speakers, listening to stories and using various media—in short, what good teachers and progressive educators have advocated all along. Getting the brain's attention is what we in education call student **motivation.** The brain doesn't thrive on textbooks and worksheets. We require students to do them, but unfortunately, little enduring learning results.

Programs

The second building block in the brain is programs, which are the brain's instructional set or actions—whether to walk, read, button a shirt, or speak. Just to say the word "hot" in a whisper or a roar or to write it requires an enormous amount of different instructions for the muscles and vocal cords. Many of these programs in the brain run almost automatically once well-learned. Still, given damage to part of the brain from a stroke, the program for walking is impaired even though the muscles of the body are intact. Analogously, if a computer's program is damaged, it will not run.

Programs are learned largely through trial and error, with increasing refinement through practice and **feedback.** Humans develop and deepen thousands, perhaps millions, of programs through the reinforcement of carrying out activities many times in various ways. Think again to the formative years when a child learns to manage a spoon and to express needs through speech. The infant with constant practice comes to master these actions, thereby establishing an efficient program for each of these activities in the brain's structure.

Research has demonstrated that a more richly woven tapestry of neuronal connections for programs occurs from stimulating, active environments. Programs develop by doing, actions, projects, and practice. Schools must be experiential; a place where students invent, try their wings, build and exercise their thinking skills, talents, and abilities.

Sitting passively in straight rows kills motivation and creates discipline problems. The brain needs, indeed craves, challenges and opportunities to apply learning. In most school settings, students are like racecars at the starting line, energized and ready to go, but the flag never falls. So, they sit and sit and sit. Students must be given and assume reasonability, be encouraged to tackle new tasks, be involved in complex interdisciplinary projects and life-linked studies—in short, contextualized learning.

As an illustration of how patterns and programs interact, Leslie Hart pointed out that the three-year-old who says, "Mommy, Jimmy hitted me," demonstrates how the child's brain has extracted the past tense ending pattern though the word "hitted" has never been heard. This remarkable achievement of the brain, erroneous as it is for an irregular verb, is surpassed by an even more amazing event. The brain self-corrects the wrong pattern with only the mildest suggestion from mommy when she says, "You mean hit." A grammar lesson on the past tense would not be nearly as efficient and probably would sail over the head of the child. The child's new speaking program will soon be, "Jimmy hit me." Two other key features support the development of patterns and programs.

Safety and Security

It seems readily apparent that a student racked by anxiety, uncertainty, or fear will not be an attentive learner. Clearly, for relaxed learning, the brain requires a sense of well-being and safety. Leslie Hart created the colorful term "downshifting," to describe the brain's response to danger as one of involuntarily shifting to preparation for fight or flight rather than openness to higher levels of thinking. It now appears that the brain blocks or shunts incoming data that threatens the person's security.

This explains why the child needs to feel safe and secure to learn. Schools must accept the child as a precious and honored person and provide a kind, orderly, safe environment. The brain does not function as well for higher level learning under threat or danger. In such settings, children will accept huge challenges, but at their own pace. If the student senses lack of trust or belief in them by the teacher, less learning is the result. The brain learns best under conditions of safety and security; and, if possible, joy.

Feedback

Feedback is how the brain determines if it is successful or unsuccessful. Students, indeed all human beings, need to know if they understand or misunderstand information. Through observation and what others tell us we receive feedback on our performance. The brain refines its patterns and programs through feedback. Every coach knows the danger of practicing the wrong action and not realizing its incorrectness. That would reinforce the wrong pattern or program in the brain and make it harder to eradicate. This is, of course, true not only of physical actions but also of thinking patterns, responses, and habits.

Feedback is the mechanism for the perfection of patterns and programs. Feedback in a practical sense means suggestions and coaching at all stages of development. Even champions have coaches! The feedback must be immediate and helpful. Reflection is a powerful form of self-feedback. Most classrooms give too little time to showing students how to improve, limiting feedback to test scores and grades. Students need to be coached, given suggestions, receive peer reactions, and see the results of their efforts in important endeavors, such as teaching a younger child arithmetic. A tutor sees if a child is interested and is learning. The tutored child receives real time, real life feedback so that adjustments can be made.

Learning can be defined, therefore, as the acquisition of patterns and the development of useful programs. This constitutes learning inside the brain.

See also: **Challenges and Enrichment; Classroom Environment; Mastery; Teaching Model for the Brain.**

Further Readings

Caulfield, J., Jennings, W. (2002). *Inciting Learning: A Guide to Brain Compatible Instruction*. Reston, VA: National Association of Secondary School Principals.

Diamond, M., Hopson, J.L. (1998). *Magic Trees of the Mind: How to Nurture Your Child's Intelligence, Creativity and Healthy Emotions from Birth through Adolescence*. New York: E.P. Dutton.

International Brain Research Organization www.ibro.org

Science Daily, Brain Center Searches for Patterns, www.sciencedaily.com/

JOAN CAULFIELD, PH.D.
AND WAYNE B. JENNINGS, PH.D.

Pedagogy

Active brain imaging techniques, advances in understanding of biochemical messengers, and the ability to analyze the function of single cells are radically and rapidly transforming our understanding of brain structure and function. We can look at which parts of the brain are engaged as learners perform different tasks. As the methodology advances, increasingly we will be able to pinpoint sequences of brain structures and processes engaged while complex cognitive tasks are performed. We are on the threshold of undreamed discoveries: We are actually beginning to watch thinking!

Contrary to protestations that brain science has not advanced to a point far enough to inform educators which instructional practices to use, active brain imaging studies do provide enough information to allow us to conclude with relative certainty that some instructional strategies align well with how the brain best learns whereas others do not. Using brain-friendly instructional strategies is like swimming with the current—students learn more, and teaching and learning are more enjoyable. Using instructional strategies that are incompatible with how the brain naturally learns is like swimming against the current— teaching and learning are more of a chore and students retain less.

Principles of Brain-Friendly Instruction

Brain-friendly instruction maximizes brain engagement, creates the conditions for optimal brain functioning, and provides the learning material in ways the brain is most likely to attend to and retain. The most important principles of brain-friendly instruction can be outlined as follows:

I. Creating Brain Engagement

II. Optimizing Brain Function

    A. Nourishment

    B. Safety

    C. Emotion

III. Providing Preferred Stimuli

    A. Social

    B. Novel

    C. Predictable, Meaningful

    D. Feedback

IV. Respecting Multi-Modal Processing

    A. Multiple Intelligences

    B. Multiple Memory Systems

Books can be written about each of these principles, so the discussion here necessarily will be brief and suggestive rather than comprehensive. Further, there are many ways to implement each of these principles. The Kagan Structures and instructional methods are aligned with how the brain best learns. Structures are relatively simple step-by-step teaching/ learning sequences designed to structure the interaction of learners with the academic content, with the teacher, and with each other.

Creating Brain Engagement

If the brain is not attending to or processing the content, little learning will occur. As obvious as this is, it is the most important of all principles of brain-friendly instruction. Instructional strategies that increase engagement with the content will increase learning.

Many traditional instructional strategies ignore this basic principle. For example, the traditional teacher wishing to create active engagement asks a question of the class. Several hands go up. The teacher calls on one. That student responds. At that moment, Broca's area is engaged in the student who is responding as the student formulates her/his response, but the brains of all the other students in the class are relatively quiescent. Using a simple structure, *Timed Pair Share,* the teacher can make the same content more engaging for all learners. In a *Timed Pair Share,* students interact in pairs, one speaking and the other listening for a specified time, and then students switch roles. Using *Timed Pair Share,* in the same amount of time that the traditional teacher requires to call on and respond to two or at most three students, every student in the class has verbalized an answer. *Timed Pair Share* is one of over two hundred carefully designed cooperative learning and multiple intelligences structures designed to maximize engagement among learners.

Active brain engagement is probably responsible for much of the well-documented gains produced by cooperative learning. Cooperative learning has an enormous empirical research base and the outcomes have been very positive, including student gains in academic achievement, social skills, race relations, classroom climate, self-esteem, and empathy. Cooperative learning consistently produces powerful gains in part because it more actively engages more brains than the traditional sequential instructional strategies. But as we will see, it relates to each of the basic principles of brain-friendly instruction in different ways.

It is important to note that simply asking students to talk or work together in pairs or groups will not lead to brain engagement and gains for all students. Group work is not cooperative learning. During unstructured interaction (group work), one or a few students can do most or all the talking; there is nothing to prevent a student from disengaging and allowing their partner or group mates to do all the talking or work. Only by carefully structuring the interaction can we be sure of engagement of all students.

Optimizing Brain Function

A. Brains Need Nourishment. Brains are small—they weigh about three pounds and are approximately the size of two fists put together. Although they account for only about 2 percent of our body weight, they consume up to 25 percent of the body's oxygen and blood glucose. When brain oxygen and glucose levels drop, so does brain functioning. Increasing the supply of oxygen and blood to the brain of students in a classroom increases student alertness, sense of well-being, and learning.

Bodily/kinesthetic structures involve movement and so help nourish the brain. Cooperative learning structures include movement, interaction among students, and hands-on manipulatives. Class-building structures all have students get out of their seats and move in the classroom. There are a host of brain-breaks and energizers that take only a few minutes but dramatically increase students' energy levels. The movement and interaction integral to cooperative learning increases breathing rate and volume as well as heart rate; which in turn increases the supply of oxygenated blood to the brain. Increased blood supply to the brain also increases the delivery of glucose, the primary nourishment that fuels cognitive activity.

Take Off, Touch Down is one of the simplest of all Kagan Structures. In this structure, students stand when the instructor says something true of them and sit if it is not true. For example, an instructor wishes to poll the class to see how many agree with four alternative actions our country can take in response to terrorism. Traditionally, we would simply have students raise their hands to indicate agreement. Using *Take off, Touch Down* the instructor announces each action and students stand to express their agreement. Everything is exactly the same except now students are using a total physical response rather than just raising their hands. Why bother with something as apparently silly as *Take off, Touch Down?* My physiology friends say there is approximately 15 percent more blood and oxygen in the brain after standing and sitting twice compared to raising one's hand twice! Thus, through the structures we choose, we actually nourish or fail to nourish the brain!

B. Brains Seek Safety. Our brains have evolved to help us survive. The amygdala fires far more in response to strangers than friends, more in response to those of other races than our own race. When the amygdala fires, our adrenal glands release the peptide called cortisol, which in turn triggers a string of physical reactions including tensing of the large muscles and increased blood pressure. Heightened firing of the amygdala is associated also with the release of adrenalin and sympathetic nervous system arousal, which predisposes us to fight or flight. This fight or flight defense alarm reaction is associated with a narrowing of the perceptual field, inability to perceive subtle internal and external cues, and a general constricting cognition that makes concentration on academic content difficult or impossible. The optimal state for learning is relaxed alertness, which is accompanied by parasympathetic nervous system arousal. Parasympathetic and sympathetic nervous system arousal are mutually antagonistic, so in the face of threat we "shut down." As our bodies prepare to meet a threat, we become narrowly focused on potential threats and less able to think broadly, creatively.

The negative effects of stress are not just temporary: chronically high cortisol levels lead to the death of brain cells in the hippocampus, a structure essential for laying down new memories. The hippocampus of Vietnam veterans suffering from post-traumatic stress disorder atrophied from 8 to 24 percent and was associated with impaired ability to recall old memories and lay down new memories.

Team-building, class-building, and community-building structures and activities are designed explicitly to create social safety. The class-building and team-building structures allow students to know and support each other and to accept individual differences. Through team-building and class-building, students drop their fear of social rejection and their worry about social acceptance—they are freer to focus on the academic content. No longer fearing rejection of their ideas, students are more expressive, offering and receiving feedback essential for learning.

For example, during a team or class discussion the instructor might use *Paraphrase Passport*. The rule is simple: The right to speak is earned by accurately paraphrasing the opinion of the person who spoke just beforehand. Because of this structure, every student knows his/her ideas will be listened to and validated, creating a caring, safe context for the exchange of ideas. *Paraphrase Passport* reduces the risk students experience for sharing a new or contrary opinion. Each student knows his/her ideas will meet a sympathetic paraphrase rather than an argument or put-down. This reduction of fear frees the brain for higher level cerebral functioning. Safe students think more clearly and more deeply.

*C. Brains Retain **Emotion**-Linked Stimuli.* Brains are exquisitely designed to respond to and remember stimuli that elicit emotions. There are receptors on the cell walls of neurons that respond to ligands, neurotransmitters, steroids, and peptides. Each receptor is a single very large, complex amino acid chain molecule—some approach 3,000 times the size of a water molecule. Seventy types of receptors have been identified to date, and each responds to only one type of ligand. For example, some receptors respond to opiates (endorphins, morphine, and heroin, which make us feel euphoric), others respond to stress peptides (like cortisol, which makes us feel stressed and anxious). A neuron may have millions of receptors on its surface, different numbers of different types—perhaps 10,000 of one type of receptor and 100,000 of another. Thus, a particular neuron may be quite sensitive to one type of chemical, but relatively insensitive to another. Just as our eyes and ears sense different types of stimuli in the external world, through the receptor on their cell walls, neurons sense different types of stimuli in the internal world of our bodies—emotional stimuli. Our brains are constantly bathed in these ligands and every neuron is responding to their presence or absence. From moment to moment in the classroom, we are changing the chemical composition of brains, releasing more stress peptides by giving embarrassing public feedback or releasing more endorphins by having students do a supportive teambuilding structure.

Why is sensitivity to emotions so crucial to brain functioning? Emotions are the primitive signals that keep us alive by motivating us to flee from being bitten or eaten, care for and protect our progeny, and hunt for a tasty morsel. It is elegantly argued by Antonio Damasio that the very origin of consciousness resides in the brain's capacity for emotion. The brain naturally focuses on and remembers stimuli associated with emotions. The ability to respond to and remember what produces pain, fear, and pleasure keeps us alive. As a nation, we pay huge sums to keep our emotional reactions in tune, if only by exercising them vicariously through spectator movies, sports, and drama. That which makes us feel, is remembered.

To better understand the link between emotion and memory, we need to take a brief detour into the nature of short-term and long-term memory systems. There is very strong evidence that short- and long-term memories are based on completely independent processes. It does not surprise us to hear we can have short-term memory without long-term memory. What is shocking, though, is to learn that we can actually have long-term memory without short-term memory. Contrary to our phenomenological experience, short-term memory does not turn into long-term memory. We have independent short-term and long-term memory systems! The long-term memory system takes a longer time to consolidate (we recall better after sleeping on it). This feature is very adaptive because it allows us to give more weight to and better remember things that are *followed by* positive or negative consequences, even if those consequences occur well after the event. Injection of certain drugs *following* learning enhances long-term (but not short-term) memory, a process called retrograde memory enhancement. Retrograde memory enhancement is adaptive: if emotion follows an experience, the brain says, "This is something worth remembering." Retrograde memory enhancement has important implications for us as teachers, indicating the need to teach with emotion. *A brain-friendly classroom is one in which emotions are not avoided, but rather elicited in service of learning.* Various cooperative learning and **multiple intelligences** structures link emotions to the academic content and help students understand and deal effectively with their own emotions and those of others.

In *Agree-Disagree Line Ups,* for example, students learn to take a stance depending on their feelings about an issue, and to listen with respect to opinions of other students who hold different feelings about the issue. The instructor simply states an opinion and the students line up to indicate the degree of their agreement with the opinion, strongly agree at one end of the line and strongly disagree at the other. Students then talk to those nearest them in the line to reinforce their position and to gain fresh arguments in favor of their opinion. The line is then folded so the strongly agree and strongly disagree students interact, often using *Paraphrase Passport.* In the constructive controversy that results, students find the content more memorable, and also learn to understand better their own emotions and those of others. Anything that elicits and allows students to deal effectively with their own emotions and those of others promotes emotional literacy and emotional intelligence while making the academic content more memorable. Many cooperative learning and multiple intelligences structures elicit and help students deal with the emotional component of curriculum and so are compatible with the finding that brains selectively respond to and remember any stimuli associated with emotion.

Providing Preferred Stimuli

A. Brains Attend to Social Stimuli. In a remarkable book, *Friday's Footprint: How Society Shapes the Human Mind,* Leslie Brothers makes the case that our brains have evolved to selectively attend to social stimuli. For example, babies at nine minutes of age are much more likely to turn their heads and eyes to follow a black and white picture if the parts are arranged to resemble a human face than if the same parts are arranged randomly. Single neurons of primates respond selectively and preferentially to social stimuli. Some neurons do not respond to an inanimate object moving, but do respond to a person moving; others do not respond to a geometric form, but do respond to a form resembling a hand—and the more the form resembles a hand, the more they respond! In *Mapping the Mind,* Rita Carter displays results of active brain imaging studies that show brains are dramatically more active when learning in interaction with others than when alone, reading or listening to a lecture. Opiate-like substances are released in mammalian brains during care giving and play, explaining why these activities are so rewarding. Our brains, to a remarkable extent, are social organs.

If we naturally attend far more to social stimuli, and our brains are more active during social interaction, it makes sense to have students interact regularly over academic content—having them discuss, debate, and work together on the content. Cooperative learning and multiple intelligences structures do exactly that.

For example, if rather than answering questions alone, the instructor uses *Numbered Heads Together* to have students respond to questions, students are far more engaged. In *Numbered Heads Together* students usually sit in teams of four, each with a number: one, two, three, and four. The instructor first asks a question. The students then think, write their individual responses, and discuss their responses in their teams. This social interaction provides the kind of stimuli that brains crave.

B. Brains Seek and Attend to Novelty. The **attention** systems in the brain are activated when novel or unexpected stimuli appear. We become more alert. We attend more carefully. The evolutionary basis for this is obvious: Those animals that did not become more alert when novel or unexpected stimuli appeared, did not survive to pass along their genes! Infants become bored, habituate, when presented with the same stimuli over and over; they instantly become alert when new stimuli are presented. One of the greatest sources of novelty is other people. When we interact with others there is always new and unexpected stimuli. Part of the reason we find it so rewarding to interact with others is because we become more alert and engaged in the face of the novel stimuli they present.

Cooperative learning and multiple intelligences structures are compatible with the brain's need for novelty in two ways: First, by changing structures on an ongoing basis, the instructor is always creating novel stimuli in her/his classroom—quite in contrast to the instructor who always lectures or only uses any other single mode of instruction. Second, the structures involve interaction, and social interaction is a primary source of novel stimuli. The input and feedback of a peer is often unpredictable and so provides novel stimulation. Students are encouraged to use new and unexpected praise, and to use different gambits as they interact to keep the stimulation high. Students in classrooms in which the structures are used regularly report the classes to be more "fun." In technical terms students are telling us that structures respond to the brain's need for a regular flow of novel and unexpected stimuli!

C. Brains Seek Predictable Patterns and Meaning. Seeking patterns is one way we make sense of the world; it is related to our need for safety. For some students, a classroom is not safe unless there are predictable routines. At birth infants show a startle reaction to novel stimuli, but quickly habituate; they are seeking patterns and forming expectations. In a classic experiment babies are presented with a ball that rolls down an incline and hits a miniature bowling pin, making a loud noise as the pin falls over. The infants show a diffuse startle reaction for several trials but on subsequent trials they simply watch with little excitement. However, when the apparatus is rigged so the ball hits the pin and there is no loud noise, the babies once again show a startle reaction. The pattern is broken; the world is no longer predictable; the babies fixate, searching to make meaning of this novel set of events. We are meaning makers. With no instruction babies learn to make sense of these funny sounds we emit called words. They convert the buzzing confusion of visual stimuli into familiar objects and predictable relations among objects.

The structures respond to the need to establish patterns and make meaning in two ways: First, the structures themselves are a predictable sequence of events. Once the students know the steps of a structure like *Numbered Heads Together,* they feel secure because they know exactly what is coming next. Second, a number of structures are explicitly designed to help students discover patterns in stimuli. This of course, facilitates learning because facts learned in isolation are soon forgotten; facts that are part of a coherent whole, which have meaning, are retained. Making meaning goes beyond seeking patterns; it involves examining relationships, relating stimuli to other stimuli and categories of stimuli, and constructing conceptual models.

One of the many Kagan Structures designed explicitly to help students make meaning of the academic content is *Team Mind Mapping*. There are many forms of *Team Mind Mapping*, but a very simple form is to have students in teams, each working with a different colored marker, create one large Mind Map of the content. They begin by putting the main idea in the center of a piece of chart paper. They draw lines out from the main idea and write or symbolize core concepts. Supporting details are added to the core concepts. Use of colors, pictures, symbols, arrows, and other graphic elements offer more ways of organizing information and creating meaning than does the traditional outline. Further, in the process of negotiating agreement on how to construct the mind map, the students are more likely to discover patterns and construct meaning than if they were to work alone. Constructing meaning by processing and interacting over the content, revealing patterns and connections, makes the content memorable. This, in part, is why structures improve academic achievement. The structures are brain-compatible because they assist the brain in its natural search to construct meaning. Instruction that promotes identification of patterns and construction of meaning is brain-friendly instruction.

*D. Brains Seek **Feedback***. The hundred billion neurons in the brain each fire not as a simple function of the amount of input they receive, but also as a function of how other neurons in the past have responded when they fired! There are feedback loops even at the neuronal level. Our brains are feedback hungry. The search for feedback is biologically rooted in our need to be an effective organism, to satisfy our needs, and to make a difference. A brain-compatible classroom is feedback rich.

The search for feedback is related also to the search for meaning. In our search for meaning, we try something and then check to see if it works. All of us are scientists from birth, conducting mini experiments to see which behavior produces which consequences.

Traditional individual worksheets or individual assignments are feedback poor. Students do not get feedback until the next day, or until after the instructor has graded the papers. But the brain seeks immediate feedback. Mastery structures like *RallyCoach* provide immediate peer feedback and are brain-compatible; they are aligned with the brain's need to receive frequent and immediate feedback.

RallyCoach is simple. Students work in pairs solving a series of problems or answering a series of questions. Student A in the pair solves or answers the first question, talking through the solution as they write it. Student B, watches and listens, and then either praises (if the answer is correct) or coaches (if A needs help). Then the students reverse roles. Student B solves or answers the second problem while A watches and listens, and then either coaches or praises. Students continue alternating roles as they work through the series of problems.

There are many advantages to *RallyCoach* over individual worksheet work, including immediate rather than delayed feedback, frequent rather than infrequent feedback, peer-based feedback, immediate and frequent reinforcement, and peer support and coaching. Students who might otherwise practice a whole worksheet wrong get immediate correction opportunities and have the opportunity to immediately practice the correct skill. Feedback-rich instruction and practice meets the basic need of all humans—to have what they do make a difference. We all need positive feedback.

Respecting Multi-Modal Processing

This last principle, respecting the ways brains process information, is the most complex. Brains are mini-modular and process different types of information with different subsystems. For example, when we engage in deductive reasoning, areas of the right hemisphere are engaged; when we engage in probabilistic reasoning, left hemisphere areas are more engaged. Further, there is almost no mutual engagement: One type of reasoning does not depend on another! To take another example, when we are asked to determine if one object is above or below another, we are categorizing objects with regard to where they are in space. This kind of categorical spatial reasoning is associated with left hemisphere activation. In contrast, when we are asked if the two objects are more or less than two feet apart, we engage in coordinate spatial reasoning that is performed in the right hemisphere. Single neurons respond to certain kinds of stimuli and not others; neuron groups are dedicated to different types of information processing. We recognize a table because of the functioning of our object recognition system; we recognize a face with face recognition neurons that are part of an entirely independent information processing system. As our understanding of brain structure and process increases, we discover the brain is incredibly differentiated, with different systems and subsystems responsible for processing different types of information. All consciousness and complex cognition is assembled.

Given the enormous complexity of the brain and the way it processes information, we might be tempted to say that inferences about the usefulness of classroom instructional strategies based on how the brain processes information are indeed "bridges too far." Nevertheless, there are a number of inferences that can be made with a great deal of certainty. The two we will examine here are the need to use multiple intelligences instructional strategies, and the need to address multiple memory systems.

A. Multiple Intelligences. Howard Gardner defined eight intelligences: verbal/linguistic; logical/mathematical; visual/spatial; musical/rhythmic; bodily/kinesthetic; interpersonal/social; and intrapersonal/introspective. Because engagement of each intelligence is associated with activity in different brain structures, we are actually developing different parts of the brain when we teach in ways that engage the various intelligences.

Brain plasticity can be summarized by the *use it or lose it* principle. The brain is constantly rewiring itself depending on which parts of the brain are frequently used and which fall into disuse. For example, when a blind person touches Braille dots, neurons in the *visual* cortex respond. As the visual cortex is not used, but touch is frequently used, the brain of the blind person rewires itself to make use of the unused parts of the brain. When a finger is amputated, within a few months neurons that received input from that finger are receiving input from surrounding fingers. Thus, it is not too much of a stretch to conclude that by using otherwise unused intelligences we are actually rewiring brains—developing parts of the brain that otherwise would be under-developed.

By engaging a range of intelligences through a range of multiple intelligences structures, we not only appeal to a far greater range of learners, we actually develop otherwise underdeveloped parts of the brain. Schools have implemented multiple intelligences theory in different ways and the academic and nonacademic outcomes have been extraordinary.

There are eighty-four established multiple intelligences structures, each designed to engage and develop different intelligences. For example, *Kinesthetic Symbols* is a simple structure in which learners use their hands to symbolize the content, often creating a sequence of hand movements to remember items in a sequence, like the steps of a math algorithm, the parts of a letter, or the steps in the scientific inquiry process. For example, when *Kinesthetic Symbols* are used, parts of the pre-motor and motor cortex are engaged in association with the content. This provides an alternative way to symbolize the content, makes the content more attractive and understandable to kinesthetic learners, and develops the kinesthetic intelligence.

B. Multiple Memory Systems. The brain remembers different types of information differently. For example, learning to ride a bike (**procedural memory**), remembering what we had for dinner last night (**episodic memory**), and remembering a list of unfamiliar vocabulary words (**semantic memory**), involve quite different memory systems. Procedures are usually learned by trial and error, with plenty of practice. Episodes are often remembered effortlessly, with little or no conscious intent, especially if they have an emotional component. Formal memory systems such as peg systems and other mnemonics can facilitate semantic memory. Semantic memory that is not related to a meaningful context can be quite difficult, but if semantic memory is embedded within memorable episodes, it can become effortless. Different structures are designed to address different memory systems. For examples, the *Flashcard Game* addresses semantic memory; *Simulations* address episodic memory; and *RallyCoach* addresses procedural memory.

Just as the brain processes different information differently, individuals process the same information differently and have preferences for how best to remember information. One student may remember information easily by using a memorable visual image, a second student might be more comfortable with a peg system, a third may need to draw the content, and yet another student may find making kinesthetic movements to be the most helpful. Because students have different preferred ways of processing information, using a range of structures is the approach most likely to reach the most students. As there are different brains in each classroom, we need a range of instructional strategies.

Toward a Brain-Based Pedagogy

As brain science continues to reveal how brains function, it will be increasingly clear which instructional strategies align with how the brain best learns and which do not. This in turn will allow us with increasing confidence to develop a brain-based pedagogy. Increasingly, we will align our instructional strategies with the findings of brain science and in the process transform how we teach and how students learn. At this point, however, we can say with confidence that teachers will be more successful with instructional strategies that include safety, movement, social interaction, emotion, novelty, predictable patterns, meaning, feedback, and with strategies that engage the multiple memory systems and the multiple intelligences. When we align our instruction with how the brain best learns, students not only learn more and learn more easily, they acquire a love of learning in the process.

See also: **Feedback; Patterns and Programs; Social Learning.**

Further Readings

Brothers, L. (1997). *Friday's Footprint. How Society Shapes the Human Mind*. New York: Oxford University Press.

Campbell, L., Campbell, B. (1999). *Multiple Intelligences and Student Achievement. Success Stories from Six Schools*. Alexandria, VA: Association for Supervision And Curriculum Development.

Gopnik, A., Meltzoff, A.N., Kuhl, P.K. (1999). *The Scientist in the Crib*. New York, NY: William Morrow.

Kagan, L., Kagan, M., Kagan, S. (1997). *Cooperative Learning Structures for Teambuilding*. San Clemente, CA: Kagan Publishing.

Kagan, S. (2000). *Silly Sports and Goofy Games*. San Clemente, CA: Kagan Publishing.

Kagan, S., Kagan, M. (1998). *Multiple Intelligences. The Complete MI Book*. San Clemente, CA: Kagan Publishing.

Marzano, R.J., Pickering, D.J., Pollock, J. E. (2001). *Classroom Instruction that Works. Research-Based Strategies for Increasing Student Achievement*. Alexandria, VA: Association for Supervision and Curriculum Development.

McGaugh, J.L. (2003). *Memory and Emotion. The Making of Lasting Memories*. New York: Columbia University Press.

SPENCER KAGAN, PH.D.

Physical Environment

The human brain is wired to be sensitive to the surrounding environment for signs of threat. When its attention is drawn to a perceived threat, the brain's ability to learn and remember new information may be minimized. In classrooms, real or imagined threats may be from a combination of social interactions, academic challenges, or physical elements. In the last thirty years neuroscientists have also shown that the brain's capabilities can be enhanced when it is exposed to novel, meaningful, interesting multi-sensory stimuli in a comfortable physical environment. Reducing student **stress** and creating enriched learning environments should be educators' first considerations.

Effects on the Brain

Physical survival and safety are the brain's primary goals so we are on constant alert and guard against possible harm. When we feel threatened, intimidated, not included, confused, incompetent and physically unsafe the brain shifts into survival mode. The brain sends chemical signals throughout the body and we go into the "fight or flight" reflex response. Even the anticipation of a stressful or dangerous situation can trigger the hypothalamus and amygdala to release an immediate overabundance of neurotransmitters such as cortisol and adrenaline. Heart rate, blood flow, breathing, and muscle strength increases, while the immune system, digestive systems, sex drive, and the ability to carefully process new information, diminishes. The brain focuses on immediate survival issues rather than on learning and storing new memories.

In addition to this rapid first response to threat, the brain also responds with a slower reflective response. We analyze the situation, connect the new stimuli to past, related experiences and plan appropriate responses. We try to detect recognizable patterns in the event. This can assist us in predicting what might happen next and determine an action we might take to avoid it if necessary. The greater the variety of effective problem-solving strategies we can draw upon, the more likely we are to override the stress reaction with reasonable solutions and thoughtful actions.

Students' interpretation of perceived threats in a classroom environment regulates their abilities to learn and think. While new learning often involves some stress caused by an element of risk and some degree of pressure, if the stress exists in an otherwise low threat environment learners can be motivated to try new and difficult tasks without ridicule or a lack of support. Memory is enhanced by an appropriate degree of stress and our ability to remember things may be interfered with if the stress is really intense and prolonged.

In addition to the potential negative effects of too much stress, educators can enhance learning by orchestrating a wide variety of multi-sensory experiences in an enriched environment. Neuroscientists have stated that by creating deliberate enrichment in the learning environment educators can promote brain growth and development. Studies reveal that input from the environment actually helps shape the human brain. Many studies suggest that by paying attention to the details of the physical learning environment educators can enhance learning and ultimately, students' success at school. When we learn, amazing changes take place in the brain. How a teacher goes about structuring learning experiences will affect the strength and duration of those changes. When assessing a physical environment for learning or play, one should consider the possible negative effects on the learner from physical elements, perceived social and emotional threats or restrictions. Orchestrating a developmentally appropriate enriched environment may include aesthetics, comfort, meeting basic needs, organization, and orchestrated experiences.

Potential Physical Harm and Distractions

A safe learning environment is largely influenced by physical attributes in the classroom. There can be negative effects on the learner's body from elements such as poor lighting, noise and acoustics, and air quality. Many other distractions can occur in classrooms such as inappropriately sized furniture, interruptions, and clutter.

Lighting

A learning environment with a lack of natural, full-spectrum lighting, and a dependence on fluorescent lights, has possible adverse effects on students' vision, general health, growth rates and concentration levels. In several studies fluorescent lights have been linked to triggering headaches, mild seizures, attention disorders, and hyperactivity. The flickering vibration of the light quality and the audible hum may contribute to the detrimental effects and add to distractibility. Research indicates providing full-spectrum bulbs can increase calcium absorption, lessen visual and physical fatigue, improve visual acuity, and decrease hyperactivity.

Carol Venolia, an architect interested in how buildings affect quality of life, emphasizes the need for people to get outside and be exposed to sunlight on a daily basis. Some people are particularly sensitive to the shortening of daylight in winter and suffer from SAD (Seasonal Affective Disorder). Symptoms include lethargy, carbohydrate cravings, being sedentary, weight gain, and avoiding social interactions. When we do not see the sunlight for extended periods of time we can become disoriented about the time of day and even lose a sense of direction. These same symptoms can be seen in people who have a lack of exposure to full-spectrum light.

First and foremost educators should utilize natural day lighting whenever possible. New buildings designed with the brain in mind should include windows on one or two walls, skylights, and provide overhangs or blinds to allow each teacher more control over the direct sunlight. Optimum lighting should include more ambient light produced from indirect sources (usually reflected off of the ceiling). This type of lighting is appropriate in classrooms using lots of technology and in commons areas. Task lighting and accent lighting can combat monotony, enliven spaces, and provide adequate light for specific activities and breakout areas.

Noise

Research studies on sound and noise in classrooms have determined that constant exposure to loud noises, "white" ambient noise, and a poor acoustical environment can hamper learning in a variety of ways. We rarely escape noise and the sound level is often physically harmful. High noise levels interfere with conversation, reading, thinking, or listening to music; just about everything that could contribute to our well-being. Sudden loud noises are registered by our bodies as warning signals and can trigger the reflex response. In addition, classrooms are often bombarded with constant white noise from air conditioning and heating systems, computer stations and monitors, overhead projectors, and light fixtures. Even students with normal tolerance levels and attention spans often have difficulty filtering out this ambient noise and complain of being fatigued, having headaches, and not being able to concentrate.

If unable to eliminate it, educators can try to mask background noise by playing soft music or introducing a small fountain or fish tank to produce some environmental sounds. Use area rugs on the floor and fabric or tapestries on walls to help soften as many hard surfaces in the classroom as possible to improve acoustics. Teachers should orchestrate a variety of times during the day for quiet reflection or silent reading and studying. Many schools emphasizing brain compatible strategies have also placed restrictions on intercom interruptions and when outdoor maintenance (such as leaf blowers) can be used around classrooms.

Air Quality and Temperature

A classroom that is either too hot or too cold may be uncomfortable to students and distract from learning. Students may be groggy or sleepy if the room is too stuffy. Good airflow and a constant room temperature of 68–72 degrees have been reported to enhance learning for most students. Consider using a room ionizer to enhance the air quality.

Aromas—Introduce some scents to make the classroom pleasant smelling. Using mild lavender, lemon, cinnamon, or peppermint aromas can reduce anxiety and encourage attention.

Visual Stimulation and Clutter—In some classrooms, teachers let the massive amount of materials, resources, and student examples become unorganized and overwhelming. There is a great concern for what the surrounding environment is teaching. While an enriched environment is conducive to learning, a cluttered classroom can harbor massive amounts of dust, mold, and even critters. The visual stimulation may be too distracting to many students. An interesting and challenging environment should not bombard young brains with too much of a good thing. Poor physical conditions in classrooms can have a negative effect on student learning and behavior and can promote absenteeism and vandalism. It is believed that approximately one-third of all public schools in the United States were in need of extensive repair. As we examine student success, and orchestrate high standards, the physical learning environment must become a greater priority.

Restrictions and Limitations

Being able to satisfy basic needs is a necessary survival strategy, and if not attended to in a timely manner, can disrupt the learning process. When students perceive that water, food, and even bathroom breaks will be limited, they may have anticipatory anxiety about when those survival needs can be met. Fresh water should be easily accessible. Scheduled times to eat healthy snacks should be consistent. Reasonable restroom breaks should be allowed.

The size of the physical classroom can have an influence on students' brains. When there is more space, teachers can design a variety of flexible areas. Smaller meeting and individualized work areas allow students to seek out comfortable safe places to work and get help. Different places for active and passive learning activities decreases rigidity and provides some choice for students. Physical activity is essential in promoting brain growth. Schools need less restrictive spacious areas where students can move. In addition to attending to form and function, the scale of the classroom design and furniture needs to be body compatible. When desks and chairs are not ergonomically correct it can affect health and cognitive functions.

Social and Emotional Threats

Bullies, "put downs," lack of inclusion, and confusion can all contribute to an insecure learning environment. Educators must attend to building a sense of belonging so that students feel supported and cared about within the classroom community of learners. Adult help and supervision should be highly visible. A high priority should be on the development of systems and procedures that alleviate ambiguity and confusion. When students know what the agenda is and what the expected behaviors are, they are able to attend to learning rather than worrying about what they should (or should not) be doing.

Enriched Environments

Brains are known to grow and develop when exposed to an enriched environment. In addition to basic needs being met and a steady source of positive emotional support, there are many qualities that teachers and parents can deliberately orchestrate. Children should have opportunities to choose from a variety of age-appropriate novel challenges. Adequate materials and resources need to be available that are appropriate to the developmental and language needs of the learner. Children should have experiences to develop mental, physical, aesthetic, and emotional skills as well as have many opportunities for social interactions. Perhaps most importantly, brain compatible classrooms should be environments that allow children to be active participants and promote exploration and the joy of learning. Enriched learning environments give children a chance to make mistakes without ridicule, assess their own results of their efforts, and to modify and try again. Deliberate enrichment includes activities that are fun, interesting, and exciting to a child. They provide challenge and stimulation and require active involvement.

Keeping kids, and their brains, feeling safe and secure has to be our first and foremost goal if we want to maximize learning. Professionals need to understand the difference between classrooms and brain-compatible learning spaces. Schools should be designed that meet the curriculum needs of students, as well as be "teacher friendly" schools. School planners should be concerned about safety and security, plenty of natural light, manageable circulation (movement) patterns, aesthetic designs, appropriate scale, access to the outside, and flexible spaces. These modifications can be made to the physical environment by providing low threat, comfortable settings where challenging tasks, curiosity, and engagement abound.

See also: **At-Risk Behavior; Attention; Challenge and Enrichment; Classroom Environment; Emotion; Proactive Classroom Management. Teaching Model for the Brain.**

Further Readings

Clayton, M.K., Forton, M.B. (2001). *Classroom Spaces That Work*. Northeast Foundation for Children, Greenfield, MA: Stenhouse Publishers.

Jensen, E., Dabney, M., Markowitz, K., Selso, K. (2003). *Environments for Learning*. San Diego, CA: The Brain Store.

Kaufeldt, M. (2005). *Teachers, Change Your Bait! Brain-Compatible Differentiated Instruction*. Norwalk, CT: Crown House Publishing.

Le Doux, J. (1996). *The Emotional Brain*. New York: Touchstone.

Sylwester, R. (2000). *A Biological Brain in a Cultural Classroom*. Thousand Oaks, CA: Corwin Press.

Wolfe, P. (2001). *Brain Matters: Translating Research into Classroom Practice*. Alexandria, VA: Association for Supervision and Curriculum Development.

Burch, L. (Architect and Vice President 3D/I). "Brain Compatible Learning Environments" www.3di.com

Diamond, M. Ph.D. (Neuroscientist UC Berkeley) Brain Connection www.brainconnection.com/topics/?main=conv/diamond

Fielding, R. (Educational planner and architect) "Lighting the Learning Environment." www.DesignShare.com

Lackney, J.A. (Professor, University of Wisconsin-Madison, architect) www.engr.wisc.edu/epd/faculty/lackney_jeffery.html
Tanner, C.K. Ph.D. School Design & Planning Laboratory, The University of Georgia www.coe.uga.edu/sdpl/sdpl.html

MARTHA KAUFELDT, M.A.

Physical Movement

Neuroscience supports the link of physical movement to learning. Important aspects of physical movement increase learning: preparing and developing the brain for learning, being physically fit to learn, and reinforcing cognition using movement designed to rehearse and anchor learning. The physical condition of the body and the way the body moves affects the way the brain thinks. The brain and body connect to navigate the environment by predicting, planning, and executing physical movements. The brain uses this framework to sequence, order, practice, and rehearse cognition. Being physically active prepares the brain for learning by increasing oxygen and glucose to feed the brain nutrients and by integrating, organizing, and energizing key components of brain function through physical activity. Learning academic concepts kinesthetically through physical movements using games, activities, and lessons reinforces memory and retrieval and allows the student to rehearse the learning in a non-threatening environment.

Physical Movement and Brain Development

Brain development corresponds to and depends on physical movement as body and brain systems connect from infancy to adulthood preparing the brain for cognition. Proper functioning, enrichment, and remediation of these systems are critical to a child's ability to learn.

Physical movement activities are designed to develop necessary components that enhance whole brain learning and to access the parts of the brain that may be otherwise underdeveloped. Each component is important to build the framework for learning. These components are described in the following passages.

Vestibular Activation and Spatial Awareness

The vestibular and cerebellum systems (inner ear and motor activity) are the first systems to mature. These two systems work closely with the reticular activation system (RAS system) located at the top of the brain stem and is critical to our attentional system. These systems interact to balance, turn thinking into action, and coordinate moves. Physical movement activities like rolling, jumping, and spinning stimulate inner ear motion. These movements aid the brain in putting numbers or letters in sequence, discriminating different sounds, placing letters and words on a page, and writing letters in proper proportion. For example, a series of vestibular balance exercises similar to those found on a typical playground during recess helped dyslexic students to improve reading skills at a greater rate. The results were said to be the closest thing to a cure yet.

Cross Lateral Movement

Crossing the midline of the brain and body facilitates neural activation allowing the brain to process information efficiently. Information in the brain travels back to front across the motor cortex, side to side across the corpus callosum, and up and down from the brain stem to the top of the frontal lobe. The action of crossing the midlines lays the framework for learning. Mastering crossing the midline can facilitate the ability to see words and letters on the page, track and trace letters and words, group like objects and organize thoughts.

Motor Skill Development

The brain uses its motor skills as a framework for learning. Motor skills enable the brain to put patterns into sequence. There are three basic human motor movements: walking (crawling is the prerequisite), rolling, and jumping. These basic motor skills simulate the way the information flows in the brain: walking sends information back to front, rolling sends information side to side, and jumping sends information up and down in the brain. When motor skills are mastered, the brain has the ability to put letters into words, numbers in sequence and groups. The motor skill of skipping signals reading readiness, indicating that the brain has mastered putting mature motor patterns into a complicated, coordinated sequence.

The cerebellum is the part of the brain instrumental in physical movement and motor skills. It is the brain region that controls balance, coordination, and agility and is also instrumental in the reading process. The cerebellum has one-half of the brain's neurons even though it is only one tenth of the brain's volume. Brain imaging shows that most of the energy from the cerebellum is output and not input. Physical movement and motor activity initiated in the cerebellum is preceded by quick thought that problem-solves, plans, and executes the movement. This ability of the brain to put patterns into an ordered sequence builds the framework for the brain to puts patterns like letters or numbers into an ordered sequence. Physical movement connects the brain and body to rehearse tasks needed for cognition.

Sensory Integration

The physical movement skills of spinning and rolling and jumping integrate the visual, auditory, and kinesthetic systems. The senses are enhanced and coordinated as students move through space at different levels, speeds, and positions. The central nervous system matures from the center of the body out to the extremities. Joint compression while jumping activates and develops the nerves along the extremities as students bounce on a hoppity hop or jump and land. This coordination of bodily systems prepares the brain to coordinate, and organize thoughts.

Eye Tracking, Ocular Fitness Exercise, and Peripheral Vision Development

Vision is affected in early brain development when physical movement is impaired causing inadequate peripheral vision function. A critical period of vision development is in the first six months of life. Some infants are kept in baby carriers or car seats for long periods of time and not given equal time to lie on their stomachs. This inhibits the ability of the infant to lift his/her head to look around to develop muscles needed for vision development.

The lack of eye fitness affects the ability to read. The average American child watches a TV or computer screen on an average of three hours a day. The prolonged staring locks the eyes into a state of constant distant vision and the muscles that control eye movement may begin to weaken. Physical movement provides an avenue for specifically strengthening eye muscles. Tracking exercises, manipulatives, navigation activities, and target games exercise the eye muscles making the eyes fit to read.

Physical Movement and Physical Activity

When humans exercise, the body/brain goes into a homeostatic state, balancing brain chemicals, hormones, electricity, and system functions. When the body/brain is out of balance because of poor nutrition and lack of physical activity, the student is not in a good learning state. Movement, physical activity, and exercise change the learning state increasing one's ability to retain or retrieve memory. The beneficial effects of physical activity may last for a thirty to sixty minute period depending on the student.

Neuroscientists recognize that students who exercise do better in school, lifelong fitness boosts brain function, movement anchors learning as more of the senses are involved, and that which makes us move is also what makes us think. Numerous studies support the link of movement and physical activity to cognition.

Exercise Grows New Brain Cells

Running and other aerobic activity promotes brain cell regeneration (neurogenesis) in the hippocampus learning and memory center. A Japanese study suggested that daily exercise can increase memory retention because exercise strengthens secondary dendritic branching, the brain's mechanism to remember details.

Exercise Boosts Brain Function

Exercise triggers the release of a brain-derived neurotropic factor (BDNF) that enables one neuron to communicate with another. Students who sit for longer than twenty minutes experience a decrease in the flow of BDNF. Educators should provide physical movement opportunities during the school day for a brain break, for consolidation and review of concepts, and to motivate students to learn.

Exercise Reduces Stress

Mental stress and anxiety can rob the brain and body of adequate oxygen by interrupting normal breathing patterns. However, studies also indicate that exercise can enhance oxygen flow, thereby reducing heart rate and anxiety. Aerobic activity releases endorphins—the class of neurotransmitters that relax us into a state of cortical alertness and reduce the symptoms of depression.

Vigorous Exercise Helps ADHD

Vigorous exercise helps students with ADHD to focus attention longer and self monitor behavior. Exercise puts the brain into optimal function and its positive effects lasted thirty to sixty minutes depending on the student.

Lifelong Fitness Makes the Young and Aging Brain More Resilient

Physical movement in the form of aerobic exercise actually slows the decline of brain density in white and gray matter areas of the brain as we age. Among older adults, aerobic exercise (activities such as walking, jogging, running in place and jumping jacks) helps preserve white and gray matter density in the brains frontal, temporal, and parietal cortexes, areas vital to higher-order thinking.

Fitness Levels Correlate with Student Achievement Levels on Standardized Tests

A 2002 California study shows that physically active kids perform better academically. The statewide study provides compelling evidence that the physical well-being of students has a direct impact on their ability to achieve academically. The results indicate that students achieve best when they are physically fit.

Proper Nutrition Improves Performance

Participation in school breakfast programs is associated with significant improvements in academic functioning. Missing breakfast may be associated with reduced cognitive performance. Schools with proportionately large numbers of students who engage in weekly physical activity and who ate nutritiously have higher Academic Performance Index scores. Good physical health improves grades, school attendance, and school success.

Investing in the health needs of early childhood students has profound effects on school readiness and early learning. Secondary students who reported recurrent health problems also reported school failures.

Recess/Play Can Increase Attention

The brain needs recess. The brain shifts its attention and focus about every ninety minutes. Even a short break from focused concentration allows the brain to consolidate information for better retention and retrieval of memory. Using physical movement in the classroom gives the brain that opportunity.

The play process uses methods of observation, visualization, communication, imagination, creativity, cause and effect, and problem-solving. Play helps to create mental pictures using different perceptions that will aid in reading and writing concepts. In play situations children often operate beyond their average age mentality or behavior. Social skills are increased among players. Using physical movement in play creates a healthy, imaginative non-threatening environment to try out higher level thinking processes.

Physical Movmement and Learning

If students learn through movement, then how does that translate to classroom practice? Teachers can incorporate activity and physical movement by using kinesthetic teaching strategies to teach academic concepts. Some of the activities may be short brain breaks that increase blood flow to the brain, while others reinforce concepts without breaking the flow of the lesson. In the same way that classroom teachers use movement to anchor learning in the classroom, physical educators integrate academic content using physical education concepts to put learning into action in the gym. Students find meaning and purpose in the learning as teachers build bridges from the classroom to the gymnasium and vice versa. For example, as the physical educator works on motor skill development, the teacher may see improvement in reading or spelling.

An example of a kinesthetic activity is "Action Punctuation" used to reinforce punctuation concepts in a fun way. Students work cooperatively to create an action and a sound for each punctuation mark. As the teacher reads a story, the students use the whole body to act out the punctuation marks.

Another example is reviewing geography map skills. Students use body mind mapping to represent a globe. They raise the right hand to represent North America, touch the nose to represent Europe, raise the left hand to represent Asia, touch the waist to represent Africa, touch the right knee for South America, touch the left knee for Australia, and waddle like a penguin to represent Antarctica singing the continents to the tune of "Are You Sleeping?"

The physical and cognitive systems interact to anchor learning. Physically fit students are more receptive to learning and physically fit students who move to learn have an advantage in learning. When healthy active students use physical movement to understand concepts, the concepts are better learned and remembered because they are processed using the whole body and the whole brain. Activity time in the classroom and reinforcement of academics in the gym involves the whole child in the learning process and does not sacrifice precious instructional time. Accordingly, schools should provide time during the school day for exercise, physical activity and movement by providing recess and physical education and add time for kinesthetic activities in the classroom. The evidence is clear. Exercise helps the brain to grow and learn and a large majority of students learn best kinesthetically.

See also: **Early Childhood Brain; Physical Environment.**

Further Readings

Ayres, J. (1996). *Sensory Integration and the Child.* CA: WPS Publishing.

Blaydes Madigan, J. (2000). *Thinking on Your Feet.* Murphy, TX: Action Based Learning.

Dennison, P., Dennison G. (1986). *Brain Gym* (Teacher's Edition). Ventura, CA: EDU-K Publishing.

Jensen, E. (2005). *Teaching with the Brain in Mind* (2nd ed.) Alexandria, VA: ASCD publishing.

Action Based Learning www.actionbasedlearning.com

JEAN BLAYDES MADIGAN

Play

One of the most intriguing questions in the study of the brain is how the play of children affects their brain development. It is well known that young animals of many species engage in play, including human young. Indeed, play is such a pervasive characteristic of children that it is the topic of many books and education texts, and its many forms have been observed in numerous research studies. While play decreases with maturity in many animal species, in humans, play extends throughout life in various forms. Researchers have seen both animal and human play as adaptive for the species; thus, the brain must be involved in this behavior. Exactly what the connections are between play and the brain is only beginning to be explored.

Many psychology theorists (e.g., Piaget; Vygotsky) have speculated on the value of play for children's development and have described ways play seems essential not only for physical development but also for the development of cognition, language, social skills, emotional regulation, and creativity. Conversely, in the formal educational system, play has often been considered an unimportant or even meaningless activity, and it is rarely included in the curriculum of the school. Recently, however, neuropsychological researchers are speculating that youthful play may be a major enhancer of brain development. Although some studies of human brain development are beginning to focus on the relationship between play and the brain, the majority of current neuropsychological research connecting play and brain development has focused on non-human animal play.

For example, animal researchers have noted that the proportionate size of the brain (in relation to an animal's overall size) is related to the amount of playful behavior observed in various species. The greater the proportion of the body devoted to the brain, the more extensive and long lasting is play in that animal species. The human animal plays more extensively, longer, and in more complex ways than do the other playful species, and of course, the proportion of overall size taken up by the brain in humans is extremely high in childhood and even in adulthood. Neuropsychological research on play now being conducted with animals suggests that during rough and tumble play (the typical play of many animals) neurochemicals associated with pleasure and excitement in humans are increased. These researchers are speculating that play may activate many parts of the animal brain and stimulate the growth of nerve cells. Play may be especially important in fostering the development of the frontal lobe. In brain imaging studies of children diagnosed with ADHD, there appear to be delays in the development of frontal lobe areas that are involved in inhibition of action, planning, and conceptualization of complex tasks. One researcher has hypothesized that these children's active behavior may be signaling a need for a longer period of rough and tumble play and that when children are given drugs that inhibit this activity the development of their frontal lobe may be further inhibited. Another type of evidence for the connection between active play and brain functioning is found in the studies of effects of school recess on children's ability to attend to school work. This body of research indicates that having an active play period at recess enhances later attention to school tasks.

Although neuroimaging studies have not yet demonstrated the specific neurological connections between play development and brain development, a comparison of these two areas of development certainly suggests that they are related. For example, in infancy the neurons of the brain are only beginning to be connected in networks. The connecting process (synaptogenesis) proceeds rapidly during the first year in the sensorimotor area of the brain. This is also the age period when sensorimotor (practice) play is most extensive. Infants explore textures and sounds, manipulate objects, and perform increasingly elaborated actions in their play. By six to eight months, when frontal lobe development begins, social games such as "peek-a-boo" become a major form of play. As frontal lobe synaptogenesis increases, children's play becomes more diverse and involves social interactions. Other areas of the brain that are developing during the toddler age include the language areas (Broca/Weirnicke), and as these areas develop, play with the sounds and symbols of language becomes extensive. The areas of the brain that are active sites of emotions (amygdala/limbic system) also gain more connections with the frontal lobe, and at this time, toddlers begin to exhibit pretense in caregiving behaviors, such as "feeding" a doll. In early childhood (age three to eight), which is the fastest growth period for the frontal lobe networks, a corresponding ability to think logically in concrete ways is observed. Children at this age engage in extensive and very complex pretend play, taking varied roles and wearing elaborate costumes to play out extended scripts for "superman" or "doctor's office" or "school." Through their play they demonstrate how elaborate their symbolic thought processes have become and they show their ability to self-regulate and work cooperatively with others. As the maturation of the brain continues during middle childhood and adolescence and pruning occurs, speed and efficiency of thought increases, planning and problem-solving skills increase, and scientific reasoning and metacognition are achieved. Play during this age period becomes increasingly sophisticated and symbolic, with pretense themes continuing for extended periods, symbolic board games and computer games becoming popular, and play that has elaborate rule systems being preferred. One view of why play continues to be an activity throughout life is that play serves to keep the frontal lobe networks active when survival-related problem-solving is not needed. That is, the rich networks in the frontal lobe are designed to deal with crises that might affect survival. In a society where such crises are less evident, play serves as a way to create challenges that keep humans prepared for action of more serious types. Older children and adults engage in symbolic games such as Monopoly, sports-related play such as golf or mountain-climbing, and socially acceptable forms of pretense through use of computer-aided virtual realties or actual role-taking in little theater. With maturity, play may still have an important role in keeping the brain active and preventing deterioration of the neuronal networks. Some studies of senior citizens are beginning to show that maintenance of brain functioning can also be enhanced through playful activities and thinking games (e.g., crossword puzzles).

Although understanding of the specific ways that play aids brain development await more neuropsychological research, and because play development and brain development seem to have many parallels, enhancing children's play skills and giving many opportunities for play is likely to be useful in helping the brain develop well. At present, there is no research that points to specific play or creative activities, such as listening to Mozart, as being especially useful to the brain. However, there are many aspects of play that are likely to enhance brain development. The most important role that play has is to help children to be physically and mentally active, to have control and choices, to solve problems, and to practice actions to mastery. Until more is known about how specific types of play might enhance particular brain structures or functions, a variety of play experiences in a wide variety of content areas is probably warranted because these will be important for the development of a complex and integrated brain. Play that links sensorimotor, cognitive, and social-emotional experiences together really provides an ideal setting for brain development. Here are some suggestions for extending play's role in enhancing children's brain development.

For infants and toddlers, the play environment should provide many safe and easily manipulated toys and other objects that are accessible to the child. Objects that encourage development of the sensorimotor areas of the brain are especially important. For example, toys with an interesting variety of sounds, shapes, sizes, colors, and textures will give young children motivation to be active and this will involve activity also in the brain. Often the best play objects for young children are adults and older children, who initiate social play, demonstrate ways to use these objects, and encourage variation and elaboration of object play. Having a variety of objects that activate sensorimotor and language areas of the brain and increasing the complexity level of toys as children grow older, will enhance the synaptogenesis process. Similarly, language, social, and emotional interactions with other people in play will help activate the brain centers related to these capabilities.

During the preschool and early elementary years, the time of greatest pretend play, having many opportunities to engage in pretense is especially likely to enhance development in higher brain centers. Providing adult models of symbolic actions and pretend roles while labeling those actions and emotions can help children expand the variety of their pretense. In peer play, provision of the time, space, and materials needed for complex and extended scripts and roles is likely to promote the development of the higher brain centers. Synapses in the frontal lobe are likely to be activated when children follow self-designed scripts and take roles that require self-regulation and problem-solving abilities. As children's pretend play skills increase, their pretense can be enhanced with books, writing, and other symbolic materials, which will be incorporated in their play.

As pruning of synapses in the brain becomes more extensive during later childhood, the pruning process may be affected by the types of play in which children most frequently engage. Playing games with rules that require higher order thinking processes, involve negotiation and problem-solving, and promote self-regulation skills are important as brain processes become more efficient. Children's processing will be slower than adults because pruning and myelination of neuronal networks are still occurring. One of the types of play that extends from childhood into adulthood is play involving symbolic games, and often it is evident how such play promotes the capability of using the control processes of the frontal lobe. In early adolescence, children's choices of play activities become more focused and intense; this may be a result of the pruning activity of the brain.

While at one time it was believed that neuronal and synaptic development ended in adulthood, some studies indicate that the brain is capable of developing new networks and strengthening existing networks throughout life. Such activity may be highly related to new and enjoyable experiences—that is, play. Thus, opportunities for play should continue throughout life to preserve creativity and innovative thought. There are now many creators of games and other play activities for adults, some of them utilizing computers and some promoting interaction through board games. There are a number of recent games specifically promoted for enhancing or maintaining effective brain activity during adulthood. In sum, play and brain functioning are related throughout life.

See also: **Early Childhood Brain.**

Further Readings

Bergen. D. (2003) *Play's Role in Brain Development.* Olney, MD: ACEI.

Bergen, D. (2002). The role of pretend play in children's cognitive development. *Early Childhood Research & Practice [Online], 4*(1). Available: http//ecrp.uiuc.edu/v4n2/bergen.html

Panksepp, J. (1998). Attention deficit hyperactivity disorders, psychostimulants, and intolerance of childhood playfulness: A tragedy in the making? Current Directions in Psychological Science, 7(3):91–98.

Pellegrini, A., Bjorklund, D.F. (1996). The place of recess in school: Issues in the role of recess in children's education and development (Introduction to theme issue, J. Johnson, Theme Coordinator.) *Journal of Research in Childhood Education* 11(1): 5–13.

Siviy, S.M. (1998) Neurobiological substrates of play behavior: Glimpses into the structure and function of mammalian playfulness. In M. Bekoff, J. Byers (Eds.), *Animal play: Evolutionary, Comparative, and Ecological Perspectives.* New York: Cambridge University Press.

http://www.cranium.com (board game for adult play)

DORIS BERGEN, PH.D.

Pleasure and Love

It is becoming increasingly clear that early sensory experiences and environments have a definite impact in determining the foundational organization and capabilities of the brain. How we experience pleasure and love plays a key role in the brain's response to its environment as well as how the brain will interpret future interactions and relationships. These early experiences define and lay the foundation for motivation, energy, and joy throughout life.

The areas of the brain that are responsible for pleasure and love will be examined. In addition, we will discuss what factors trigger the pleasure pathway of the brain as well as the implications for school success.

The Limbic System and The Pleasure Pathway

The brain's pleasure pathway was discovered in the 1950s by James Olds. He inserted electrodes into the limbic system of rat brains. The electrodes were connected to a bar that sent a small charge of electricity to stimulate the pleasure pathways of the rat brains. The research showed that the rats would push the bar nonstop. So often in fact (up to 5,000 times an hour) the rats went without food, water, and sex until they collapsed from exhaustion.

Every brain has an area that responds to pleasure. The pleasure pathway, located in the limbic system, makes us repeat behaviors by giving us charges of emotional energy that range from powerful highs and satisfaction for doing a good job to powerful lows that cause depression, anxiety, and impulsiveness.

The limbic system is the emotional seat of the brain and responsible for our social world. It is where we learn to make friends, bond with our primary caregivers and handle our anger. The limbic system is located in the center of the brain and is about the size of a walnut. This area of the brain is also thought to store extremely charged emotional memories. The brain makes associations from a specific event and generalizes that event to other situations. Hearing the growling of a saber tooth tiger and its association with danger should only take one experience. However, the generalization from the embarrassment caused by one teacher is stored and processed over numerous years. This experience then provides the context for that student to feel anxious in all or many learning environments. An experience in the classroom can trigger a strong emotional response to the past experience, thereby causing the student to re-live that past experience of being embarrassed by a teacher. This process of association and generalization literally can alter the way future experiences are perceived and processed.

The pleasure pathway is fueled by neurotransmitters and endorphins with dopamine playing a key factor. When a human experiences pleasure, these neurotransmitters and endorphins are released into the pleasure pathway of the brain and our emotions take over.

Powerpacked with functions critical to human behavior and survival, the limbic system's functions include the capacity for problem-solving, planning, organization, and rational thought. These functions correlate directly to the early sensory experiences that define what gives us pleasure, passion and the emotional desire to complete a task. It is largely developed by the age of four years and is dependent upon our early experiences with primary caregivers. It is in these experiences that we define pleasure.

The pathway is involved in movement, cognition, **emotion, motivation,** and **addiction.** There is a direct link between the brain chemicals and the physical and emotional sensations of the body, for example, the experience of different states of euphoria through praise, finding a dollar, sex, laughter, alcohol, and drugs, and even the chemicals found in chocolate.

Research has suggested that if these pleasure pathways are not stimulated or do not receive differing amounts of pleasure, we can become depressed, bored, function poorly, or die. The brain needs positive interactions to function appropriately. Activities that stimulate the pleasure pathways can be both positive and negative and include eating, drinking, sex, drugs, and anything else that gratifies us. For example studies show that animal and human babies who do not receive appropriate amounts of nurturing and physical touch after birth have stunted growth and may even die.

The brain develops through sensory experiences: touch, taste, smell, sight, and sound. Whether it is pleasurable or not, we learn through our experiences and interactions. Imagine how the loving touch of our primary caregiver translates to the desire and passion to do well on a spelling test. It is the pleasure of external feedback that translates to internal motivation. We have to have pleasure and stimulation from daily activities put into our bodies to power our brains to think, interact, and engage with others. Without these experiences the brain experiences a pleasure deficit that translates to depression and a lack of drive to complete a task, learn, or engage with others.

The brain wires itself in the context of relationships. These relationships build the neuronal networks that interpret how we will interface, connect with, and relate to others. We are pleasure-seeking creatures that need the joy, touch, and love of others to sustain both our physical and mental health.

Experiencing love outside the family and learning mating rituals is considered a normal part of adolescence. Some neuroscientists and educational psychologists hypothesize that the teenage years are the **critical period** for learning these skill. Typically, boys and girls experience their first puppy love at age ten and it is thought the brain, not hormones, initiates this happening.

Further evidence of the brain's role in love can be seen by research conducted at University College London. Scientists performed neuroimaging on the brains of young adults who were in love. Pictures of boyfriends or girlfriends were shown to participants while their brain was being scanned. At the sight of their love interest four regions of the brain lit up—the medial insula, associated with emotions, the anterior cingulated gyrus, involved in feeling good, and the putamen and the caudate nucleus related to positive experiences and addiction.

As was mentioned earlier, dopamine plays an important role in feeling pleasure, so it is no surprise it is involved in love. When an individual falls in love dopamine is released, and a person feels satisfaction, contentment, and joy. The brain interprets these positive emotions associated with love as a reward and wants the feelings to persist so it pursues the stimuli, love.

Love is only one of many strong emotions students experience. A teacher's praise, the classroom bully, or the smell of crayons can elicit a strong emotional response. The pleasure pathway in the limbic system provides the filter through which we interpret the events of the day. Sensory stimulation is the nutrient that is essential for normal growth, development, and brain functioning. Positive experiences matter; they define and frame what will drive and motivate us, and ultimately what we find pleasurable.

Humans do not learn only with their minds. Some psychologists believe as much as 80 percent of human learning is unconscious and registered through sensory and emotional neural pathways. The brain relies upon specific learning behaviors and possesses specific beliefs regarding learning, challenges, problem-solving, and motivation based on the surrounding sensory experiences.

Implications

Experiencing pleasure is key in motivating children to learn. Experiences such as hunger, lack of appropriate feedback, the wrong temperature, uncomfortable seating, unsuitable learning styles, and flickering lights cause students to lack feelings of pleasure, thus creating an environment not conducive to learning. The learning environment must meet the needs of every student and provide experiences that elicit pleasure.

Reward is another component that should be considered when discussing pleasure and learning. As discussed previously, the brain produces its own internal rewards. Because the brain does produce its own rewards, it raises the question of the effectiveness of external rewards. Educators have observed that external rewards are effective with some students and ineffective with others. Every student responds differently to external rewards based on genetics, life experiences and brain make-up. Research has demonstrated that students who receive external rewards for a job well done will expect an increasingly valuable reward every time they do a good job. Therefore, external rewards withhold lasting pleasure for the student.

To provide an environment that elicits pleasure, experiences need to be nurturing, comfortable both emotionally and physically, nonthreatening, and intrinsically motivated. As educators, it is imperative that we treat students with respect and encourage them to discover the pleasure and intrinsic rewards of learning. Teachers have the opportunity and the responsibility to provide students with the fuel to seek pleasure in learning by motivating, praising, and recognizing students as the individuals their brains have defined them to be.

See also: **Emotion; Emotional Intelligence; Depression; Stress.**

Further Readings

Kotulak, R. (1997). *Inside the Brain: Revolutionary Discoveries of How the Mind Works.* Kansas City, MO: Andrews McMeel Publishing.

Ratey, John J. (2001). *A User's Guide to the Brain: Perception, Attention, and the Four Theaters of the Brain.* New York, NY: Pantheon Books.
Corante Brain Waves http://www.corante.com/brainwaves
International Brain Research Organization www.ibro.org

LYNETTE POOLMAN AND
LAURA CRAWFORD, MA.

Poverty

Poverty affects millions of students each day in the United States. It is a risk factor impacting one in five children, making it a serious and pervasive school issue. Poverty is defined as an income below $19,350 in 2005 for a family of four. This economic status has a high incidence of unemployment, violence and neglect, substance abuse, and homelessness. The culture of poverty impacts school success in a variety of ways, academically and behaviorally. Educating children of poverty requires meeting basic needs first and then tending to educational requirements.

The Brain and Poverty

Babies are born with approximately hundred billion brain cells. During the first year of life the human brain develops quickly and is eager to learn. The hardware, neurons, is present at birth, but the software, massive dendrite production and synaptic connections, is yet to be developed. Experiences, both positive and negative are the primary influence in creating these neural networks. Poverty undermines the quality and number of experiences an individual has and so impedes brain development. Medical care, safety, nutrition, maternal depression, stress, substance abuse, and violence are additional remnants of poverty that impact the brain throughout the lifespan.

Educators and child care providers have long been aware of the importance of early language activities and rich experiences in developing cognitive skills and thinking patterns. Now neuroscience is providing insights that confirm this viewpoint. Unfortunately, an impoverished environment is not conducive for growing dendrites and making synaptic connections. Children born into poverty are immediately at a disadvantage; their mothers tend to have less prenatal care, putting them at risk for birth complications. The expense of medical care continues to haunt them into adulthood, as they are frequently not able to afford proper medical attention. Not only is their physical well-being problematic, but the emotional setting is complicated. These infants' and children's mothers are often dealing with depression. The children of depressed mothers have more stress hormones and receive little stimulation. The lack of interaction between infant and mother inhibits cognitive growth as does the activation of stress hormones.

In addition, parents living in poverty tend to be less equipped with parenting skills. This results in reduced social interaction between parent and child, which limits language growth. The intermittent language the children are exposed to tends to be simply structured and does not exhibit higher order thinking skills such as critical thinking, problem-solving, and synthesis. Homes are often not equipped with computers. Visiting science museums, parks, and libraries are a rarity. The majority of preschoolers in poverty do not attend preschool and quality child care is lacking. All of these experiences have the potential to add to cognitive growth. The lack of initial neural networking makes academic readiness an issue. The less you know, the more difficult it is to learn new information. In other words, the more dendritic branching and synaptic connections an individual possesses, the easier it is to produce more.

The amygdala and hippocampus work together to store memories. The aymgdala is the emotional center of the brain and the hippocampus plays a major role in storing memory. The hippocampus identifies the person or event and the amygdala interprets how we feel about it. The involvement of the amygdala allows emotional experiences, good and bad, to easily be stored in long-term memory.

Unfortunately, the primary emotions children in poverty experience are fear and stress. When the brain is under intense stress it is more difficult to pay attention, learn, and retrieve information. The person feels helpless and takes no academic risks, all creativity is hindered. When individuals are under chronic stress cortisol is released into the system. One of the effects of cortisol is a reduced immune system, making not only the cognitive system shutdown, but also the physical.

Dopamine is the neurotransmitter that helps us feel happy, motivated, and attentive. The body releases it when we feel good about something such as winning the race, seeing a good friend, or eating a delicious meal. Unfortunately, fear of failure, isolation and trauma, often present in poor children, causes dopamine to be converted into norephinephrine. Norephinephrine energizes an individual and under adverse conditions results in aggression and agitation. This makes it difficult for the individual to tolerate frustration and stress. Students may become belligerent or apathetic. In school this is the student that flies into a rage over a simple comment such as, "Where's your homework?" or falls asleep during class.

Serotonin, a calming agent, is naturally produced in the body. Low levels are associated with depression and low self-esteem and conversely high levels are associated with tranquility and positive self-esteem. Poverty has been correlated with depression and low self-esteem. Researchers have found that individuals in poverty have less serotonin in their bodies, contributing to feelings of unrest and agitation.

Nutrition goes first to vital organs, then to muscle and skeletal growth, and finally to cognition. The more poverty an individual faces, the lower the nutritional value in their food. Nutrition delivers a two-fisted punch to the brain. First, people in poverty are not receiving the necessary nutrients to support cognitive growth. Second, chronic stress, frequently found in poverty, prevents the body from properly absorbing the nutrients which then inhibits the growth of dendrites and synaptic connections.

Basic Needs

Resources most people take for granted are not present in an impoverished environment. Basic needs such as food, physical and emotional safety, and community connections are all in jeopardy. The theorist Abraham Maslow's groundbreaking research brought to the forefront the understanding that basic needs must first be met before learning can take place.

Too often children in poverty come to school hungry. To counter this, federal hot lunch/breakfast programs provide free and reduced meals for low-income families. Teachers may act as facilitators, encouraging and assisting families in receiving and filling out the necessary forms for these benefits. Food feeds the brain and gives the students the edge they need for optimum learning. But it is not just the physical that needs to be tended to in the lunchroom. Creating a pleasant atmosphere by greeting students and letting them know their absence is missed conveys the message that you care about their mental as well as their physical well-being.

The homes and communities where poor children sleep are not always safe environments. School may be their one safe haven. Feeling threatened can produce emotions of depression and anger. Teachers need to be attentive to these emotions and help students press through or diffuse these feelings so the focus can be on education.

Teachers need to provide a community in which all children can learn. Living in poverty can isolate a family and student. Nurturing a class where everyone feels like they have a place and purpose gives courage to students. A sense of belonging is created by using competition carefully and promoting noncompetitive group activities, offering academic support outside the classroom, and getting to know each individual and their interests. Realizing that many students need added support outside the school, teachers can act as a liaison with community and school services. Community health and dental clinics are available in most counties, cities, and states. Bringing in the school nurse to share hygiene and good health practices can influence the home life for children.

Some students are parents themselves, trying to raise a child of their own. Connecting them to the Special Supplemental Nutrition Program for Women, Infants, and Children, better known as WIC, can provide necessary nutrition for the entire family. School in-house daycare may make the difference between teenage moms dropping out of school or continuing their education. Keeping the parent and the child close together and available for nursing and noon-time meals create an incentive to stay in school.

Finally, the dream for higher education often seems impossible for students of poverty. Teachers can connect their students with career counselors and college representatives. Oftentimes students who have nothing expect nothing. They are unaware of how to navigate the post-secondary scene. Knowing how to apply for technical schools or four-year colleges and availability of student loans and grants is outside their radar screen. A high school diploma is no longer sufficient to support a family of four. A high school dropout is expected to make $16,000 annually, a GED $18,000, and a high school diploma recipient $20,000; all incomes at or below the poverty line. The reality is that in this age of information students need an advanced degree. A one year post-high school program acts like an economic rocket, propelling an individual above the poverty line.

Educational Needs

Families in poverty are often transient; frequently moving from place to place. Children are enrolled and re-enrolled in different schools throughout the course of their K-12 education. Each move creates a learning gap. For instance, one school may be in the midst of teaching long division while the next has already completed this unit. Therefore, the child has missed a fundamental concept. Teachers can not make assumptions about the academic background of a student that has frequently moved. Identifying where the student is and then providing ample opportunities to learn and practice missed skills is necessary. Regular review of all major concepts provides an educational framework that is beneficial for all students. At the same time a curriculum totally based on repetition and drill will quickly lose interest for students and motivation to learn will cease. A balance must be found.

Poverty creates absenteeism. For example, the car breaks down, younger siblings need to be watched or parent(s) or guardian may need to appear in court. Teachers need to be prepared for the academic inconsistencies this presents by having the day's assignments available and attainable. Be flexible whenever possible; explore alternative ways for assignments to be completed that will be practical for the students' erratic lifestyles. When dealing with at-risk students, understanding is important, but pity is misdirected. This is a time to assist and support their success. Hold all students accountable and provide clear guidelines for absences.

Common knowledge, prior knowledge, and background knowledge is often lacking for poverty students. Language and literacy-rich classrooms provide an academic setting for learning. Real vocabulary, not just lists of words to be defined, boosts their academic foundation. Crossword puzzles, sharing current events and numerous field trips will bolster background knowledge which is the springboard for continued learning.

One of the best practices for meeting the needs of all students is differentiated instruction. This consists of giving students multiple options for learning and showing their academic progress. Differentiated instruction provides students with curriculum that best meets their ability to grasp the concepts being learned. Most lessons can be adapted to meet the specific learning level of all students in the classroom. Because of the gaps in education and the need to scaffold the learning of students born and living in poverty, differentiated instruction can provide the necessary elements in the learning cycle: instruction, content, and product.

Meeting basic needs first and then meeting educational needs will nurture and encourage students disadvantaged by poverty. Teachers can then provide an equal and fair chance at an education that may break the cycle of poverty. Poverty is not destiny.

See also: At-Risk Behavior; Beverages; Nutrition.

Further Readings

Banks, J.A. (2006). *Cultural Diversity and Education* (5th ed.). Boston, MA: Allyn and Bacon.

Kozol, J. (2005). *The Shame of the Nation*. New York, NY: Crown Publishers.

Payne, R. (2005). *Framework for Understanding Poverty*. Highlands, TX: aha! Process, Inc.

Poverty and Race Action Research Council http://www.prrac.org

SHERYL FEINSTEIN, ED.D. AND
EVIE J. BROUWER, M.A.

Prenatal Brain

The prenatal brain develops in three basic ways: the expanding basic structure of brain regions, multiplication and pruning of individual neurons available for synaptic connections, and finally, the wrapping of an insulating myelin sheath around the axons allowing transmission of electrochemical signals that produce abilities and functions.

The sensory pathways available for systematic stimulation are limited in utero, but are demonstrably effective according to scientific studies. Stimulation effects during the prenatal period can be profound (a result of nature plus nurture, rather than Nature vs. Nurture). For example, Wolfgang Amadeus Mozart grew up in the home of the premier music teacher in all of Europe where lessons were given and live music was performed daily during his prenatal period. Mozart had both musical genes and a musical environment from conception, along with a loving mother and an eight-year-old big sister who practiced the keyboard daily. The prenatal brain is plastic and is fashioned by the environment either accidentally or intentionally.

Growth and Development

Prenatal care, including examination and supplemental nutrition are essential. The building blocks of the brain are protein for essential amino acids, beneficial fats (Omega-3) for fatty acids and myelin, carbohydrates for glucose, and oxygen. Enzymes and neuro-growth factors guide these basic brain-building nutrients, along with vitamins and minerals, to specific construction sites. Nutritional deficiencies cause the body to take nutrients from the mother's body tissue to supply fetal needs.

Neuronal growth increases at phenomenal rates to more than 100,000 cells per minute in the ninth month. Cells are overproduced and then pruned, with about one-third of the cells trimmed in the final weeks prior to birth. Certain cells physically migrate up to a millimeter in the cerebral hemispheres unless disturbed by alcohol, at which time organization and symmetry of cell formations are scrambled and disconnected. By contrast, babies born to mothers addicted to crack cocaine have normally constructed brains but with extreme oversensitivity to environmental stimuli.

The prenatal brain is plastic and subject to influences beyond merely adding growth weight. Prenatal stimulation studies were conducted by Brent Logan, and Rene Van de Carr, and Marc Lehrer, beginning in the 1980s. The processes are simple and somewhat mechanical. The impact of repeated stimuli over days and weeks has immediate and long-term implications for cell organization and later preferences, abilities, and behavior. Principles of prenatal stimulation are those universally applied in childhood: systematically increase the frequency (how often), intensity (how loud, how fast, how strong), and duration (at least twenty seconds or longer). Soothing stimulation shuts down cell activity while arousing stimulation increases electrical activity at an exciting level to produce growth and development. Regular, daily, systematic stimulation establishes and maintains connections and expectations. Stimulation should always be at pleasant (but exciting and challenging) levels.

Insulation of neuronal axons in the spinal cord begins in the fifth month with the process of upward myelinization. The myelin sheath allows cells to conduct electro-chemical activity through axons to dendrites, producing the first reflexive physical movements in response to sensory stimuli. The myelin (Schwann cell) is a beneficial form of cholesterol that wraps around the axon, becoming thicker with increased stimulation to facilitate faster and more efficient transmission. The spinal cord and axons are fully covered by an initial myelin wrap at birth and the visible functions of a newborn derive from the extent of the progression of myelin. The medulla is also myelinated to some extent at birth.

Fetal brain functions at eleven weeks involve only slight movements of arms and legs, and some slight abdominal reflex. With the beginning of spinal cord myelinization, by eighteen weeks the functions include differential movement of arms and legs easily felt by the mother, thumb sucking and face scratching, motions of crying, reception of sounds, opening and closing of hands, and movement of lips and tongue. By twenty-eight weeks, survival of premature birth is possible because the spinal cord is myelinated sufficiently to produce function and reflexes, including extensive physical movement and reactions, sucking, grasping, sound startle, and opening and shutting of eyelids. Prenatal stimulation is possible through vestibular, auditory, and vibratory senses. At full term of thirty-eight weeks the spinal cord is fully myelinized, producing light, sound startle, grasp, foot Babinski, sneeze, Moro, and asymmetrical tonic neck reflexes.

Once myelinization has begun in the spinal cord, reception of stimuli and motor responses become evident with kicking reflexes in response to sound and movement. Mothers have reported that the fetus can habituate to a time schedule in which movement is expected at certain times of the day and kicking can indicate desire for stimulation.

Primitive reflexes are established in the spinal cord prenatally and are available and visible at birth, including the Moro, sound startle, asymmetrical tonic neck reflex (ATNR) (fencer arm extension), Babinski big toe extension, grasp reflex, rooting reflex, pupillary reflex, sucking reflex, and many more. The fetal position is a flexor position and reflex actions are extensor reactions. The newborn is a bundle of primitive reflexes at birth as only the spinal cord and medulla are myelinated and operational. The ATNR is considered to assist in the movement through the birth canal. The Apgar rating at one and five minutes following birth includes the nasal sneeze irritability for tactile sensitivity, cry for respiration effort, pink skin color for circulation, and active motion of all limbs.

Systematic procedures for prenatal nurture of brain development are well-known and accepted for active stimulation by parents. Interoceptors are the physical/biochemical emotional senses of fear, anger and joy; proprioceptors are internal bodily sensors of balance and vestibular swinging/spinning movements, and exteroceptors include the prenatal sound and touch senses.

Biochemical nurture is produced through aerobic physical activity by the mother that increases oxygen supply to the fetal brain; wholesome nutrition provides nutrients, including calcium for bone-building and neuronal synapses, a variety of proteins for amino acid production and healthy fats for production of myelin; spring water rather than caffeine and sugar drinks for hydration and evacuation of toxins; the joyful and secure mother habituates the desirable happy parasympathetic acetylcholine biochemical state in the fetus.

Sensory nurture utilizes the myelinized and available exteroceptors by playing pleasant loud music in the environment or through earphones on the mother's abdomen, loud talking and reading to the fetus, playing tapes of foreign languages, dancing/moving to loud music, swinging, twirling, singing to the fetus, and touching the foot as it kicks. The sounds heard by the fetus are similar to those heard while swimming under water so the speech must be louder and intentionally pleasantly lilting, happy, and playful. The sound of the mother's heartbeat is a constant rhythmic stimulus. Recognition of specific parent and sibling voices has been observed at birth by the newborn turning the head toward the familiar voice. Quieting of crying has been observed when familiar prenatal music is played. A variety of auditory stimuli are produced, including those produced by the preferences of the mother including singing, humming, talking, talking on the telephone, environmental sounds (ticking clock, animals, traffic), music, songs, reading to the fetus, birds, instruments during music lessons or practice. Movement choices include spinning, dancing, swaying, swinging, sliding, upward/downward, acceleration, deceleration, and vigorous rocking. Effects of stimulation are noticeable in the infant and produce enthusiasm for nurture in parents and siblings.

Threats to the Fetus

At conception, the developing brain is dependent on the health of the egg and sperm, influenced by the prior **nutrition** of each parent and limited exposure to toxins and/or other substances, including medications, radiation, and allergies. The presence of genetic threats from family heredity, toxic exposure, aging mother, and Rx factor (blood type incompatibility) suggests seeking genetic counseling to determine the probability of a positive pregnancy. Toxic threats include alcohol, nicotine, drugs, tobacco smoke, exposure to toxins from building materials and home chemicals, ambient tobacco smoke, caffeine from chocolate, coffee, and tea, and the obvious heavy metals such as mercury and lead. Agricultural pesticides and herbicides, plastics (vinyl), wood treatments, construction and carpet installation compounds, radon and fuel gasses, traffic fumes are also possible threats to the fetus.

Following conception, the neural tube forms during the first weeks, eventually becoming the spinal cord and complex brain levels and regions. The placenta acts as a barrier for some toxins, and as the brain develops, the blood–brain barrier increases defense against toxins. The brain is vulnerable in spite of these barriers, however, including threats of alcohol, rubella, toxoplasmosis parasite from cats, tobacco, and nutritional deficiencies such as folic acid/folate (causing spina bifida). Natural chemical threats include negative maternal emotions precipitating habitual sympathetic autonomic nervous system stressors of fear and anger/frustration (high epinephrine and norepinephrine states) and estrogen effects on males. Negative effects of anesthesia, ultrasound, and radiation have been noted. Avoidance of biochemical and emotional stress at birth is accomplished by using spinal block in place of anesthesia and low-stress birthing such as Lamaze, LeBoyer, water birthing, and a pleasant delivery room,

Premature birth (low birth weight) is implicated in numerous difficulties, including learning problems, cerebral palsy, health problems, dyscoordination and impaired intellectual development. Diet and supplementation are especially important; lack of omega-3 fats (canola, fish, flaxseed, olive oils) have recently been linked to prematurity. The effects of poverty on pregnancy and delivery result from convergence of several variables producing increased proportions of prematurity. African American premature births, for example, are at twice the rate of premature births in Africa because of the high American poverty rate and malnutrition. In the United States about 8 percent of births are premature with more than 15 percent of low birth weight births being African American children. Miscarriages, at 30 percent of conceptions, are much more common than previously thought, and indicate chromosomal abnormalities in half the cases.

The prenatal brain has plasticity and is eager to learn. We have a unique opportunity to begin creating an active and responsive brain before birth.

See also: **Beverages; Fetal Alcohol Syndrome; Gender Differences; Infant Brain; Music.**

Further Readings

Fleming, A.S., O'Day, D.H., Kraemer, G.W. (1999). Neurobiology of mother-infant interactions: Experience and central nervous system plasticity across development and generations. *Neuroscience Behavioral Review* 23(5):673–685.

Jefferis, B., Power, C., Hertzman, C. (2002). Birthweight, childhood socio-economic environment and cognitive development in the 1958 British birth cohort. *British Medical Journal* 325:305–308.

Logan, B. (1992). Prelearning; trials and trends. *International Journal of Prenatal and Perinatal Studies* 4:67–69.

http://www.asoundbeginning.com

http://www.ecobaby.com

http://www.thesmartbaby.com

LYELLE L. PALMER, PH.D.

Proactive Classroom Management Strategies

Fear, apprehension, discomfort, lack of understanding, and loneliness: just a few of the emotions students battle daily when entering the classroom/school. Consciously or unconsciously, our emotional reactions determine our behavior, our health, our learning, and our memory of past experiences. Emotions literally drive attention, learning, memory, and how we go about the day: emotion is the gatekeeper to learning and performance. Creating a brain-compatible classroom and school is within our reach Providing a safe and predictable environment, consistency and continuity, adults as role models, common expectations of personal interactions, and a commitment to meaningful curriculum that leads to responsible citizenship will make a difference in the lives of our students.

The past twenty-five years of research into the physiology of the human brain have provided an abundance of vital information relevant to educators. A most consistent message is the enormous and all-encompassing power our emotions have in every aspect of our lives. This information is critically important to educators as they facilitate and orchestrate effective learning communities. Creating a positive and productive emotional tone in our schools and classrooms is a number one priority for academic achievement. Both the physical space of the school/classroom and the personal interactions within that space contribute to the overall emotional tone.

Creating the Space for Learning

The effects of space on our emotional wiring can be illustrated by the difference between walking through Disneyland, a space uniquely orchestrated for enjoyment and efficiency; and walking through a carnival midway with people yelling for our attention and a cacophony of sounds coming from many directions. Our bodies respond to each space differently. The goal in a school is to create an academic learning space that is safe and predictable, both in the design of the classroom and in the interaction of all those in the building.

The emotional and visual appeal of a learning community begins when parents and students approach the building. The outside of the school provides the invitation and the school entryway reflects what we think of our clientele. We all have had the experience (feeling) of knowing ahead of the actual experience that something was good or bad. You never get a second chance to make a first impression. A school should welcome and invite students and their parents into the building. Adequate signage directing students and parents to their destination alleviates worry and confusion. Evidence of the mission of the school in language that is understandable and specific provides confidence that the educators in the building are committed to the task of educating the students in their charge. The academic content goals and the social skills necessary to accomplish these goals, clearly displayed, allow a measure of confidence for those who enter, stating that a successful and productive learning experience is expected here and that the educators have the necessary knowledge and skills to reach that goal.

Solid academic achievement can be orchestrated when all adults in the building recognize the power of a safe and predictable environment and work toward establishing consistency and continuity for all students, thus allowing the brain to stay focused on the learning at hand. The teacher sets the tone at the classroom door by greeting students and calling their attention to the entry procedures. Being well planned and organized allows students to have confidence in their teachers as they direct their attention to the learning goals of the day. It is clear to the students the decisions for which they are responsible. Decision-making, both personally and within the group, leads to independence and a sense of authonomy, important in building positive self-esteem.

Creating the Climate for Working Together

A classroom, by design, illustrates the expectation for the year, both socially and instructionally. A productive learning environment provides physical and emotional space for learning to occur. It is free of clutter, toxins have been removed, it is well ventilated, well lit, has ambient temperature, and the furniture is appropriate for the age of the students. A healthful and aesthetically pleasing setting contributes to a relaxed and positive learning environment. The room must reflect a conscious intent for collaboration. Furniture is arranged in clusters so students can interact in learning groups and have a support group. Their materials are within close reach so they do not have the distraction of having to leave their desks. Group procedures clearly state the expectations of how to best work together in a variety of situations. Written procedures provide detailed guidelines about how to go about daily activities. They are used to describe what to do when you enter the room, go to the library, the restroom, recess, what to do when you have finished your work, how to head your paper, and how to work in a group. A copy of the procedures is placed within each cluster, freeing the teacher from answering the same questions countless times, while building confidence and responsibility in the students, thereby providing another level of consistency.

To assist students in mentally preparing for their day, a daily agenda is clearly visible for all students to read. A daily agenda defines the flow of the day and the personal responsibilities of the students and the teacher. A yearlong curriculum theme posted in a prominent location indicates the curriculum content for the year. Meaningful curriculum includes activities that are emotionally engaging, academically challenging, community based, and that lead to responsible citizenship. By implementing agendas and themes, students need not worry about the direction of their learning as they can readily see the big picture of how all aspects of the classroom come together to create a meaningful learning experience.

Creating Classroom Behaviors for Learning

In orchestrating a brain-compatible environment there must be agreed-upon behaviors valued by all; thereby allowing students the freedom to learn. Creating the emotional safety necessary requires agreement on how people, students and staff alike, treat one another. Behavior modeled by adults within a school should be of the same quality expected from students. In contrast to a punitive model of discipline, which depends upon fear and threat, a brain-compatible environment is built upon civility and respect. Especially challenging today is exposure to extreme behaviors modeled in our visual world of television and the computer and their influence in the everyday behaviors of children. In a flash of images children view content that is negative and regularly focusing on survival at any cost. Often these scenarios spill over into the school and classroom. The result of these constant visual messages is costly to the learner. These negative images can create dysfunctional circuits within our emotional wiring. Students must understand cause and effect to comprehend the differences between the surreal actions they are watching and the real life they are living.

Implementing a Positive Model of Behavior

The Lifelong Guidelines and LIFESKILLS, as coined by the integrated thematic instruction model (ITI), identify character behaviors needed for a solid working relationship between friends, spouses, employees, teachers, and students. The Lifelong Guidelines are the foundation for what makes a community work and the LIFESKILLS are the specific actions we should expect from our peers within the community. The Lifelong Guidelines include: Trustworthiness, Truthfulness, Active Listening, No Put-Downs, and Personal Best. When presenting these Guidelines to students, the following questions help form a deeper understanding: What is it? Why practice it? How do you practice it? What does it look, sound, and feel like in the world beyond the classroom? How do you know when you are successful?

A learning community is only as strong as the everyday behaviors all people within the building routinely demonstrate. LIFESKILLS are consciously taught to provide students with the social and character behaviors that will support their cognitive development. We cannot separate cognition from emotion, as each influences the other. Emotions are the glue that hold us together; whether good, bad, or indifferent, we become part of the emotional tone of the school. The eighteen LIFESKILLS are easily recognizable daily behaviors that enhance our ability to work together. They include: Caring, Common Sense, Cooperation, Courage, Curiosity, Effort, Flexibility, Friendship, Initiative, Integrity, Organization, Patience, Perseverance, Pride, Problem-Solving, Resourcefulness, Responsibility, and Sense of Humor.

Throughout the day, all activities have the potential to illustrate a necessary or missing LIFESKILL. The broad use of these skills begins first thing in the morning as students select and record in their journal the LIFESKILL they personally want to work on. Additionally, each learning group chooses a LIFESKILL they will practice during the week. The LIFESKILL or lack thereof can describe characters in a story, the newspaper, or a television show. LIFESKILLS can set the parameters for working on a project, having a guest speaker, attending a performance, or having lunch in the cafeteria. Beginning in the faculty room, the use and practice of the Lifelong Guidelines and LIFESKILLS form the basis of school and classroom interaction and are the foundation for orchestrating a brain-compatible learning environment.

In the coming years we will learn more of how the brain learns; in the meantime we have enough to begin creating a proactive brain-compatible learning environment that acknowledges the importance of emotion in all that we do. Aristotle said, "We are what we repeatedly do. Excellence then, is not an act, but a habit." We will continue to learn more each year about the physiology of learning and to build on what is known of the powerful effect emotions have on all we do.

See also: **Classroom Management; Handling Specific Problems in Classroom Management; Pleasure and Love, Social Context of Learning; Visuals and Classroom Management.**

Further Readings

Damasio, A. (1994). *"Thinking about Emotion," Descartes' Error: Emotion, Reason, and the Human Brain.* New York: Grosset/Putnam Sons.

Kovalik, S.J., Karen D.O. (2002). *Exceeding Expectations: A User's Guide to Implementing Brain Research in the Classroom* (2nd ed.). Kent, WA: Susan Kovalik & Associates, Inc.

LeDoux, J. (1996). *The Emotional Brain.* New York: Simon and Schuster.

Pearson, S. (2000). *Tools for Citizenship & Life: Using the Lifelong Guidelines & LIFESKILLS in Your Classroom.* Kent, WA: Susan Kovalik & Associates, Inc.

Ratey, J. (2001). *A User's Guide to the Brain.* New York: Pantheon Books.

Sylwester, R. (1995). *A Celebration of Neurons.* Alexandria, VA: ASCD.

Thompson, J.G. (1998). *Discipline Survival Kit for the Secondary Teacher.* Hoboken, NJ: Jossey-Bass.

Education World www.educationworld.com

SUSAN J. KOVALIK

Procedural Memory

Once a child learns how to ride a bike, it is highly unlikely that he would have to relearn it. This is because of procedural memory. Procedural memory is remembering how to do things. Virtually every subject in school can use this type of memory: music, orchestra, athletic programs, science, social studies, language arts, math, driver's education, and more. Procedural memory strategies are easy to use, easy to master, and are an enjoyable way to learn.

What Is It?

Procedural memory is often called muscle memory, body memory, motor memory, or kinesthetic learning. This memory lane stores habits, learned skills, and how to do something. It stores processes that the body does and remembers involuntarily and automatically. Some examples of information that you might store within this memory lane would be: riding a bike, rollerblading, driving a car, reading, following lab procedures, writing a letter, cheerleading, and more.

Neuroscientist Larry Squire found that amnesic patients, who had temporal lobe damage, would succeed or fail on a word retrieval task depending on the specific instructions given. The patients performed poorly when asked to list words after given some time to review the words. They performed better when given a cue and then asked to say the word. The conclusion of this piece of research was that the ability to recall something depended on which pathway the person used to retrieve the information. The information was within the brain, but the research participants just donít know it (procedural/automatic memory lane). Educators need to aid students in storing information in the strongest memory lanes so retrieval will be successful.

Brain Location

Procedural memory is stored within the cerebellum, the back part of the brain that controls movement and balance. The cerebellum has many neurons within it. It helps with memory formation. Automatic memories that are not associated with muscles are also stored within the cerebellum. For example, multiplication tables and the alphabet are stored within the cerebellum. Kinesthetic information is temporarily stored in the motor cortex (top portion of head) and then when the information is mastered; it is permanently stored within the cerebellum. In other words, once a procedure becomes a routine or habit, then it is stored within the cerebellum.

Declarative vs. Nondeclarative

Memory can be categorized as declarative (explicit) or nondeclarative (implicit). Declarative memories, or conscious memories, can be recalled and reported. They contain two types of memory: **semantic**, or word memory; and **episodic**, or location memory. These explicit memory lanes take effort and much practice to get information into them. Explicit information is first stored within the hippocampus.

Declarative knowledge must precede procedural knowledge. A learner needs to know the steps of how to do the procedure. For example, to read fluently and automatically, the student needs to know several sight words quickly. This requires accessing decoding skills that use the semantic memory lane. The more words that students know automatically, the more the brain can be free to comprehend or think about the text or words as a whole. Students that have difficulty decoding words, use all their working memory space just to decode words and are unable to use memory for comprehension. If an unknown word is come upon while reading, automatic processing is disrupted while the reader tries to decode the word. The processing within the brain goes from reflective to reflexive or automatic.

Pros and Cons

There are pros and cons when learning information that is stored within any of the memory lanes. One huge benefit of storing information within the procedural memory lane is that it gives students the ability to essentially do two things at once. Motor neurons may become so used to being activated in a particular sequence that they fire automatically with little or no conscious processing. For example, holding a conversation and driving can be done simultaneously because these two functions activate two different areas within the brain. They do not compete with each other. Doing two things at the same time is different from consciously processing two inputs at the same time. A person can do two things at the same time if one of them is stored in the automatic or procedural memory lanes. Driving a car and holding a conversation at the same time is fine for adults who have been driving for quite some time, but not for an adolescent who is still learning these motor skills.

Classroom teachers can help students make procedures more routine so that the information can be recalled automatically, freeing the brain to think and focus on something else. For example, while students are in their morning routines (putting homework in bins, hanging up coats, etc.), the teacher could have a question written on the chalkboard that the students are thinking about.

Procedures and routines decrease stress and allow the mind to more actively focus on conscious learning. The more automatic learning is for students, the more they free up their working memories to focus on deeper, higher-level tasks. Working memory overload can cause great stress, and could make learning very challenging. Think of the stress involved with a student who is doing long division and has not put the multiplication facts within her procedural or automatic memory lane.

Procedural memory skills are so memorable that they are the most often used methods for early childhood learning. A child's life is filled with standing, running, playing, building, and riding. All of these actions create a more complex and over-all greater source of sensory input to the brain than just cognitive activity. Unfortunately, this memory lane is used less as students proceed to higher grades. This continues to happen even while there is a host of research out there that says that procedural knowledge is easier to master, more easily remembered, and full of fun memories of the learning episode.

A con of the procedural memory lane is that it takes much practice and effort to ingrain the information into the memory lane, but once it is learned, it is in that brain for a long time. Distributed practice is the key when it comes to strengthening the connections between the neurons. For example, while learning vocabulary words by attaching a body movement to represent the meaning of the word, students should review these words and their definitions right after the lesson. A second review should take place twenty-four hours later since about 90 percent of information is forgotten within twenty-four hours, and a third review seven days later as the hippocampus (brain part with the role of cataloguing memories and transferring them to long-term storage sites) makes a decision to keep or discard the information. While reviewing this pattern of numbers (10-24-7), students should use the body movements associated with the sequence so they are stored in both the semantic and procedural memory lanes.

Another con of procedural memory is that the information takes time (anywhere from Four to six hours) for the learning to consolidate. Researchers at the Massachusetts Institute of Technology Department of Brain and Cognitive Sciences have observed that learning a motor skill sets in motion neural processes that continue to evolve even after practice has ended. When subjects learned a second, different motor skill immediately after a first skill was learned, the consolidation of the first motor skill was disrupted. However, if four hours elapsed between learning the first and second skills, this disruption did not occur. Researchers suggest that motor skill consolidation relies on the same structures in the medial temporal lobe that are necessary for the consolidation of explicit memory tasks. When teaching a procedural movement skill, it is important not to teach a new and different skill immediately following the initial skill taught. Teachers should give the initial skill time to consolidate.

Accessing the Procedural Memory Lane

There are two ways that will help students access the information from their procedural memory lanes. One way is to have students perform or use the information enough so that it becomes a procedure. With enough repetition and practice, the procedure can be stored permanently so it can be accessed with a cue. This is why schools have fire drills and tornado drills—so that these procedures can be performed automatically under stress when the fire alarm sounds, a time in which thinking is much challenged.

A second way to help students access the information from procedural memory lane is to invent procedures with the students so that the subject area is cemented with a movement into this memory lane. Connect the content to be remembered to movements. Some examples are: role-playings, simulations, school plays, dances, debates, puppet shows, hands-on manipulatives, choral reading, and games. Tying movements with vocabulary words can be very useful and memorable. For example, when the word "noun" is said, all of the students jump out of their chairs and point to objects in the classroom and chant, "A person (point), a place (point), a thing (point) or idea (palm out by brain)." The word "noun" is the cue for the body and brain to define it.

How to Teach Procedural Knowledge

There is a process for teaching procedural knowledge. In the early stages of procedural learning, there are three brain parts that are involved in forming the new pathway. The prefrontal cortex, parietal cortex, and cerebellum allow a person to pay attention to the tasks and ensure correct movements. This is why perfect practice needs to be a priority. How a person practices is how the information will be remembered. The bottomline for storing information into this lane is the amount and type of skill practice. As students practice skills, the memories become more efficient and can be performed with little conscious thought or recall. Eventually after lots of distributed practice, all of these brain areas show less activity. In other words, as a skill is mastered, there is less activity within the brain.

For procedural knowledge to become part of long-term memory, there are several processes or steps that must be present in the lesson. First, the teacher should model the process by talking through the process aloud so that students can visualize it. For instance, while reading aloud, the teacher might come across an unknown word. The teacher would think aloud the steps to solving this context clue mystery. She might say: "I have never heard or seen this word before. I wonder what it means. I'm going to reread the paragraph before the unknown word to see if there are any clues for this unknown word." The teacher takes the time to model and talk through how to find context clues. Students are more apt to visualize the process in this situation.

Second, the teacher should provide a written set of steps for the procedure so that students can see and review the steps. For example, there are four steps that aid students in finding context clues:

1. Box-in the unknown word.
2. List words or phrases that are clues to the meaning of the unknown word.
3. Mentally think about what the unknown word might mean.
4. Guess the meaning of the unknown word. Check in the dictionary if the guess is correct.

Teachers should take the time to teach the students to talk through the process. Teachers should make time for guided practice and independent practice. For example, the teacher could provide time for students to pair up and talk through finding context clues.

Finally, teachers should provide time for students to practice enough so that the steps are mentally rehearsed. Encourage students to mentally rehearse the steps involved within the process so that eventually, the process becomes automatic. Eventually, each step will no longer be a separate step, instead, the brain will be able to complete the process quickly, automatically, and unconsciously while looking at it all as one whole process.

Once the procedural knowledge is automatic, it is extremely challenging to consciously express the skill while performing it. If this is tried, the performance may be impaired. For example, once a piano song is learned automatically or by memory and the pianist tries reading the song by looking at each note, the song will sound slow and may not be played the same way at all.

Procedural memory lane is a fun, valuable, and highly memorable lane to use in all subject areas.

See also: **Information Processing Model; Mastery.**

Further Reading

Jensen, E. (1998). *Teaching with the Brain in Mind.* Alexandria, VA: ASCD.

Sprenger, M. (1999). *Learning and Memory: The Brain in Action.* Alexandria, VA: ASCD.

Squire, L., Kandel, E. (2000). *Memory: From Mind to Molecules.* New York: Scientific American Library.

Walker Tileston, D. (2004). *What Every Teacher Should Know About Learning, Memory, and the Brain.* Thousand Oaks, CA: Corwin Press.

LEANN NICKELSEN, M.ED.

Processing Time

The time required for the brain to neurologically process and encode newly acquired information is often referred to as *processing time*. This critical aspect of the learning process allows new ideas to settle into memory and become easily retrievable. Brain research even reports that perhaps the most significant period of learning frequently occurs not when learners are paying attention to external stimuli, but in fact when they are allowed time to mentally process new information. Educators who handle these moments correctly can allow learners to encode and understand new content, and create a strong foundation upon which to build further related concepts.

Simply stated, to "learn" new information the brain needs to build connections between brain cells. This occurs when the dendrites of one brain cell approach the axon of another brain cell. They get close, yet don't quite touch. The dendrites then secrete chemicals—neurotransmitters—which the axon of another brain cell detects. If the information being passed is sufficiently "interesting" to the receiving brain cell, it will pass it along to yet another brain cell nearby. This process continues extremely rapidly, between millions of brain cells nearly simultaneously. Connections are made between brain cells as incoming information is sorted, organized, and stored for later recall.

For these connections to be strong, myelination must also occur. This is the process by which fatty tissue forms around the axons being used most often. This layer of tissue functions much like rubber insulation on electrical cords. The result of myelination on these axons is the more rapid and reliable transmission of electrical impulses, thus creating better communication between and among neurons. Perhaps this description of how the brain biologically learns can be summarized by saying it is a *bio-chemical process stimulated by electricity.*

Brain researchers will recognize this as a fairly simplistic explanation of a vastly complex process, one they are learning more about every day. However, for the purposes of this discussion it is more than adequate because for educators the key lies not in understanding the technical terms, nor even in fully grasping how the processes actually happen. Rather the most important aspect of this description to a practitioner—someone who plans on *using* this information in a classroom—lies simply in that fact that encoding new information is a *process.* For this process to be effective, it must have sufficient time to work. Essentially, for learning to effectively occur, these processes—as well as many more complex yet related biological ones—must be given an appropriate amount of time to accomplish the tasks for which they were biologically designed by nature.

Interfering with the process, whether through an overload of information or by competing stimuli, causes the process to either never finish as energy in the brain moves on to a new task, or in some cases simply abort. The result is a series of incomplete connections between brain cells, causing learners to develop hazy memories of new information. Consequently, little or no learning will have actually occurred. Building further upon this ill-constructed foundation only complicates the multiple problems that have already been created.

Understanding this critical need to allow the brain to complete building these neural connections naturally leads to the question of how educators should handle facilitation of the learning process. However, the optimum learning sequence can be stated in a fairly simple manner. New content should be presented in brief bursts, possibly between ten to fifteen minutes, followed by a period of time allowing learners to process the newly acquired information.

How long an educator chooses to allow for processing will depend on a wide variety of factors. If the recently presented information is entirely new to the learners, the necessary processing time may be significantly greater than if what was just taught was closely related to previous material, or even a straightforward review. The length of time may also be influenced by the depth of the new information. If the content is dense with important facts, critical concepts, and possibly even new terminology, learners may need a lengthy amount of time to fully encode and store the information. On the other hand, if the content section was somewhat lighter, the processing time required might be significantly less. In general, however, after ten to fifteen minutes of presenting new information, educators can expect to allow from two to five minutes for processing, and then adjust the time appropriately given these various factors.

In addition to deciding how long to allow for processing, educators must also make another critical choice regarding what learners will actually be doing during their processing time. One way to process the information verbally might be to have learners form dyads or small groups, and simply discuss their reactions to the material in an open-ended manner. At the conclusion of the processing time, they could even be invited to share their thoughts, ideas, and insights. Educators might also allow more directed verbal processing time by providing each dyad or group with a pointed question that they will respond to, again based on their reactions to the material.

Another direction educators might pursue could be to allow learners to process the material in some written manner. Perhaps they are given time to review the notes they have already taken and make clarifying notes to themselves. Perhaps they are directed to write on a piece of paper at least three questions from their notes regarding any aspect of the presentation where they would like further clarification. Another choice might be to again form groups, and this time each group must generate a paragraph that summarizes the key aspects of the information.

There is even a wide range of highly creative choices that an open-minded educator might choose to explore. For example, perhaps small groups of learners could each be given one key aspect of the new information. Their assignment would then be to present this idea to the rest of the class in a nonverbal manner, perhaps by acting it out, by telling a story about it, or maybe even drawing a picture of it. A further choice related to drawing might be to have all learners review their notes, and then allow them a specified number of minutes to add creative doodles around their notes. For many students, the related visual stimuli will provide a more powerful memory clue to the content than the written words.

These are only a few of the many ways in which an educator might chose to allow for processing time. Given that there is usually a wide variety of preferred **learning styles** in most classes, the best classrooms frequently allow for a mixture of these strategies. Any of these options would allow the brain to continue to build and solidify connections between brain cells without the adverse effect of competing stimuli.

This idea connects directly to one of the most dangerous phrases in education, "Time On Task." Brain research clearly indicates educators should not want learners to always be "on task." Consider a situation in which the task given to the students was to process new information by discussing the material in groups, and then drawing images in their notebooks. This clearly might be valuable processing time for some learners. However, an outside observer might view this activity as frivolous and "off task," when in fact learners are doing exactly what they should be doing to fully understand and remember the information.

Many word pairs could possibly be used to express the strategy discussed here, where new information is presented followed immediately by processing time. It might be referred to as "ebb and flow," or "focus and diffuse," or "press and release." All of these are indeed appropriate descriptions of how the brain processes information and its need for adequate processing time. A final metaphor to consider might be the manner in which bread is baked. After the dough has been prepared, it must be allowed to sit for a period of time while it rises due to the reaction of the yeast. Baking dough too soon creates a "flat" result. The same situation applies as the brain attempts to process new information. After it has taken in a certain amount of information, the "dough" has been created, and the chemical processes in the brain must be allowed to act upon the content, just as the yeast acts upon the dough, so the information is processed and stored correctly. When educators provide learners with appropriate periods of processing time, they are essentially using the correct recipe for creating solid learning.

See also: **Attention; Learning Cycle; Information Processing Model; Learning in a Social Context.**

Further Readings

Allen, R. (2002). *Impact Teaching: Ideas and Strategies for Teachers to Maximize Student Learning.* Boston, MA: Allyn and Bacon.

Hart, L. (1999). *Human Brain and Human Learning.* Kent, Washington: Books for Educators, Inc.

Philp, R. (2005). *The Engaged Brain.* San Diego, CA: The Brain Store, Inc.

Sapulsky, R. (1999). *Why Zebras Don't Get Ulcers.* (4th ed.) New York: W. H. Freeman.

Sylwester, R. (2000). *A Biological Brain in a Cultural Classroom.* Thousand Oaks, CA: Corwin Press.

RICHARD H. ALLEN, PH.D.

R

Reading and Comprehension

That reading happens in the brain is obvious. However, how this occurs has been a focus of scientific investigation for over hundred years. What do we really know about how the brain learns to read? We know that whereas speaking is natural, reading is not. Children do not automatically read. They have to learn how to do it. Reading in its simplest form is a process of decoding and comprehension. The ultimate goal of reading is for children to become sufficiently fluent to understand what they read. Reading begins when someone unlocks the code of a written language system. And the "someone" to be a reader needs to know how this system works. Where does this knowledge reside? It resides in the brain. However, the neuroscience of reading is much more complex than this simplistic view. Reading is an elaborate process that involves decoding abstract symbols into sounds, then into words that generate meaning.

In particular, the past decade has experienced amazing progress in our understanding of the brain and its impact on reading and comprehension. Never before have neuroscientific studies and classroom instruction been so closely linked. Educators can now refer to carefully designed research studies to determine the most effective ways to teach reading. What does this evidence tell us? Several studies have found that reading originates in and relies on the brain systems for spoken language. The major findings of the National Reading Panel indicate that in order to read, children need to be taught alphabetics (phonemic awareness and phonics); reading fluency; vocabulary; and strategies for reading comprehension. These components of the reading process need to be taught comprehensively, systematically, and explicitly.

Another important question about recent research findings is whether teachers can implement these findings in their classrooms. The connection between theory and practice remains paramount in the minds of educators concerned with the issue of reading and comprehension. Reading is very likely the one area of the school curriculum where neuroscience has made its greatest impact. Educators have been well aware of the difficulties involved in learning to read and have long debated the best methods to teach beginning reading. Reading proficiency depends on expert teaching so that the reader learns how to access print accurately and fluently.

Brain researchers have developed new technologies for looking inside the brain and analyzing functions and process. These technologies fall into two major categories: those that examine brain function and those that focus on brain structure. Different technologies are utilized to look at how the brain works. These procedures can be used to isolate and identify the areas of the brain where distinct levels of activity are occurring. Using these technologies, researchers have been able to determine how different brains function when conducting certain activities, including reading. Some of these discoveries include:

- Novice readers use different neural pathways while reading than skilled readers.
- Individuals with reading difficulties access different brain regions to decode text than proficient readers.
- The brains of people with reading difficulties are working harder than those of skilled readers.
- With proper instructional intervention, the brains of young, struggling readers can be rewired to use different cerebral areas that more closely align with those of typical readers.

Clearly, we have a lot to learn. Investigators and researchers have worked hard to understand reading and now with the ability of new technology to observe the brain in action, they have a place to focus their research.

The ultimate goal of reading is for children to become sufficiently fluent to understand what they read. Reading comprehension depends heavily on spoken language comprehension. Reading comprehension is a complex cognitive process that relies on several components to be successful. To comprehend a printed word, we first need to decode it. However, much more is involved. To develop these comprehension skills, students need to interact with text to derive meaning and develop vocabulary and linguistic knowledge.

An area of the brain that primarily has to do with this meaning-making process is the temporal lobe of the brain. The temporal lobes are located on each side of the brain just behind the ears. Looking through this new focus on brain imaging, we can see how some children experience greater challenge and struggle in becoming readers. It is important to look at appropriate interventions for these children. Some students can read and not understand a word, and yet others seem to understand everything but struggle with decoding the words. Because of this discrepancy, educators are vitally interested in information and strategies that are brain-based and can assist them in reaching all students and engaging them in the reading process.

From this research, applications for instructional practices that are brain-compatible have been developed. These strategies also take into consideration how to build the reading brain and how to differentiate instruction.

Understanding Text

How do good readers derive meaning from text? Good readers are constantly monitoring their own comprehension and are thinking what they need to do to understand the text. They are metacognitive and aware of their own comprehension. Text comprehension occurs when the brain's frontal lobe is able to derive meaning by processing the visual and auditory input with the reader's prior knowledge.

What do good readers do when they read?

- Good readers are active readers.
- They have clear goals in their mind as they read and constantly evaluate while reading the text.
- Good readers skim the text to preview before reading, noting structure and format.
- Good readers make predictions as they read.
- They read selectively—making decisions about their reading—what to read carefully, what to skim quickly, what to re-read, etc.
- Good readers construct, revise, and question as they read.
- They draw upon, compare, and integrate their prior knowledge with the material in the text.
- They think about the author's craft—their style, beliefs, intentions, etc.
- They monitor their understanding of the text, making adjustments of their reading as necessary.
- Good readers try to determine the meaning of unfamiliar words and concepts in the text.
- They evaluate the text's quality and value and react to the text in a range of ways.
- Good readers read different kinds of text differently, using distinct approaches for narrative and expository text.
- For good readers, comprehension is a consuming, continuous, and complex activity that is both satisfying and productive.

Explicit instruction is important for all learners as they engage in the meaning-making process interacting with text. Some tested, brain-compatible and research-validated strategies include:

Predicting—Preview the title, pictures, headings, connecting student experiences to story themes or topics of informational text. Have students make "informed guesses." Help "fill in the gaps" in their prior knowledge. This stage is critical for students to construct meaning.

Questioning—Have the students ask and answer questions. Use higher order thinking strategies for questions based on Bloom's Taxonomy (application, analysis, synthesis, and evaluation). Teach students to generate good questions. This process helps set a purpose for reading: to read, discuss, and investigate.

Clarifying—It is important to note the big ideas and to assist students with comparing and contrasting their understandings. Establish the common base of understanding and fill in the gaps.

Summarizing—It is necessary to assist the students to synthesize the big ideas, key events, and critical themes. They can write their summary or share it verbally with a partner.

Imagery—Help students form pictures in their minds, making "mental movies." Assist them in techniques to visualize the action.

Teachers need to keep in mind some specific components that are important to build comprehension strategies in students. These strategies are best taught through "reciprocal dialogue." Dialogue moves from teacher-directed to student-directed. An explicit description of the strategy and when and how it should be used needs to be shared. Teachers should model the strategy in action with specific examples. The use of mental modeling and thinking aloud provides a "window on the thinking" for the student. Collaborative use of the strategy in action should follow, so that students are able to cooperatively share their application of the technique. Practice and feedback within an interactive social setting is essential. This should be followed by guided practice using the strategy with gradual release of responsibility. The final stage should be independent use of the strategy on the part of the learner.

Think Aloud Strategy

Specific approaches to comprehension instruction that are brain-compatible involve teaching multiple strategies simultaneously. A technique that teachers can use to help all students become more metacognitive is the Think Aloud strategy. Comprehension strategies to model during Think Alouds include: activating prior knowledge; building vocabulary; determining importance; questioning and clarifying; inferring; synthesizing; summarizing.

When a teacher introduces Think Aloud, some techniques need to be considered. Before reading the book to the class, decide which strategy will be the focus of the session. Preview the text to determine appropriate places to pause for personal commentary related to the focus strategy. Plan how you will demonstrate the use of that strategy. When introducing the book, explain that you will be stopping to share your thoughts. During various think alouds focus on different strategies. If focusing on background knowledge, select parts of the story or text that connect with your personal experiences (text-to-self connections), that connect with other literacy works (text-to-text connection), and that connect with events and life in general (text-to-world connection). Pause at chosen spots and share with the students. When the reading is complete, invite the students to share their thoughts. When the students are engaged in their own independent reading, guide them to use these strategies that have been modeled for them.

Visualization

Proficient readers create images in their brains as they read. Visualization is a natural part of reading for them. Struggling readers, for various reasons, are not able to connect to the text in this way. They have not learned to make "movies in their mind." To help students visualize as they read, start with a simple sentence and ask the students questions that help create images.

Guiding students with detailed questions that lead to open-ended answers helps them create their own visual interpretation of the sentence. It transforms a simple image into a complete setting. This activity not only encourages students to create imagery, but also encourages them to think about questioning and generate questions themselves.

Graphic Organizers

Graphic and cognitive organizers can help students to consolidate and elaborate their understanding of what has been read. These strategies are usually best done in small collaborative teams using the principles of cooperative learning. The goal is to get students to process the information at a deeper and more meaningful level. This in turn will facilitate increased retention and recall of information.

Scaffolding instruction with cognitive organizers is important. The teacher needs to model the filling out of the diagram during the lesson. The student follows along. Then the teacher fills out only the first part of the diagram and the students work in pairs to complete the rest, using their notes and texts. Then the teacher hands out blank diagrams for the students to complete. The final stage is when the students create their own diagram, map, or graphic and complete it based on the reading.

Graphic organizers are brain-compatible tools for comprehension and help students gather data, organize, and categorize information and create points of comparison. Graphic organizers appeal to various learning styles and help students learn concepts because they are able to order the information in a pattern for the brain to make the information more memorable.

Reciprocal Teaching

Reciprocal Teaching is a research-validated intervention strategy designed to assist less capable readers in developing powerful reading comprehension strategies as they gain more control over their reading. This technique helps students focus and monitor their reading to achieve higher comprehension. The process involves structured dialogue in which the teacher begins by being the leader, modeling the strategies, guiding student responses, and taking care to "think aloud" during modeling. The students then move into guided practice in four areas: predict, question, clarify, and summarize.

As students take on the roles in Reciprocal Teaching, they predict content, question and clarify their understanding of the content, and then summarize what they have learned.

Directed Reading-Thinking Activity

Directed reading-thinking activity (DRTA) has many facets that support and extend the student's reading and thinking. The components that support comprehension include: activating prior knowledge through brainstorming and providing an anticipatory set of questions to create a need to know, predicting the content that will be covered in the reading using a cloze procedure so that students will make appropriate predictions around key concepts of the story utilizing syntactic and semantic cues; reading and revisiting predictions to compare and contrast with the actual events of the story or chapter.

This is a powerful brain-compatible strategy to help students activate prior knowledge as they brainstorm words and phrases they associate with the topic. At the predicting stage, students are establishing their own purposes for reading. When they select appropriate words and phrases for the cloze procedure of a passage from the text, they are building their word bank and anticipation of the actual content. Finally, when students are given the opportunity to reflect, collaborate, confirm, and revise predictions after the reading, they are practicing active engaging strategies for comprehension.

In conclusion, reading and comprehending well is an instructional imperative in our schools. Certainly, there is more to developing better comprehension than just memory. Research on how the brain reads has produced impressive progress. There is still a lot to be learned about how the brain implements the cognitive processes of reading. Teachers need to provide an enriched brain-compatible environment to foster the meaning-making process. It is important to display learning resources throughout the room. Provide opportunities for interaction among students, because the human brain is a social communicative brain. Guide students, through brain-based practices, to help them master important skills and strategies.

See also: **Reading and Fluency; Content Area Literacy.**

Further Readings

Jensen, E. (1998). *Teaching with the Brain in Mind.* Alexandria, VA: ASCD.

Shaywitz, S., Shaywitz, B. (2004). False claims about literacy development. *Educational Leadership* 60:6–11.

Sousa, D. (2005). *How the Brain Learns to Read.* Thousand Oaks, CA: Corwin Press, Inc.

Wolfe, P., Nevills, P. (2004). *Building the Reading Brain, Pre k-3*. Thousand Oaks, CA: Corwin Press, Inc.
The Brain Store (Eric Jensen): www.brainstore.com

KATHERINE D. PEREZ, ED.D.

Reading and Fluency

According to the 2000 National Reading Panel report fluency is acknowledged as one of the five basic components of a good reading program with the others being phonemic awareness, phonics, vocabulary, and comprehension. Traditionally the fluency piece of the reading puzzle has been left to develop on its own or as a side effect of the oral reading component associated with phonics and vocabulary. A clearer definition of fluency leads to a better understanding of how students acquire fluency.

Fluency is the ability to read text automatically, accurately, and with expression. When fluent readers read, it sounds as though they are speaking. The reading is fluid and accurate, with appropriate speed, appropriate phrasing, and correct intonation. Fluency becomes the puzzle piece placed between word recognition and comprehension. In independent leveled text and with practice, word recognition and comprehension occur simultaneously. With rereading and good strategies, readers are able to develop a sense of knowing how and when to pause within sentences and at the ends of sentences, and when to change tone and emphasis within sentences.

Accurate Letter and Word Decoding

Reading fluency has three important stages that lead to full comprehension of text. The first stage of fluency is accurate letter and word decoding. This group of readers is putting the phonics puzzle pieces together to sound out the words in a text with minimal errors. Although sometimes fluency and automaticity are used interchangeably, they are not the same thing. Automaticity is the fast and accurate recall of words and phrases. This begins to occur when students' brains are establishing the visual patterns within written language. Students first recognize high frequency words and then process other words that may be less familiar by following known patterns. The more times that students see words separately and within text, the better chance that they will be able to read those words accurately, automatically, and fluidly. Rehearsal is a critical component in transferring new information from working memory to long-term storage in their brains. It is important to devote adequate time to the practice and to make sure that the rehearsal is positive. The **feedback** that the students get during this learning stage must be specific, quick, and supportive. The structure of the fluency puzzle piece is teaching the predictable patterns in the written system to give the readers the code necessary to learn to read.

Automatic Processing

The second stage of fluency uses automatic processing. In this stage readers are more ready to consolidate and automate basic decoding skills and give more attention to making sense and meaning of the text. Fluency is that bridge between word recognition and comprehension. Because fluent readers do not need to spend so much time laboring over decoding words, they can focus on the sense and meaning of the text.

Using strategies that good readers employ for comprehension purposes, students have a head start in making sense of the text through strategies such as previewing the book to see what it is about and connecting the topic to what they know in their own lives. Then regardless of the strategy chosen by the teacher to instruct fluency, the students have a head start in understanding the text.

Reading requires the brain to perform in many areas for readers to be successful. The visual cortex is involved in recognizing the visual pattern of the word and the angular gyrus translates the written word into sounds. Wernicke's Area and Broca's Area are located in the left hemisphere and are the two language processing centers of the brain. Wernicke's is involved in the comprehension of words, while Broca's is involved in the processing of syntax, which is the area that helps us understand language. If the spoken sentence structure is complex, more areas of the brain are activated, including areas in the right hemisphere. Reading is complex and not linear and singular. Many processes including decoding, word identification, vocabulary, reasoning, concept formation, and sense/meaning are going on at the same time.

Automatic processing can be increased through strategies that use guided, modeled, and repeated oral reading. There are many structures for teaching fluency, but all include using a "perfect" model for the student. In one instructional model students hear the text read aloud by a teacher first. The second time the teacher reads the text again with the students joining in when they can. After the second reading the teacher and the students discuss any words that are unfamiliar or patterns that might be troublesome. The passage can be reread a third time. The following day the same passage is read first by the teacher and then followed by reading by the student or students with the teacher fading the voice until only the students' voices are heard. Passages can then be practiced with a reading partner, read silently, and read alone to the teacher to get a scoring on rate or accuracy.

Flashcards with irregular words or familiar regular high-frequency words that students have mastered can be used in games that encourage them to read as many words as possible in thirty seconds. Words that are correct are placed in one stack, while words missed are placed in a second stack. Obviously, feedback for both students playing should be provided to increase the accuracy, but their mission is to improve their own goals.

Letter naming is included in fluency activities and can be addressed through activities that involve students using plastic letters or letter tiles randomly drawn out of a bag. Place the five or ten tiles on the table top and model naming the letters (or sounds of the letters.) Rapid automatic naming of objects is shown to be a precursor to reading with fluency. The brain can use the practice in naming familiar objects such as colors, numbers, animals, household objects, or toys within a given time. The brain is working at developing connections to identify items rapidly, disengaging from that category, and moving to a new category then identifying the new set. Flashcards with pictures categorized in groups can be used to encourage accuracy and speed.

Prosody

The third stage of fluency has readers sounding the way "good readers" sound. In this stage the reader reads with "prosody," a term that describes reading with accuracy, speed, and expression. Readers, who read with the same intonation on each word, who pay little or no attention to surface punctuation, and who stop and start at inappropriate times throughout the text, will have little understanding of the meaning of the piece of text.

Inefficient word recognition and poor decoding skills lead to a slow, halting pace, poor phrasing, careless mistakes, and little expression. This lack of skill affects comprehension as well as the ability for the readers to self-monitor and self-correct their own reading.

Students benefit from appropriate texts and activities that have been structured to allow for success and enjoyment. Many of our struggling students who are pulled out for the flashcard repetitive activities often miss the fluency activities that include the Readers' Theater, the choral reading, the partner reading, and other activities that are more passion-filled, theater-like, "why-we-read" parts of the class.

Fluency can be developed through instruction. When students are working alone or with peers on activities to foster reading with expression, they should be working with independent level texts. If working with teachers, then instructional level texts are appropriate to use, however frustration level text should not be used to develop prosody. For the purpose of developing fluency, students should read and reread text that they have already read as they are trying to improve speed, accuracy, intonation, and expression.

To sound like good readers, students need to hear what good reading sounds like. In its simplest form, teachers must provide various models of good reading. Teachers reading picture books aloud, guest readers reading favorite books, books read on tape, and teachers sharing chapter books are all examples of modeling good reading. Teachers who partner together to model Readers' Theater for groups of students are wonderful examples of enthusiasm for reading. The key to making this component of fluency work is repetition. The students need the opportunities to experience the same text multiple times. Too often we present them with new material and rush them through the work without providing them the time necessary to manipulate the rhythm, the tone, the expression, and to dig into the deeper meanings of the work.

Fluency at Work

Using appropriately leveled text that is of high interest to the reader will assure success with building fluency skills. Students need guided, repeated oral reading that has been modeled along with independent silent reading at their appropriate levels. There are many reading strategies that can improve fluency. Echo Reading allows the students to listen to the teacher read part of a text while following along, and then "echo reading" the same text, trying to repeat the teacher's rate and expression. The teacher begins by reading only two or three sentences of the text fluently. In echo reading the text can be available to each student individually, or can be shown on an overhead or chart paper. Text can be from a story, a poem, or even a song.

With Choral Reading students again use a variety of text either individually or as a class, but in this format the reading is done a little differently. The teacher models the task by reading the first part of the text out loud, setting the pace and reading with proper phrasing, rate, and expression. On the second reading, the students read along with the teacher trying to match the pace, phrasing, rate, and expression of the teacher. With each following reading, the teacher begins to lessen the support until the students sound more in control. On subsequent days for most of these strategies, the teacher can assess small groups or individual students for pace, phrasing, rate, and expression.

Partner Reading has several variations but is often used in pairing a higher performing student with a lower performing reader for fluency practice. Each pair of students has texts at the lower performing reader's instructional-reading level. Partner A being the stronger reader reads the text aloud modeling fluent reading for one minute. Partner B follows along while A reads. Then Partner B reads for one minute. Partner Reading needs to be modeled for the entire class several times before everyone begins the process. Students are not told that Partner A is the stronger reader.

Readers' Theater is one of the most enjoyable fluency activities for students. Students are given a reading passage in script format. This passage often comes from a favorite book that the class has read and that the teacher has adapted or a text that has been commercially adapted. Copies of the text are given to each student depending on the number of characters in the script. The text for each character is highlighted, and parts are modeled and practiced. This type of production is performed for an audience; however it does not require students to memorize their parts as reading is the key. Costumes and props are not necessary, but a set day and time for the reading performance is important.

Through brain compatible instructional strategies this piece of the puzzle can be taught and facilitate reading comprehension.

See also: **Patterns and Programs; Reading and Comprehension; Reading Vocabulary and Word Recognition.**

Further Readings

Lyons, C., Clay, M.M. (2003). *Teaching Struggling Readers: How to Use Brain-Based Research to Maximize Learning.* Portsmouth, N.H.: Heinemann. (2000). *Report of the National Reading Panel: Teaching Children to Read.* Washington, D.C.

Rhodes, L. (1996). *Readers and Writers with a Difference.* Portsmouth, NH: Heinemann.

Sousa, D. (2004). *How the Brain Learns to Read.* Thousand Oaks, CA: Corwin Press.

Vaughn, S., Linan-Thompson, S. (2004). *Research-Based Methods of Reading Instruction Grades K-3.* Alexandria, VA: ASCD.

Wolfe, P., Nevills, P. (2004). *Building the Reading Brain, PreK-3.* Thousand Oaks, CA: Corwin Press.

LINDA G. ALLEN, M.ED.

Reading in the Content Area

Content Area Reading is the use of language—reading, writing, speaking, and listening—to learn subject matter. Teachers of content who embrace this concept understand how students learn and reflect this in their instruction. They not only teach content, they teach students how to read, write, speak, and listen in the language of the content area in their efforts to help students become independent, lifelong learners.

Recent research with the use of functional magnetic resonance imaging (fMRI) has led to a better understanding of the reading process. No one area of the brain specializes in reading, rather, various areas of the brain work together to make sense of and construct meaning from text. Being able to read and make sense of what we read is predicated on our knowledge of previously acquired spoken language. Our brain must first "know" its abc's so that the brain can connect letters to sounds or phonemes. Children who have already been successfully using spoken language, a natural development, must now learn to read, an unnatural activity . Our language is a complex one and letters and groups of letters often represent different sounds. For example, the "a" sound in water differs from the "a" sound in cake. While some come by this naturally, most will have to be taught how to read and make meaning of text.

During the reading process, text is processed by the brain's right hemisphere where the visual cortex of the brain first "sees" the word. This information is then transferred to the brain's left hemisphere where the brain's language areas help to sound out words and make meaning from text. In the Angular Gyrus, the word is phonetically decoded as this area breaks the word down into its basic sounds or phonemes. This sounding out process activates Broca's area of the brain where the word is identified. Finally, through the brain's higher level functions of reasoning and concept formation in Wernicke's area, we are able to think about and understand what the word means or represents.

The brain is a pattern seeking device and this quality is fundamental in teaching reading in the content areas. As the student reads content in science, math, or social studies it is seeking patterns to connect it with stored knowledge. Every area of the content has its own distinctive patterns of information. The brain must find the pathway to the prior knowledge to make sense of the reading text.

Neuroscientists discovered through positron emission tomography (PET) scans that the brain stores related words together. Verbs are in one area, nouns in another, and then further desegregation of nouns between tools and animals. Proximity between bits of information enables them to quickly activate each other aiding in retrieval and storage. For instance, biology investigates cells and mitosis; this information is stored near each other.

When reading a passage, students must be able to hold one paragraph in their memory and associate it with the next. Working memory must link paragraphs together so that the main ideas can be understood at the end of a reading. Text comprehension occurs when the brain's frontal lobe is able to derive meaning by processing the visual and auditory input that resulted from the reader's prior knowledge.

During elementary school, reading instruction focuses on narrative text rather than informational text, and tends to be fiction rather than nonfiction. In addition, the typical textbook for the high school level classroom is much more sophisticated and complex than the type of texts students encounter during elementary school. Secondary students are expected, all of a sudden, and in most cases without instruction, to be able to read and understand vast amounts of complex material. However, reading is much more than simply sounding out or being able to pronounce words. Being able to read difficult text material requires advanced reading skills. In addition, reading tasks vary and do not always require the same types of thinking skills. Reading a chapter from a physics text requires a different approach to reading than one would use when reading a short story, for example. According to the national assessment of education progress (NAEP) 60 percent of secondary readers are able to read at a basic level but only 5 percent of these same readers can interpret what they read. In other words, while most secondary students may be able to decode written text, the vast majority of them are not able to make sense of what they read. Perhaps more alarming is the fact that this statistic has remained constant over the past twenty years.

We know what characterizes good, active readers. Good readers are able to construct meaning from what they read. They know how to monitor and adjust their reading and when done, to reflect upon what was read. Good readers take time before reading to set a purpose for reading, to preview and make predictions. During reading, good readers stay focused and know how to monitor and regulate understanding, to ask and answer questions, to stop, slow down, or re-read. Good readers strive to make connections, to consider how new information fits with what is already known. After reading, good readers take time to summarize and reflect upon what was read, to revisit predictions, and make adjustments to their understanding of subject matter. Good readers will often seek out additional information beyond what was just read.

Poor readers, on the other hand, are passive. They are often overwhelmed and plunge into a reading task without any thought from beginning to end. Easily distracted, poor readers make no effort to monitor their reading, and when finished, are often not sure what they just read. Most often, they are relieved to have finished the assignment.

Good readers, then, are strategic. They are deliberate and thoughtful in their approach to a particular learning task. These readers are able to apply strategies to construct meaning as they read. Somewhere along the way good readers acquire the tools to enable them to make meaning of what they are reading. Although some students seem to intuitively figure out how to be strategic, most of our students need to be explicitly taught how to be strategic. Eventually, applying the strategies becomes automatic but not until we, as content area teachers, model for our students how to read, learn, and be strategic in meaningful, authentic ways. Secondary teachers should provide students with the tools to strategically approach reading tasks. Content area teachers can be more effective when they purposefully incorporate strategies into their instruction.

The National Reading Panel reports that most secondary teachers do not use content area strategies in their instruction. Many teachers feel they do not have the time or expertise to teach their students how to read. They view their role as that of content area specialist, not reading teacher, and feel that the teaching of reading is something that elementary school teachers were supposed to have done. Reading instruction should, however, continue after elementary school and be integrated with the teaching of content. As today's secondary teacher often feels pressured to cover content and teach a prescribed set of standards, many secondary content area classrooms continue to be characterized by the assign and tell method. These students, having spent hours in these classrooms, are rarely actively involved in their learning. In fact, they are quite comfortable being told what, not how, to think by their teachers. It is time for a change and a shift from teaching students how to read to teaching students how to use reading as a tool to learn.

If our students are to be strategic in their learning, we must be strategic in our teaching. Content area teachers should adhere to an instructional framework, a guide or outline, to facilitate the teaching of lessons. The instructional framework reflects what we know about good readers: they prepare to read, they are actively engaged while they read, and they take time to reflect upon what they have read when they are finished. If we utilize a consistent approach to instruction in our classrooms, our students will be more likely to internalize it and apply it in their own learning.

Strategies can be plugged into the stages of the instructional framework to provide students with the tools they need to be good readers. As teachers, we need to model strategic reading and teach our students strategies with the same deliberateness and passion as we teach our content. In addition, we must deliberately and purposefully inform students what the strategy is and why they are engaging in it so that students have an understanding behind the strategy and when it can be useful. Finally, we need to incorporate a variety of strategies so that students are able to select the strategy that works best for them and for a particular academic task. Content area teachers can play a vital role in teaching their students how to read to learn by incorporating strategies in a purposeful, meaningful manner. It is essential that teachers take time to inform students what the strategy is, why they are engaging in it, and to model the strategy for students.

In the first phase of the instructional framework, the pre-reading phase, the teacher's job is to prepare the students for learning. During this phase teaching goals include determining and building upon students' background knowledge, setting a purpose for reading, getting students motivated or curious about the reading, and creating a need to know. This pre-reading phase is perhaps the most critical as research has shown that the strongest factor in learning new information is the ability to connect it to existing knowledge. Schema theory explains how prior knowledge plays a role in comprehending new information. As we present our students with new information, we must create ways for them to connect the new ideas with their prior knowledge. Tapping into students' background knowledge is a key aspect of comprehension and helps students to be prepared for the reading ahead.

Consider having students engage in the following types of activities to facilitate the pre-reading phase of the instructional framework and to make an initial connection to the topic being studied:

- Describe in writing or share with the class what they know or think they know about the topic and what they want to know about the topic (KWL).

- Incorporate **writing** to learn and have students respond to a specific teacher-created prompt related to the topic (Quick Write, Admit Slip).

- Show a video clip, take a field trip, or visit web sites to spark students' curiosity about the topic or simply write a question on the board to get students thinking about the lesson.

- Share key vocabulary words students will encounter in the reading, ask students to decide if they know the word, have heard of the word, or have no idea about the word (Knowledge Rating Scale).

- Have the class generate a list of ideas related to the topic, record on the board or overhead (Brainstorming, Factstorming).

- Share visuals related to the topic, have students record their thoughts in writing or share with a partner or the class (Journal, Log).

- Fill in a Graphic Organizer as a class to help students see relationships and connections among ideas related to the topic.

- Have students agree or disagree with teacher-created statements related to the reading (Anticipation Guide).

- Preview the text, have students look for its organizational features such as headings and bolded terms (Text Preview, Skim Away).

- Generate a list of questions by turning section headings into questions (SQ3R).

In the second phase of the instructional framework, the teacher's job is to support the students while they are engaged in the reading process and facilitate student comprehension of text. One of the most effective ways teachers can do this is by demonstrating or modeling their own thought processes by thinking aloud for their students. Teachers can walk students through the thought process of figuring out an unfamiliar word or verbalize how to use a graph or read a chart. The during-reading phase of the instructional framework is directly related to a student's ability to be strategic while reading, to monitor understanding of what is being read, to be megacognitively aware. Megacognitively aware readers are able to monitor their understanding by asking questions to determine if what they are reading is making sense. These readers have self-knowledge of how they learn and they know how to regulate their understanding.

Consider having students engage in the following types of activities to facilitate the during-reading phase of the instructional framework as they work to understand ideas and concepts:

- Teach students to stop, think, and ask questions while they read, such as: Do I understand what I am reading? What is the main idea of what I am reading? Or create questions starting with Who? What? When? Where? How? and have students record answers as they read (Self-Questioning).

- Take turns posing questions to your students and having them pose questions to you while reading; model the types of higher level thinking questions they should be asking themselves (ReQuest).

- Ask students to think of personal experiences they have had that help them connect to what they are reading, have them close their eyes and try to get a visual image as they read (Visualization, Imagery).

- Create statements for students to respond to on the literal, interpretive, and applied levels of thinking (3-Level Reading Guide).

- Incorporate writing to learn and have students stop from time to time while reading to take notes or record questions they are having or thoughts that come to mind (Journal, Log).
- Have students keep running lists of new or confusing vocabulary as they read (Vocabulary Self-Collection).
- Create data charts or information tables and have students fill them in with information as they read (Jot Chart, Story Map, Think Sheet).
- Working in partners, have students take turns reading aloud and questioning one another about the reading (Paired Reading).
- Have students use post-it notes to mark areas in the text they agree with, disagree with, question, or do not understand OR create a system of symbols to correspond with categories of information such as "!" Significant Information "?" Unclear Information and "=" Information I Can Connect With; have students use the symbols to mark text as they read (X Marks the Spot, SMART/Self-Monitored Approach to Reading and Thinking).
- Add to the Graphic Organizer started prior to reading.

In the third phase of the instructional framework, the teacher's job is to determine comprehension by helping students to summarize, reflect, and evaluate, in essence, to think critically about what was read. Consider having students engage in the following types of activities to facilitate the post-reading phase of the instructional framework and to act upon or apply what they have just read about:

- Incorporate writing to learn and have students write a summary, in their own words, to reflect their understanding of what they just read (Summary Microtheme, One-Sentence Summary); have students write a letter to the editor of the school newspaper to express their opinion related to the reading or write a patterned poem to reflect their understanding of the reading (Cinquain, BioPoem).
- Students could further explore the topic area by completing a research paper or project and presenting the findings to the class (Research Paper).
- Have students participate in a discussion about what was read, use the questions generated prior to reading to get the discussion going (Reaction Guide).
- Revisit the statements students reacted to prior to reading to see if thoughts have changed and discuss why or why not (Making Predictions).
- Have students discuss both sides of an issue, identify rationale points for each, and take a stance (Discussion Web).

- Incorporate writing to learn and have students complete a ticket out of class where they indicate what they learned or what they are still unsure about, collect and use to start the next day's lesson (Exit Slip).
- Finalize the Graphic Organizer.

There is perhaps no other skill that pervades our daily lives as much as our ability to read. Most of us could not get through our day without being able to make sense of the written word. Reading is a continuously developing skill, requiring constant practice, development and refinement, much as one learns to play a musical instrument or excel in a particular sport. It is learned through and improves with practice. As teachers of content, we can be a tremendous resource and model to our students for how to use reading to learn.

See also: **Patterns and Programs; Reading and Comprehension; Visual Brain; Writing.**

Further Readings

Lenski, S.D., Wham, M.A., Johns, J.L. (2003). *Reading and Learning Strategies Middle Through High School.* Dubuque, IA: Kendall/Hunt Publishing Company.

Manzo, A.V., Manzo, U.C., Thomas, M.M. (2005). *Content Area Literacy Strategic Teaching for Strategic Learners.* Hoboken, NJ: John Wiley & Sons, Inc.

Meyer, A., Rose, D.H. (August 21, 2000). *Learning to Read in the Computer Age.* retrieved June 28, 2004 from http://www.cast.org/udl/index.cfm?i=18.

NAEP 1998 reading report card for the nation and states (NCES 1999500). (1999). Washington, DC: National Center for Educational Statistics, U.S. Department of Education.

National Reading Panel (NRP). (2000). Teaching children to read: An evidence-based assessment of the scientific research literature on reading and its implications for reading instruction. Washington, DC: National Institute of Child Health and Human Development.

Sousa, D.A. (2001). *How the Brain Learns.* Thousand Oaks, CA: Corwin Press.

Stephens, E.C., Brown, J.E. (2000). *A Handbook of Content Literacy Strategies: 75 Practical Reading and Writing Ideas.* Norwood, MA: Christopher-Gordon Publishers, Inc.

Tovani, C. (2000). *I Read it but I Don't Get it. Comprehension Strategies for Adolescent Readers.* Portland, ME: Stenhouse Publishers.

SHARON E. ANDREWS, ED.D.

Reading Vocabulary and Word Recognition

Having reading class perceived as not only pleasurable but also as appropriately challenging or strenuous ensures continual growth and independent application of literacy skills. Viewing reading and literacy as a contact sport calls on students to become engaged and actively participate as they develop the capacity to use reading as a multifaceted tool for learning. Teachers are called on to design instructional days based on student need, content standards/benchmarks, and the current research regarding best-practice, brain-compatible learning.

Research about how the brain learns to read is informing teacher decisions with respect to meeting student needs, materials used, and teaching strategies employed. The classroom teacher using a balanced approach takes the best from several philosophic or program models and develops learning experiences that are an optimal match for students as they journey toward literacy.

Current brain imaging studies indicate that effective reading instruction not only improves reading skills but also changes the processing in the brain that in turn makes the task of reading easier. Data now supports the assertion that teaching matters and good teaching prompts changes in the brain that can increase learning. Scientists studying the brains of poor readers who participate in intensive reading programs have documented increased brain activity in the areas used by good readers. After the intervention of strong phonemic awareness lessons, words are recognized instantly, and this is evident in brain-imaging studies. Their newly developed ability to recognize words without decoding or reinventing them each time they appear in a text allows for increased fluency, comprehension, and accuracy.

The beginning reader uses a portion of the brain that involves both the parietal lobes, involved in information processing, spatial orientation, and visual perception, and the temporal lobes, linked to emotional responses, hearing, memory, and speech. These two areas are put to work to identify new words. Broca's area, involved in speech and understanding language, also plays an important role in making word/sound association. With repetition the beginning reader begins to identify patterns between the sounds of spoken language and the letters of the alphabet. They learn to read one letter at a time, just as they learn to utter one sound at a time. As they blend phonemes they begin to decode words. For instance, when a child sees the word "dog" they first connect it to the spoken da-au-gu. As the reader sounds out the word the information then goes to the occipital area where a mental image of a dog develops. This is time consuming, hard work, exasperated by the fact that often the word must be read and reread multiple times before all the associations are made.

As a reader becomes more skilled, a different pathway in the brain is used for reading. In the proficient reader the occipital lobes and the temporal lobes store word forms. Identifying the form of the word facilitates quick recognition; the word no longer needs to be analyzed bit by bit. The form of the word is not the only information stored in these two areas of the brain. An abundance of information about each word is warehoused, including meaning and pronunciation, making it very efficient for the brain to identify the word. Broca's area, that played a key function in the beginning reader identifying words, now has a nominal role. The ability to decode words cannot be underestimated; research shows that decoding abilities are the best predictor of reading comprehension. In addition the skilled reader is able to identify words without any conscious effort, aiding in fluency.

How vocabulary and word recognition/identification are taught has changed drastically. Teachers are asked to consider how students learn new information, how they retain it, and how they can apply these skills to the larger job of being literate. An important part of a quality literacy program is the students' work with vocabulary and word recognition/identification as both have a longlasting impact on their success with literacy. Students with larger vocabularies are more capable readers and they use more strategies to determine unknown words. Word recognition/identification includes all the strategies students employ to decode words, including phonemic analysis, analogies, analysis of syllables, sight word mastery, and analysis of morphemes.

Educators know that retention rates after twenty-four hours for a Lecture mode class= 5 percent, Reading about a topic= 10 percent, an A.V. presentation= 20 percent, Demonstration= 30 percent, A Discussion Group= 50 percent, Practice by Doing= 75 percent, and Teaching Others= 90 percent. This dictates that teachers move away from the lecture or *look it up in the dictionary* methods for vocabulary instruction. Meaningful vocabulary instruction calls for teachers to be aware that connecting to past schema or prior experiences is critical as students store new information by similarities but retrieve it by differences. Good vocabulary and word recognition instruction then will group words to teach by similarities (i.e., vocabulary words to talk about your siblings). This also means that assessments for vocabulary and word recognition/identification need to test distinctly different groups of words not similar groups of words.

Vocabulary and Word Recognition/Identification instruction needs to ask learners to do something significant with their newly learned data or their brain will discard the information within eighteen seconds of processing it. Learning activities need to be purposeful, specific and integrate reading, writing, speaking, listening, and viewing. Reader's Theatre, visual pictures to trigger understanding, pantomime, and paraphrasing are examples of doing something significant with new words or vocabulary. Eight to ten repetitions are necessary for most students to recognize words automatically and the instruction needs to be more than just writing the definition. Knowing the etymology, synonyms, antonyms, multiple meanings, and making a personal connection to the word ensures carryover. New vocabulary should be reviewed in centers, posted on word walls, and used frequently by the teacher in a supported context if we want students to "own" them. By pairing a new, harder word with a known word the teacher can stretch the students without straying from the focus of the lesson. For example, narcissistic could be paired with thinking too much of themselves to let students infer what the hard term means as it relates to a known concept.

Programs of vocabulary and word recognition/identification should provide formative assessments so that students can correct their misconceptions. Summative evaluations come too late in the learning process to inform student learning and a teacher's instructional decision-making. Conversely, immediate or timely feedback helps students and teachers identify strengths and areas needing growth.

If reading is a tool for learning, a process skill and not a content area in and of itself then our instruction needs to mirror this belief by structuring activities and materials so students will not only learn to read but simultaneously read to learn. Consequently, instruction of vocabulary and word recognition/identification needs to occur in the context of real books and authentic printed materials. Isolated, before reading, vocabulary lists are rarely effective. Implanting vocabulary as the class previews a chapter or a new text is more meaningful and more likely to be remembered and used while reading.

Effective literacy teachers provide many, many demonstrations of how to do reading, writing, speaking, listening, and viewing. They design multi-sensory experiences with real books and authentic tasks, maintain a classroom atmosphere that is intense but not pressured, and provide timely and meaningful feedback. Meaningful challenges and an optimal match between readiness and curricular materials and methods allow every student to grow and develop as lifelong readers.

See also: **Challenge and Enrichment; Reading and Comprehension; Reading and Fluency; Content Area Literacy.**

Further Readings

Fountas, I., Pinnell, G. (2000). *Guiding Readers & Writers 3–6*. Portsmouth, NH: Heinemann.

Shaywitz, S.E., Shaywitz, B.A. (2003). Brain scans show dyslexics read better with alternative strategies. *Biological Psychiatry* 54:25–33.

Tompkins, G. (2005). *Literacy for the 21st Century: A balanced approach* (4th ed.), NJ: Prentice Hall.

National Reading Panel 2000. Teaching Students to Read. www.ncrel.org/rf/sbrr/five.htm

LAURIE WENGER, ED.D.

S

Schizophrenia

Schizophrenia is a disease of the brain that affects approximately 2.2 million Americans. Symptoms usually begin between ages sixteen and thirty and include hearing voices (auditory hallucinations), delusions, and disordered thought patterns. In the past two decades, there has been an outpouring of research on the brains of individuals who have schizophrenia showing that such brains have abnormalities in both structure and function. This has conclusively proven that schizophrenia is a brain disease in the same way that multiple sclerosis, Parkinson's disease, and Alzheimer's disease are brain diseases.

Abnormalities of Brain Structure

Research on the structure of brains of people with schizophrenia is done using imaging techniques (e.g., magnetic resonance imaging, MRI) on living individuals and also by studying the brains of individuals with schizophrenia after they have died. At first glance, such brains appear to be normal except for slight shrinkage in some cases. On closer examination, however, a number of structural abnormalities become apparent. These abnormalities can best be measured on individuals with schizophrenia who have not been treated with antipsychotic medications, commonly used to treat schizophrenia, because these medications themselves may cause some structural brain changes, thus creating confusion regarding which changes are disease-related and which are medication-related.

The most consistently replicated structural brain change in schizophrenia is enlargement of the brain ventricles, the fluid-filled spaces in the middle of each half of the brain. This is illustrated by identical twins, one of whom has schizophrenia and has enlarged brain ventricles and the other of whom does not have schizophrenia and has normal ventricles. It is thought that the enlargement of the brain ventricles is caused by a disease-related loss of brain tissue in the brain areas immediately adjacent to the ventricles.

In addition to the enlarged brain ventricles, abnormalities in never-treated individuals with schizophrenia have been reported for a variety of brain structures thought to be involved in schizophrenia. These include the hippocampus, amygdala, cingulate, frontal cortex, temporal cortex, thalamus, and cerebellum. The hippocampus is thought to be especially important in schizophrenia and has been more carefully studied than any other brain area. In addition to having a slight reduction in its overall volume in individuals with schizophrenia, the hippocampus has also been reported to have subtle disease-related differences in its shape.

Abnormalities of Brain Function

The types of brain functions that have been most extensively studied in schizophrenia are the neurological, neuropsychological, and electrophysiological functions and brain metabolism. In each of these, there are well-documented abnormalities in individuals with schizophrenia who have never been treated with antipsychotic medication.

Neurologically, individuals with schizophrenia may have abnormalities in spontaneous movements called dyskinesias. For example, they may show sudden involuntary movements of their tongue, facial muscles, shoulders, or arms. Such movements may also be a side effect of antipsychotic medication, but at least eleven studies have demonstrated that these movements also occur more often in never-treated patients than in normal controls.

Seven recent studies have also shown that individuals with schizophrenia who have never been treated with antipsychotic medication may have more rigidity, tremor, and slowing of their movements, similar to what is seen in individuals with Parkinson's disease. These symptoms may also occur as side effects of antipsychotics used to treat schizophrenia.

A third type of neurological abnormality found in some individuals with schizophrenia is what is commonly referred to as neurological soft signs. These include activities such as being able to identify the type of coin put in your hand while your eyes are closed. Neurological soft signs involve impairments in the integration and coordination of complex sensory functions. At least seven studies have reported more neurological soft signs in individuals with schizophrenia who have never been treated with antipsychotic medication compared to normal controls. Taking antipsychotic medications, in fact, appears to decrease the neurological soft signs and improve the person's neurological function.

Still another type of neurological dysfunction found in some individuals with schizophrenia is decreased perception of pain. This occurs in only a small subset of patients, but when it does occur, it can be very dramatic. There are reports, for example, of individuals with schizophrenia undergoing surgery, such as the removal of their appendix, without requiring any anesthesia and claiming that they felt no pain. The brain abnormality in such cases almost certainly involves the thalamus, which is the part of the brain that plays a major role in the perception of pain. Multiple studies have suggested that the thalamus is involved in schizophrenia.

The second major type of brain dysfunction commonly found in individuals with schizophrenia is neuropsychological dysfunction, especially verbal memory, attention, and planning (also called executive function). Verbal memory, for example, is tested by reading a list of objects to the individual and then asking them to repeat the list. Planning (executive function) may be tested by asking the person to match colors and shapes of objects in a test in which the rules for matching are constantly changing (the Wisconsin Card Sort test).

In the past two decades, over two hundred studies have been published reporting neuropsychological abnormalities in individuals with schizophrenia; in eight of these studies, the individuals had never been treated with antipsychotic medications when tested, but the outcome of these studies showed just as many abnormalities as in the studies in which the individuals had been treated.

One particular type of neuropsychological abnormality commonly found in individuals with schizophrenia has drawn much attention in recent years. This is self-perception, the ability of the person to step back and objectively look at him or herself. The ability to do this reflects complex brain functions that involve the frontal and parietal lobes as well as other areas. Neurologically impaired individuals, especially those who have had strokes involving the right side of the brain, are sometimes observed to lose this ability to perceive themselves. For example, people with a stroke-caused paralysis of their left leg will sometimes adamantly deny that anything is wrong with their leg.

This is not merely denial, a psychological stratagem we all use occasionally. This is instead an anatomically based loss of self-perception and is technically called anosognosia. In recent years, research has demonstrated that approximately half of all individuals with schizophrenia have partial or complete anosognosia, meaning that they do not realize that anything is wrong with them. They therefore commonly refuse to take medication, and a disproportionate of these untreated individuals end up among the homeless population.

The third major type of brain dysfunction seen in individuals with schizophrenia is electrophysiological abnormalities. Electrical impulses are one way that neurons and other brain cells communicate with each other. One means of measuring electrical impulses in the brain is by electroencephalogram (EEG), commonly used to detect abnormalities in brain diseases such as epilepsy. EEG studies of individuals with schizophrenia also have shown abnormalities, although these are much more subtle than those seen in epilepsy.

Another technique used to measure electrophysiological function is called evoked potentials. A loud sound, for example, elicits a brain electrical impulse (the evoked potential) that is then measured. Many studies, including some done on patients who have never been treated with antipsychotic medications, have demonstrated electrophysiological abnormalities in individuals with schizophrenia.

The final major type of brain dysfunction seen in individuals with schizophrenia is abnormalities of brain metabolism. These studies are typically done using advanced imaging techniques for studying the brain, including positron emission tomography (PET) and functional magnetic resonance imaging (fMRI). As it is known that antipsychotic medications can affect these tests, it is important to use never-treated individuals whenever possible.

Since 1991, more than twenty studies have measured brain metabolism in individuals with schizophrenia who have never been treated; all except one of them found more abnormalities of brain metabolism in the individuals with schizophrenia compared to normal controls.

Evidence has accumulated in recent decades that the brains of individuals with schizophrenia have abnormalities in brain structure and function. Studies done on patients who have never been treated with antipsychotic medications have proven that these brain abnormalities are disease-related and are not a consequence of having been treated with antipsychotic medications.

It should be cautioned, however, that these abnormalities of brain structure and function are nonspecific, that is, none of them are specifically diagnostic for schizophrenia. In other words, abnormalities such as enlarged brain ventricles, neurological soft signs, and electrophysiological abnormalities may also be found in many other brain diseases and occasionally in people who are otherwise normal. All of these abnormalities, however, occur statistically more commonly in individuals with schizophrenia than in individuals who do not have schizophrenia and, as such, provide the basis for categorizing schizophrenia as a brain disease.

With regard to what causes schizophrenia, a definitive answer to this question is not yet known. There are many theories and much research is taking place. It is widely assumed that genes play some role, although probably as predisposing genes rather than directly causative genes. It is also known that brain neurochemicals are involved, including the chemicals that transmit messages from neuron to neuron (neurotransmitters), such as dopamine, glutamate and GABA. Many of the medications used to treat schizophrenia target these neurotransmitters, and that is thought to be one of the reasons why they are effective in improving symptoms. Another current research approach is examining the possibility that infectious agents, such as viruses and protozoa, play a role in causing the disease; this research appears promising.

Instructional Strategies

The following strategies have been found to be effective with schizophrenic high school and college students:

- Spend extra time with the student as needed
- Teach study skills and time management
- Give direct instruction on target behaviors
- Clearly define expected behaviors, requirements, and assignments
- Allow students to tape-record lectures
- Make available a note-taker
- Provide hard copies of notes, and assignments for later reference
- Create an absence of background noise

- Allow them to work on computers and on-line from home when possible (reduces stress)
- Be aware of emotionally sensitive course material and discuss it privately prior to class
- Establish a behavior management program that includes positive behavior supports, immediate consequences, consistency, and a cool-down area.
- Give extra time on exams
- Be flexible
- Don't single them out
- Ask them what they need from you to concentrate and be productive.

See also: **Adolescent Cognition Development; Adolescent Social and Emotional Development.**

Further Readings

Deveson, A. (1992). *Tell Me I'm Here.* New York: Penguin Books.
Sheehan, S. (1982). *Is There No Place on Earth for Me?* Boston: Houghton, Mifflin.
Torrey, E.F. (2002). Studies of individuals with schizophrenia never treated with antipsychotic medications: a review. *Schizophrenia Research* 58:101–115.
Torrey, E.F. (2006). *Surviving Schizophrenia: A Manual for Families, Consumers, and Providers* (5th ed.). New York: Harper Collins.

E. FULLER TORREY, M.D. AND
MICHAEL B. KNABLE, D.O.

Self-Efficacy

Much has been said, in the last century, about the need for students to have a positive self-image. How we feel about ourselves is paramount to how we tackle problems, how we persevere, and to our own mental well-being. While a positive self-image is important, self-efficacy may be even more crucial to academic and social success. It is thought to be the gate-keeper to **motivation** and it has a significant impact on our **self-esteem**. In reality an individual may not be able to sustain positive self-esteem over time without self-efficacy.

Self-efficacy differs from self-esteem. Self-efficacy is built on fact: "I know that I can be successful in this subject, class, or endeavor because I have been successful before." Self-esteem is built on "I think and I feel," not necessarily on fact. While self-esteem is a judgment of self-worth based on how I feel about myself in comparison to the value put on my perceived abilities; self-efficacy is a judgment of my ability to succeed based on past experience. This is one of the reasons that it is so important to provide students with the opportunity to be successful: success really does breed success.

A meta-analysis study, conducted through the Mid-continent Regional Educational Laboratory, found self-efficacy to have one of the highest effect sizes on student learning. When teachers reinforced self-efficacy in students (as opposed to control groups in which self-efficacy was not addressed), there was an effect size of eighty, which translates to a percentile gain of 29 points. This means that a class average at the 50th percentile where self-efficacy is properly incorporated can increase to the 79th percentile in learning.

Origins of Self-Efficacy

The basis for the idea of self-efficacy came from a Stanford psychologist, Albert Bandura, in the 1950s who believed in a social learning theory that was an extension of the classical behaviorist principles related to modeling, imitation, and reinforcement. Bandura published *Social Foundations of Thought and Action* in 1986 in which he outlined his belief that self-efficacy was critical to human behavior and motivation. Bandura would later comment that self-reflection is the most distinctively human characteristic. Self-reflective judgments include perceptions of self-efficacy—the beliefs that we hold about our capability to organize and execute a course of action required to manage prospective situations. In essence, self-efficacy is the confidence that we have in our own abilities. Without positive self-efficacy, people tend to have a low locus of control and a feeling of helplessness. For students with inner-city **poverty** characteristics, being able to tap into the self-system of the brain, and in particular, self-efficacy is a positive start in changing defeatist behavior.

Connection to Brain Research

An individual's positive or negative self-efficacy is determined by the storage of long-term memories created by past experiences. The self-system of the brain houses the memories of what constitutes our self-efficacy. This is not a singular place but is composed of the attitudes, emotions and beliefs that are at the heart of self-efficacy. An area in the left hemisphere of the brain manages the inner sense of self, while the right hemisphere controls the outer impressions of the environment.

Memories are initially stored in working memory and then may or may not be moved into our long-term memory (LTM). Working memory connections between neurons are temporary and wear off in minutes or hours. The hippocampus, Greek for seahorse because of its shape, stores temporary memories and then decides which information will be turned into long-term memory. LTM storage is influenced by information that is repeated, meaningful, or filled with emotion.

Long-term memory (LTM) storage is relatively permanent and anatomically changes the brain. LTM requires the synthesis of new proteins. CREB, a protein, becomes active with LTM storage; it signals other proteins that aid in assisting the growth of new synaptic connections between neurons. For instance, students that are learning to read new words are growing dendrites and making new synaptic connections with each bit of learning. In reverse, if CREB is not activated it stops production of other proteins and actually prohibits long-term memories from being formed. Once synaptic connections have been formed (evidence that you have learned something new) you no longer possess the same brain.

It is the self-system that engages the brain in what must be attended to in all facets of the learning process and then becomes dedicated to the work at hand. Self-efficacy, how we feel about the learning and the personal relevance of the learning, determines our willingness to engage.

Instructional Strategies that Enhance Self-Efficacy

First and probably the most common way that students establish self-efficacy is through positive mastery experience. Strong personal performance that is positive and satisfying leads to a belief in one's abilities to be successful again. Teachers should provide opportunities for all students to be successful. Begin with simple tasks and questions and build to more complex tasks and questions.

Self-efficacy is greatly influenced by the **feedback** that we get from others, especially teachers and other influential individuals in our lives. Feedback should be both positive and prescriptive and it should be deserved. Just saying, "good job" is not what is meant by feedback. Students need to know specifics: how they are doing; what they are doing right; what needs work; and how to make adjustments. Writing personal goals for learning and then revisiting those goals allows students to see their progress. Never give praise that is undeserved; students quickly see through this and will learn not to trust what you say.

Provide ample wait time after questions. There is a tendency in all of us to move on too quickly when we fear that the student does not know the answer. Allowing sufficient wait time conveys confidence in your student's abilities. Other ways to communicate positive teacher expectations are by giving cues and prompts, monitor your nonverbal communication (smiling, tone of voice, proximity), flexible grouping strategies, believe all your students can learn and deserve to be challenged.

From the works of Bandura on the effects of self-efficacy beliefs we can conclude that consciously or unconsciously students do make choices based on their self-efficacy beliefs. They will take part in those tasks in which they feel confident and will avoid those in which they lack confidence. Once students begin a task, their willingness to complete the task is based, in part, on self-efficacy. Students with a low sense of efficacy will acquiesce when they confront obstacles to the work. As we all know, stress and anxiety are increased when we lack the confidence to engage and complete a task.

See Also: **Information Processing Model.**

Further Readings

Bandura, A. (1994). Self-efficacy. In V.S. Ramachandran (Ed.). *Encyclopedia of Human Behavior* (4), pp. 71–81. New York: Academic Press.

Marzano, R.J. (2001). *Designing a New Taxonomy of Educational Objectives.* Thousand Oaks, CA: Corwin Press.

Tileston, D.W. (2000). *What Every Teacher Should Know About Motivation.* Thousand Oaks, CA: Corwin Press.

Belief and Brain Research, www.control-z.com/pages/bbr.html

DONNA WALKER TILESTON, ED.D.

Self-Esteem

Self-esteem is one of the most misused, misunderstood psychological terms in today's world. The self-esteem industry has made millions promoting the quick fix, all the while supporting superficial and shallow self-esteem. Countless people have been led to believe that the memorization of *"I'm Special"* and *"Yes I can"* poems and similar incantations will lead to inner security and strength, and a new life.

On the other hand, *authentic self-esteem* results when people reach an emotional–cognitive balance that allows them to feel honestly good about themselves and be quietly confident in taking these "selves" to the outer world. They enjoy who they are, are willing to take calculated risks, able to acknowledge their large and small successes, willing to accept responsibility, able to give themselves to others without fear of loss, and while they appreciate honest feedback they are not dependent upon the applause of others.

It is critical that we understand that our self-esteem is a developed emotional–cognitive interaction that exists between the limbic areas and frontal cortices of our brain. The word "emotional" is placed before cognitive because authentic self-esteem is highly dependent on one's emotional neural networks and corresponding memories. These networks and memories are normally influenced by controlling messaging from the cognitive, prefrontal cortex. This desired emotional–cognitive balance may be more difficult to achieve if the developing brain has been negatively impacted by excessive stress or trauma.

There are a number of brain facts that should be understood. First of all, material that is memorized in rote format tends to be stored only as language in the left frontal cortex. Unless efforts are made to apply the message within the language to gain increased understanding or to process it in other ways the material will remain as language. In other words, for this material to become useful more neural connections and neural integration *must* be formed. The impact of most motivational speeches tends to be short-lived unless the person makes an immediate, concerted effort to enhance their own skill set using this information.

The limbic area, primarily the amygdala, continually focuses on our survival and unless the frontal cortices are able to generate stable plans and send soothing messages to this area, the amygdala, overcome by fear, will inhibit or even sabotage the growth of self-esteem. The amygdala does not have the capacity to form or reframe memories based on language alone as emotional memories tend to be episodic in nature. Some of these memories may have reference values, "right and wrong," empathy, success, and community. For example, if a person has a fear of not being accepted by others, it is necessary to provide safe environments and activities where that person can, over time, gain certain social skills and learn how to read the actions of others. Activity is critical.

The cognitive neural networks associated with self-esteem are built over time through language, reflection, building on previous learning, and again activity. The ability to process is critical. This may include processing data, thinking in conceptual terms, projecting in an abstract manner, and being emotionally committed to the activity. The person who learns that he or she can be self-dependent, has the capacity to make choices, can take calculated risks, care, and can take a position that may be inconsistent with that of their peers.

Through practice and supportive experiences the brain becomes increasingly comfortable in sharing this state of mind with the community at large. Although we cannot give a person self-esteem, we can coach the person to reach this state. This coaching must include teaching, modeling, and evaluation.

Characteristics of People with High Self-Esteem

- Act with integrity including acting responsibly, with psychological harmony, sincerity and consistency, possessing inner delight, being trustworthy and able to stand tall.
- Are most likely to have emotional bonds with one or more adults and possess "memory banks" full of positive affirmation experiences.
- Have an increased sense of purpose.
- Are accepting of others.
- Have the capability to laugh at themselves and have a healthy sense of humor.
- Are willing to seek out help from experts or colleagues.
- Perform better academically.
- Are more motivated in school.
- Have fewer classroom management problems.
- Get along better with teachers and peers.

Characteristics of People with Shallow Self-Esteem

- Place great reliance upon material possessions.
- Denigrate others for their own personal gain.
- Cling to fashion statements, social or cultural status for self-definition.
- Rely on "quick fixes" or applause.
- Are excessively focused on instant gratification or egocentrism.
- Develop an artificial persona or try continually to "play a role."
- Use chemical substances to enhance feelings of self.
- Are more at-risk of dropping out of school.
- Experience more depression.

The primary purpose of our brain is to keep us alive. However, "staying alive" also includes the maintenance of a positive sense of self. We all want to be somebody and hopefully this can be accomplished in a profound, honest manner, rich in value and emotional security.

The Problems of Shallow Self-Esteem

Many people base their self-identity on their car, clothes, holidays, brand of alcohol, work, office size, parking spot, physical size or shape, power over people, snow board, family status, children's accomplishments and the size of their bank accounts. Maintaining this sense of self requires a constant struggle to "keep up appearances."

The hyper vigilance of shallow self-esteem leaves the bully prone to acts of violence, disrespect toward authority, extreme sensitivity to criticism, and other negative behaviors. Their emotional memories tend to be those of fear, failure, and helplessness. Many bully to bolster their own self-esteem.

Shallow self-esteem leaves individuals vulnerable to be used and abused by others. I think of Jack, the overweight outsider who gained a group of friends when his Dad let him bring the family car to school. His "new buddies" were happy to have Jack drive them all over town. Jack told me, "I didn't used to have any friends but now I have lots of friends."

Disparity within a school usually leads to the forming of informal clusters of students. In addition, subtle differences occur within each of the subgroups as individuals vie for status. Special shoes or clothes often become the currency to "buy" their self-esteem. It is extremely difficult for most adolescents to say "I don't need special shoes to allow me to feel good about myself."

Behavior can be a self-esteem item. Some students take a perverse pride and gain self-esteem by being an "active slacker." They are generally afraid to put forth an effort and their self-esteem rests with being successfully unsuccessful. Other students act outside of the rules to get applause. This feedback re-enforces their behavior and it satisfies their need to feel good right here, right now.

Teenage self-esteem is often shaped by the intense marketing and media imaging that is fostered and supported by teen magazines, electronic media, advertisements, TV sitcoms, teen music, and associated peer pressure. This superficial approach to character development leaves these teens vulnerable to incredible self-obsession and poor decision-making that can have serious short and long-term effects on themselves and others.

Some people have suggested that children who are successful "car thieves" or "drug dealers" are held in high regard in their "communities" and may have good self-esteem. While these individuals may feel a momentary sense of pride they constantly need to have "criminal hits" to maintain that feeling. This also applies to seemingly "popular" students who harass others.

Even under normal conditions teenagers may feel "they're not good enough" or "smart enough" and that they have failed. They are likely to feel they have failed yet again when they are unable to meet the artificial expectations of today's pressure-ridden teenage world. Teenagers are extremely vulnerable to **depression**. Authentic self-esteem will not prevent a person from becoming depressed but it is likely to help the person regain good mental health.

The power of positive thinking (POPT) is largely a left brain activity. Readers of POPT literature are often left feeling empty, perhaps even failures, when they are unable to convert POPT messages into reality. In fact, authentic self-esteem is the outcome of the integration of many brain areas and a multitude of cognitive and emotional memories.

Cautionary Points

Sociopaths, psychopaths, and persons with antisocial personality disorder usually present a strong sense of self. This pattern of behavior is, however, devoid of most emotions such as fear, empathy, and social conscience. Blatant egocentric behavior should not be confused with authentic self-esteem. Such behavior is sometimes exhibited by one-dimensional star athletes who are overidolized both inside the school and the community at large.

See also: **Addiction; Adolescent Social and Emotional Development; Emotion; Episodic Memory; Trauma; Processing Time.**

Further Readings

Branden, N. (1995). *Six Pillars of Self Esteem* (1st ed.). New York, NY: Bantam Books.

Dacine, R.N., Caine, G. (1997). *Unleashing the Power of Perceptual Change: The Potential of Brain-Based Teaching.* Alexandria, VA: ASCD.

DeMoulin, D.F. (2000). I Like Me!: Enhancing Self Concept in Kindergarten-age Children Through Active School/Business Partnerships, *NASP Communique* 27(8).

Reasoner, R. (2000). *Self-esteem and Youth: What Research Has To Say About It.* e-book on International Council, www.self-esteem-international.org

DAVID HALSTEAD, M.ED.

Semantic Memory

In 1972, the psychologist, Endel Tulving, used the term semantic memory to describe this memory for organized world knowledge. Semantic memory is considered one of the Explicit, or Declarative, memory capacities. These memories can be consciously retrieved and can be "declared" or put into words. It is the long-term memory for facts and includes words, symbols for words, meanings, rules, formulas, and general knowledge. Much of this information is organized into categories, such as: Fido is a sheepdog, sheepdogs are dogs, dogs are animals. This factual information is stored through a structure in the brain called the hippocampus, which is found in the medial temporal lobe. If incoming sensory information contains facts, it will trigger the hippocampus to search its files for matching information. This information will then be brought into temporary storage areas to be examined. The brain will try to make connections between previously stored facts and new information. In this way, new long-term memories can be made.

The hippocampus is essential to the storage and the retrieval of semantic memories. The memory itself is distributed in various brain areas, but the hippocampus keeps track of it and pulls it back together. A person who has recently seen a movie stores visual memories of the faces and objects in the temporal lobe; landscapes and patterns in the parietal lobe; and social interaction is stored in the frontal lobes. As the movie is reflected upon, the components of the memory are pulled together by the hippocampus. The memory is reconstructed, so therefore, it may not be completely accurate. To recall memories without the hippocampus, a process that neuroscientist Daniel Siegel refers to as "cortical consolidation" must occur. It is believed that memories become self-sufficient after multiple repetitions of the memory. At that time, the memory becomes independent of the hippocampus. This process, however, can take years. The evidence of this presents itself in individuals who have hippocampal injuries due to an accident. The damage prevents them from storing new memories, but many memories prior to the accident are retrievable.

It was through surgery on a young man known only by his initials, H.M., that much was discovered about memory and the hippocampus. H.M. suffered a fall as a child and many years later began to have seizures. Medication could not control them, and eventually they became so severe that surgery was suggested. On August 23, 1953, Dr. William Scoville performed a bilateral resection of the medial temporal lobe, in hopes that it would alleviate H.M.'s seizures. After the surgery, the seizures had decreased significantly; however, so did H.M.'s ability to form new memories. His doctor had to reintroduce herself to him each day. Sadly, if she stepped out of the room for mere minutes, upon her return he did not remember ever having met her. Even though his I.Q. remained normal, his recall ability was absent.

Semantic memory is used extensively in school. The difficulty lies in the processes the brain must use to store these memories. Semantic information must go through short-term memory processes. Information is received into sensory memory. If it is attended to, it begins the immediate memory process. This fleeting memory lasts only four to twenty seconds. The information must then be rehearsed in the process called active working memory. This memory can hold information for extended periods of time, but it will remain a temporary memory until connections are made. When a student "crams" for an exam, information is stored in working memory and is quickly forgotten after the test.

Using either recognition or recall usually tests semantic information. Authentic assessment may be used, but most standardized tests rely on these two types of assessment. Recognition tests include multiple choice questions, matching, and true – false. Recall tests are essay questions that involve retrieving information from long-term memory, manipulating it in working memory, and producing written answers. Recall tests are thought to utilize more brainpower because only one cue is given to trigger the memory. Recognition tests offer at least two cues. For instance, a recall question might be "Describe the main character." For a recognition test, the question could be multiple choice as in "The main character has the following characteristics: (A) charming, kind, and patient; (B) hostile, angry, and sullen; (C) kind, patient, good-natured. The answer selections in the multiple-choice question provide more cues to trigger the memory.

Researcher Howard Eichenbaum refers to the commonly held belief that our semantic memories are born out of our **episodic memories**. Our lives are a series of experiences or episodes. The brain takes the repeated bits of information out of the experiences, and those become our semantic memories. As an example, consider what you might know about apples: (1) they are different colors including red and green, (2) they grow on trees, (3) they are a fruit, (4) they are somewhat round and can roll, (5) most smell sweet, (6) some grandmas make apple pies, apple crisp, and apple cider. Even this limited information was probably derived from many "apple" experiences. The experiences themselves may have escaped our memories so that we no longer know the time and the place that these events occurred, but the distinguishing characteristics of apples stay with us due to the repetition of those features. Hence, the episodes contained some repetitive information that eventually became facts that are stored in long-term semantic memory.

Multiple rehearsals are necessary for semantic information to be stored in long-term memory. The more varied these rehearsals are, the more brain areas will have access to the memory. Each rehearsal helps to organize the information for later retrieval.

Instructional Strategies to Make Semantic Memories

As semantic memory for facts and concepts is most often assessed in school, it behooves educators to have a toolbox of strategies for processing new information. Keep in mind that information is more easily remembered if it can be attached to prior knowledge.

Graphic organizers help students access previously learned information. They help form a picture of information for the students to remember. One popular example for accessing prior knowledge is a K-W-L chart. Three columns are drawn on a paper with one initial in each. The K is for what the students already Know about the topic. This information is brainstormed by the class or in small groups. Then the W column is utilized, which stands for What you want to know. Students discuss this. Then the subject is researched or taught. The final column, L, allows the students to determine what they have Learned. Other graphic organizers include concept maps, mind maps, and webs.

Comparisons, examples, and associations often activate semantic information. Identifying the similarities and differences in a topic may be helpful. This scientifically based research strategy includes metaphors, similes, and analogies. Allowing students to create their own metaphors, like "The brain is a motorcycle," encourages the student to examine the attributes of each and determine how this statement is true. In so doing, the student learns about the brain and connects that information to previously stored motorcycle knowledge. Higher level thinking skills are used when identifying similarities and differences.

Semantic strategies include emotional situations such as debate and role-playing. Defending one's stance in a debate demands that the participant know the information well. Role-playing adds the dimension of movement and emotion. Students who participate in role-playing often remember information through their bodies and through the feelings they experienced.

Repetition is essential for some semantic learning. For students to learn the multiplication tables, they must be rehearsed extensively. This repetition strengthens the connections being formed in the brain. Although this type of repetition may be rote rehearsal, applying the facts and making them meaningful is a way to elaborate. Elaboration provides more meaning to the content.

A powerful semantic memory strategy is teaching. Research suggests that teaching allows us to store and recall more information than simply seeing it or hearing about it. For students to teach concepts and facts, they must first understand them. A useful practice is to pair students and have them take turns teaching each other the concepts just covered.

Questioning sessions may emphasize significant pieces of semantic information. Asking open-ended questions that begin with How? or Why? often permits students to think seriously about the question and access prior knowledge to answer it. Eventually the goal is to have the students asking and answering their own questions. Applying questions from the various levels of Bloom's Taxonomy can increase critical thinking about the topic and aid in creating long-term semantic memories.

Outlining, summarizing, creating timelines, and giving practice tests may all encourage the formation of semantic memories. As most state assessments are paper and pencil tests, practice tests may help transfer information to the semantic test format.

See also: **Episodic Memory; Forgetting; Information Processing Model.**

Further Readings

Eichenbaum, H. (2003). Speaker. *The Neurobiology of Learning and Memory. Learning and the Brain Conference.* Cambridge, MA.

Siegel, D. (1999). *The Developing Mind.* New York: The Guildford Press.

Sprenger, M. (2005). *How to Teach So Students Remember.* Alexandria, VA: ASCD.

Squire, L., E. Kandel. (1999). *Memory, From Mind to Molecules.* New York: Scientific American Library.

MARILEE SPRENGER

Sexual Learning

A common understanding of sex education is that it reveals the secret of how babies are conceived and then born into the world. In the past, boys and girls would be separated for a short lecture on physiological changes during puberty; and then exposed to this big secret. But the domain of sexuality is broader and more pervasive than the mechanics of reproduction. Sexual development during puberty is nothing less than a complete transformation of the biological, hormonal, emotional, cognitive, and social being. It is much more than being male or a female. Sexuality is at the heart of our identity as a person.

The neural map of masculinity and femininity is constructed in the womb. The moment of conception begins the initial trajectory of gender but this differentiation is not evident until the sixth week. The basic ground plan of the fetus is female and it continues to grow as a female unless the chromosomes produce the primitive gonads that release high levels of testosterone and another hormone that impedes the growth of the female reproductive system. Testosterone not only animates the development of the male reproductive system, but it "masculinizes" the neurological system and begins to form the male brain.

By adulthood the male brain is about 10 percent larger than the female's, but the female brain contains about 10 percent more brain cells in the cortical layers. Research suggests that the corpus collosum, which facilitates communication between hemispheres of the brain, is larger with more connections in women. This may in part explain why women are more adept at processing feelings and recognizing feelings in others. The male brain has more fluid and fat, which seems to speed communication, while the female brain has larger structures to impede aggressive impulses. **Gender differences** are evident in sensory acuity, brain size, and specific cognitive abilities.

Masculinity and femininity develop out of an interplay of both genetics and experience. It is difficult to single out one or the other as a cause. However, neuroscience is giving us added insight into sexuality.

Puberty

During puberty, the process of sexual differentiation that began in the womb is completed. Neuroscientists believe that the brain is actually what triggers puberty. It is speculated that the massive pruning of dendrites and synapse during puberty prompts the maturation of the hypothalamus that initiates a carefully orchestrated set of neurological and hormonal growth patterns.

Androgens in males, in particular testosterone, and estrogen in females are released at higher levels. Once it was believed these hormones only impacted the hypothalamus, however, researchers recently discovered androgens and estrogen were sprinkled all over the brain, including the cortex and cerebellum. They set into motion the development of the primary sexual characteristics, the testes and ovaries, and the secondary sexual characteristics, lowered voices in males, pubic hair and breast development.

During puberty testosterone levels in young males are the highest they will ever be. They are ten to twenty times higher than females and one thousand percent higher than levels during childhood. Testosterone is associated with dynamic, impulsive, and aggressive behavior, along with an increased sexual appetite.

Estrogen levels in females are ten times as high as in males. The hormone patterns of females take them through monthly fluctuations that can spawn depressed and irritable moods. Norepinephrine (energizes), serotonin (soothes), and dopamine (pleasure), are neurotransmitters normally found in the body. Beginning with puberty they are mixed with fluctuations of estrogen causing girls to feel lonely and sad one moment and gregarious and happy the next.

While it is possible to measure physiological growth during puberty in terms of inches and pounds, the impact on the personality and psychological profile of young people is difficult to quantify. Puberty launches the child on a journey of self-discovery that moves toward autonomy and self-sufficiency. The transition from childhood to adulthood requires mastery of a complex set of cognitive, emotional, and social competencies.

Gender or biological sex: There is no single biological parameter that makes one male or female. Gender is determined by the interaction of chromosomes, hormones, and the growth of internal and external genitalia. In approximately one out of one hundred births, physiological differences deviate from the standard male or female with regards to chromosomes, hormones, genitalia and/or reproductive ability. This condition of gender ambiguity is known as inter-sex.

One variable is the hormonal environment of the womb. A genetic female exposed to high levels of androgens in the womb may have female reproductive organs yet appear male externally. Conversely, a male who is underexposed to androgens may not develop a penis. In other words, the gender that becomes hardwired in the brain may be different than the genitalia that develop. Every year, about one in four thousand children are born whose gender is ambiguous. Typically, prompt surgery has been used to assign a gender along with hormone therapy to "masculinize" or "feminize" the brain. Currently, the trend is to wait until the child reaches puberty to allow the individual to develop an internal sense of being male or female before determining gender.

Gender identity: Gender identity is the subjective aspect of sexuality, a distinct feeling of being male or female. Awareness of gender seems to begin at a very early age and develops over a lifetime. With the rapid physiological and sexual growth during puberty, the internal sense of being male or female comes into sharp focus. There is a sense of urgency in the hormonal rush of young boys, a growing awareness of sexual power. A young girl realizes that her developing figure generates new and unfamiliar attention from men. These new feelings must be negotiated and integrated into the personality. For most people gender identity is consistent with their biological sex. The further away from the cultural norm of masculinity and femininity a youth finds him/herself, the more difficult the challenge.

Gender roles: These describe the acceptable roles and behaviors assigned to females and males by a particular culture. They are the learned behaviors and attitudes about how men and women are expected to act. The manner in which a culture defines acceptable male or female behavior changes over time. In the past century, the parameters that define gender roles have shifted. There are more options for the type of career choice, acceptable modes of parenting, and how men and women relate. Much of the learning of attitudes about gender roles comes from modeling and is not always taught overtly. This learning is a process that begins at birth and continues throughout a lifetime.

Gender Expression: This refers to the way a person's sense of maleness or femaleness is expressed through behavior, manner of dress, hair style, and mannerisms. Gender expression may conform to socially sanctioned gender roles, deviate somewhat or deviate to a marked degree. Youth may choose to defy accepted gender expression as a way to rebel or establish independence. The use of jewelry; earrings; short, long or colored hair; tight, baggy or revealing clothing; tattoos and body piercing; are popular ways to flaunt accepted gender expression or establish a unique look or identity.

Sexual orientation: This describes the pattern of romantic, emotional and sexual attraction. Sexual orientation can be a predominant attraction to the same sex (lesbian, gay), a relatively equal attraction to both sexes (bi-sexual) or to the opposite sex (heterosexual). Sexual orientation seems to be influenced by a variety of genetic, hormonal, and environmental influences. Sexual orientation defines the nature of sexual relationships. Adolescents sometimes struggle with the acceptance of sexual orientation and periods of experimentation are not unusual.

Though the dynamics are not clearly understood, sexual orientation seems to be well established by the age of five. Recent evidence demonstrates a difference in the size of the hypothalamus in gay men as compared to heterosexual men. Sensitivity in the inner ear in lesbian women is closer to that of men than women and seems to result from higher levels of testosterone in the womb. These differences are examples of increasing evidence that sexual orientation is a predisposition that is hardwired into the brain.

Transgender. When someone's internal sense of being male or female (gender identity) does not match their biological genitalia, this condition is referred to as transgender. Such a discrepancy is frequently accompanied by distress as a person tries to establish a healthy sexual identity in a culture that only officially recognizes male and female expressions that match biological sex. For some children, this awareness manifests as a feeling of "being different" from same-sexed peers. Some transgender individuals choose to undergo a process of hormone therapy and sex reassignment surgery to have their biological sex match their gender identity. The shifts are referred to as male to female (MTF) or female to male (FTM).

Adolescents must navigate all of these domains of gender to develop a healthy sense of self. There are many permutations of gender roles, gender identity, gender expression, and sexual orientation. They are an essential part of the adolescent quest for determining "who am I?" Just knowing that one is male or female is only the beginning.

Sexual Behavior

Adolescents live in a culture that exposes them to highly sexualized images on a regular basis. Of all industrialized nations, the United States has the highest rate of teen pregnancy and sexually transmitted diseases (STD). This is still true even though teen pregnancy declined 28 percent between 1990 and 2000. Nearly four out of every five teen males and females have had sex by age twenty. By this time, those who are sexually active have had two or more sexual partners. Teen sexual activity can be sporadic. While approximately half of high school students have had sexual intercourse, at any one time 66 percent are abstinent, that is, not having had sex in the past three months. Each year, one out of four sexually active teens will get a STD with half of all new HIV infections occurring in youth under the age of twenty-four.

The average age of marriage in the western world hovers around twenty-five. This means that there is a thirteen year span between the onset of puberty and the typical age of marriage. This is also a period of dramatic personal and social growth. There is no cultural consensus as to the guidelines for sexual behaviors and relationships that guide young men and women through this period. Perspectives range from complete abstinence until marriage to the view that what does not harm oneself or another is acceptable.

Social/Emotional

Fulfillment in life cannot be measured by money, career status, or the number of possessions. The biggest predictor of happiness and fulfillment is the quality of emotional well-being and personal relationships. Adolescents must learn to develop a set of emotional and social competencies that are essential for the broad range of relationships that adulthood requires. Some relationships will be intimate and sexual, while others will be familial, professional, or based on friendship.

The growth spurt of puberty is accompanied by a growth in the emotional life. The surge of hormones creates a range of new feelings that must be managed and integrated into the personality. Emotional intensification is the natural companion to physical awkwardness. Managing the flow of powerful sexual feelings and impulses can be challenging for young adolescents due to a lack of experience with such feelings.

Children are taught to share toys, make friends, play nice, and get along. These relationship competencies are sufficient until sexuality enters the picture and complicates the arena of human relationships. Simply distinguishing between the flush of infatuation and an enduring love is challenging even for adults. Cultivating a range of healthy relationships requires a new set of skills.

The social and emotional competencies that adolescents must master include the ability to develop a healthy body image, identify a broad range of feelings, delay gratification, and manage sexual impulses, identify with the feelings of others (empathy and compassion), and manage conflicting emotions. Skills needed for establishing healthy relationships include the ability to communicate feelings appropriately, set clear and appropriate boundaries, manage and negotiate interpersonal conflicts, and be open to feedback from others.

Experimentation and Risk Taking

The brain undergoes a period of remodeling during the teen years. New neural connections are formed while other connections are pruned away. The prefrontal cortex continues to grow but will not be fully developed until the mid-twenties. When it comes to social and emotional responses, the reactive and sometimes impulsive amygdala continues to overshadow the well-planned thinking of the cortex. Rather than well-formed rational thought, the adolescent struggles with planned decision-making. A mindset focused on the present moment makes it difficult to predict consequences and plan for the future.

The growth and restructuring of the brain during adolescence makes this an ideal time to form new attitudes. The brain is poised and ready for this period of profound learning and adaptation. There is a shift from concrete to abstract thinking. Rather than complying with the guidance of parents and other adults, the adolescent is learning to make independent moral and ethical judgments. There is a fresh optimism and idealism that animates attitudes and thinking.

Two hallmarks of adolescence—experimentation and risk-taking—are the way in which adolescents accomplish the developmental tasks that they face. Creating an independent life and autonomous identity requires trying on new attitudes and behaviors, braving new challenges, and learning from mistakes. The successful mastery of the competencies related to sexuality requires active learning, and pushing outward beyond the comfort zone of safety. Experimentation involves not just physical intimacy, but exploring the boundaries of emotional intimacy.

There is a dark side to adolescent experimentation. Real and permanent harm is the ever-present companion to risk-taking, particularly when combined with the adolescent's penchant for feeling invulnerable to consequences. The effects of STDs and unwanted pregnancy are not the only dangers. The impact of sexual violence or abusive relationships on the emotional life can be equally damaging. Adolescents must be mentored to experiment and take risks within a protective environment that will minimize consequences. The best medicine is to prepare adolescents to face the developmental challenges well in advance, engage in active decision-making, take calculated risks, and generalize from baby steps.

Sex Education

Adolescents learn about sex from many sources: parents, teachers, peers, and the media. The physiology of adolescents is no different than it was thousands of years ago, but the world they will grow into is highly sexualized. The span of time between the onset of puberty and settling into enduring relationships (thirteen years) makes this an especially vulnerable period. Preparing adolescents to navigate these growth challenges must be a deliberate and comprehensive effort.

Research repeatedly demonstrates that a comprehensive approach to the sexual education of youth does not increase sexual behavior. In fact, comprehensive education is associated with postponement of initiation of sexual behavior, lower rates of unwanted pregnancy and STDs. Parents of adolescents in the United States overwhelmingly support sex education in schools although there remains some disagreement about the topics that should be addressed.

The traditional approach to educating adolescents about human sexuality is cognitive, imparting the information necessary to understand sexual development, anatomy and physiology, and reproductive health. Learning contraceptive methods and those that reduce the risk of infection are important to preventing unwanted pregnancy and STDs. Sex education should be more than preventing disasters or reducing the risk of harm, but about the creation of healthy and fulfilling intimate relationships of all kinds. This means addressing the many social and emotional competencies that adolescents must master. Learning these competencies requires skill development and practice.

Sex education for adolescents is everyone's responsibility. Parents exert a major influence over the sexual attitudes and behavior of their children and remain their primary sex educator. To adequately address all of the domains of sexual learning and prepare adolescents for the challenge of being healthy sexual adults, the partnership of schools and the larger community are essential. This will ensure that the healthy sexual learning necessary for adulthood is not an accident.

See also: **Adolescent Social and Emotional Development; Emotional Intelligence; Prenatal Brain; Self-Esteem.**

Further Readings

Allgeier, E.R., Albert R. (2000). *Sexual Interactions*. Boston, MA: Houghton Mifflin Company.

Gay Lesbian Straight Education Network (GLSEN), (2004). *Safe Space Training Materials*. www.glsen.org.

Kaiser Family Foundation, U.S. Teen Sexual Activity, January, 2005, www.kff.org.

Sexuality Information and Education Council of the United States www.siecus.org

JOHN ELFERS

Sleep

The function of sleep is not known, though it has been a target of sleep research for decades. For example, Allan Rechtschaffen of the University of Chicago began studying the function of sleep in the 1970s. His research was driven by his conclusion that sleep was a vital biological function. The evolutionary conservation of sleep in virtually every animal species—despite costs associated with prolonged intervals in an unresponsive and vulnerable state—suggests that sleep indeed serves a critical adaptive function. One such possible function of sleep is to facilitate learning, an idea fostered by many anecdotal reports of discoveries or insights gained during sleep. For example, Friedrich Kekule's discovery of the ring-like structure of benzene was said to have appeared to him during a dream about six serpents chasing one another in a circle.

Before discussing the association of sleep and learning, let us first clarify the meaning of both terms. As noted below, sleep can be defined by behavioral and electrophysiological criteria that establish it as a defined state, distinct from rest or waking. Different types of task-dependent learning (i.e., spatial, motor, perceptual) may be enhanced by different types, or stages, of sleep.

Definitions of Sleep

To study sleep in animals that are very small or difficult to monitor, behavioral requirements are necessary. Irene Tobler is a Swiss scientist who studies common lab animals, and she has also studied such animals as cockroaches, scorpions, and elephants. Tobler uses a set of behavioral criteria to determine if an animal sleeps. These criteria include having a (1) specific sleeping site (e.g., cave or bed), (2) typical body posture (e.g., lying down), (3) physical quiescence (e.g., lying still and quiet), (4) elevated arousal threshold (e.g., not responsive to soft noises), (5) rapid state reversibility (wakes up quickly from a big enough stimulus, unlike coma or hibernation), and (6) regulatory capacity demonstrated by compensation after deprivation (i.e. sleeping more after a time when sleep is prevented). When these criteria are used to evaluate sleep-like behavior, all must be met to classify the behavior as sleep. Yet, this system cannot make finer distinctions about the type of sleep occurring at a specific moment.

Specificity of sleep states and stages is defined based on electrophysiological criteria from recording brain waves, eye movements, and muscle tone, chiefly for birds and mammals. The transition from wake to sleep is accompanied by brain wave changes from irregular, low-voltage fast waves seen with waking to higher-voltage and slower waves characteristic of sleep. The sleep state with high-voltage slow waves is called non-rapid eye movement (NREM) sleep or slow wave sleep (SWS). The other sleep state, REM (rapid eye movement) sleep, is characterized by irregular, low-voltage, fast frequency brain waves, in conjunction with muscle paralysis and bursts of rapid eye movements. These two sleep states alternate cyclically during an animal's sleep, with NREM typically accounting for three to six times more of sleep than REM sleep.

In summary, sleep can be defined based on electrophysiological criteria providing state distinction (NREM/REM), or sleep can be determined more generally based on behavioral criteria without distinguishing states. Both sets of criteria have been used in the study of sleep and learning.

Learning Facilitated by Sleep

Many experiments have shown that sleep in general or specific states of sleep appear to improve learning in animals and humans. Types of learning that seem to be most affected involve basic brain changes after exposure to enriched environments, visual perceptual tasks, motor tasks, spatial tasks, and more complex types of learning including acquisition of bird songs and attainment of "insight." Evidence for the role of sleep in each type of learning is summarized below.

Basic Brain Changes

A fundamental requirement for learning is for the brain to undergo changes reflecting plasticity in neural structure and function. NREM and REM sleep may play roles in the neurological processes and brain changes underlying learning. One demonstration of sleep directly affecting neuronal structure was a study of how the brain's visual system grows when kittens are denied sleep and undergo monocular visual deprivation. Monocular deprivation, when one eye is covered to prevent visual input, causes a rapid remodeling of the visual cortex during the critical period of development (a time of enhanced brain change). Varying sleep in kittens undergoing monocular deprivation (some were kept awake in the dark, others were allowed to sleep in the dark, and others were kept awake in the light), demonstrated that sleep enhanced the brain changes in ocular columns that occur after monocular deprivation. Although not strictly speaking a study of learning, one interpretation of the study was that sleep and sleep loss modify experience-dependent neuronal changes. The brain changes were correlated with the amount of NREM sleep that occurred in the animals allowed to sleep, arguing against the possibility that the stress of sleep-deprivation might have inhibited development rather than sleep enhancing the process.

Evidence for the involvement of REM sleep with basic brain changes underlying learning comes from examining rats living in enriched environments. Brains of such rats show increases in the numbers and sizes of neural connections compared to rats living in impoverished environments. These brain changes are required to process and learn about the new environment. When sleep states are examined in these animals, those in an enriched environment show an increase in the amount of REM sleep, perhaps because REM sleep contributes to neural changes that underlie learning.

Perceptual Learning

Additional studies on visual processing and learning have been done with visual perceptual task learning. For example, a visual discrimination task has been used to assess a type of perceptual skill acquisition thought to rely on neural changes in the visual cortex. This task requires subjects to report if either a "T" or "L" appears in the foreground and if horizontal or vertical bars appears in the background of the screen. Human performance on this visual discrimination task improves after sleep, specifically due to the amount of deep NREM sleep in the first part of the night in combination with the amount of REM sleep in the second part, and does not improve simply with the passage of time. This research indicates that the progression of NREM to REM sleep across the night (not just one or the other) is necessary for the neurological processes underlying the visual perceptual task learning to occur.

Motor Task Learning

Motor task learning may require other processes than are needed for visual or perceptual processing, and NREM sleep has been implicated in enhancing motor task learning. Finger-tapping tasks have been used in humans to assess the effect of sleep on the acquisition of a motor skill that relies mainly on primary motor cortex plasticity. Participants trained on the task either in the morning or evening showed improvement after a night of sleep and no improvement after twelve hours of wakefulness. In this study, the amount of a particular type of NREM sleep (stage 2) was correlated with the amount of improvement, which may mean that stage 2 sleep is important in facilitating motor learning.

Spatial Learning

In addition to facilitating visual and motor learning, sleep has been implicated in spatial learning based on recordings from the hippocampus in rats during waking and sleep. During waking, "place cells" in the hippocampus fire together when the rat is in certain locations in its environment. These cells that fired together when the animal was in specific locations while awake were more likely to fire together during subsequent sleep. In addition, cells that did not actively fire while the rat was awake did not show an increase in firing during sleep. These findings provide evidence that experience or information acquired while awake may be repeated during sleep, perhaps as part of a consolidation process.

Song Learning

Such sleep-related replaying of waking brain activity during sleep for spatial memory consolidation is similar to that seen in a very different type of task: bird song learning. Firing patterns of neurons in sleeping birds closely parallel waking patterns, indicating birds spontaneously replay fragments of songs while asleep.

Neuronal replay demonstrated by bird song neuronal firing during wake (mot.), are replayed during sleep (spon.). For each spontaneous sample, a corresponding sample of the waking neuronal activity, indicated by "mot" is given, both under a color spectrograph of the song the bird sang. Both neurons simultaneously fire during sleep, with complex firing structures that match waking activity.

One interpretation of this result is that birds' songs experienced during the day are consolidated during sleep when the neuron firing activity mimics waking activity associated with the song. This avian research did not identify sleep stages, thus it is not clear if the replay activity occurs during NREM or REM sleep, and studies using electrophysiological techniques to identify sleep-stages are necessary for further clarity.

Insight and Creativity

Evidence for sleep facilitating learning comes not only from studies on basic brain mechanisms and simple motor and perceptual skills, but also from more complex tasks requiring higher level thinking. In one experiment, the role of sleep and insight was examined by having participants perform a cognitive task that required them to learn stimulus–response sequences. Their performance improved either gradually or came abruptly, when they gained "insight" into a hidden abstract rule. At retest, greater than twice as many subjects gained insight into the hidden rule following a night of sleep than after a night of sleep deprivation or after normal daytime wakefulness. Thus, sleep may facilitate extraction of factual knowledge and insightful behavior.

Criticisms

Other scientists have criticized research on sleep and learning for several faults. In the first place, they say that the stress and emotional effects of sleep deprivation may interfere with the learning process rather than sleep facilitating it. Second, some scientists believe that the theory of sleep and learning predicts that humans with greater intelligence or more intelligent animals sleep more than others, but this is not the case. In addition, humans taking medications that inhibit REM sleep do not have learning deficits as might be predicted. The inconsistency of findings from one experiment to another also warrants concern. The final question is whether sleep is necessary or simply advantageous for learning.

Strategies

When choosing strategies, educators should consider two things: (1) lack of sleep may interfere with acquisition of new material and (2) lack of sleep may hinder consolidation. The studies described in this article were all performed with humans or other animals where sleep was normal before they were exposed to the new material. Many other studies show that not getting adequate sleep, that is, having a "sleep debt," will interfere with acquiring new information. Sleep loss impairs alertness and attention, hindering a student's ability to learn while in the classroom. Thus, sleep not only affects learning consolidation during sleep, but also has consequences on daytime functioning and alertness. In some cases, the learning process is compromised simply because the student cannot stay awake and pay attention. In addition, emotional consequences of inadequate sleep, such as decreased behavioral inhibition and increased irritability and emotional instability, may cause classroom behavior problems that interfere with information acquisition.

To promote optimal acquisition of new material, students need to know the importance of getting a full night's sleep to help them study better and to help the information they study to "stick." Then, of course, they need to sleep. Students worried about not having enough time to finish homework if they sleep more, may be reassured to know their concentration and focus are much better with adequate sleep. They may also learn more efficiently, taking full advantage of sleep's facilitating power.

Data from a number of studies also indicate that, while pulling "all-nighters" may be sufficient for short-term memorization and regurgitation, the information will not be retained long-term. Finally, students with inadequate sleep find it difficult to pull together the facts into comprehensive themes, and therefore their papers and essays may suffer.

In summary, students who have a regular sleep pattern that allows plenty of sleep, have a learning advantage over those with poor sleep habits.

See also: **Adolescent Social and Emotional Development; Animal Studies.**

Further Readings

Carskadon, M.A. (2002). *Adolescent Sleep Patterns: Biological, Social, and Psychological Influences.* Cambridge, NY: Cambridge University Press.

Dave, A.S., Margoliash, D. (2000). Song replay during sleep and computational rules for sensorimotor vocal learning. *Science* 290(5492):812–816.

Frank, M.G., Issa, N.P., Stryker M.P. (2001). Sleep enhances plasticity in the developing visual cortex. *Neuron* 30(1):275–287.

Rechtschaffen, A., Kleitman, N., & Dement, W. (1961–1986). Association for the Psychophysiological Study of Sleep Records, *Psychophysiology* 6, 68–69.

Siegel, J.M. (2001). The REM sleep-memory consolidation hypothesis. *Science* 294(5544):1058–1063.

Vyazovskiy, V., Borbely, A.A., & Tobler, I. (2000). Fast track: Unilateral vibrissae stimulation during waking induces intermispheric ##G asymmetry during subsequent sleep in the rat. *Journal of Sleep Research.* (9)4 367–376.

Wagner, U., Gais, S., Haider, H., Verleger R., Born, J. (2004). Sleep inspires insight. *Nature* 427(6972):352–355.

Walker, M.P., Brakefield, T., Morgan, A., Hobson, J.A., Stickgold, R. (2002). Practice with sleep makes perfect: Sleep-dependent motor skill learning. *Neuron* 35(1):205–211.

Wilson, M.A., McNaughton, B.L. (1994). Reactivation of hippocampal ensemble memories during sleep. *Science* 265(5172):676–679.

Stanford University Center for Human Sleep Research, med.stanford.edu/school/psychiatry/humansleep/

**TRACY L. RUPP, M.S. AND
MARY A. CARSKADON, PH.D.**

Social Context of Learning

The common perception is that learning is something that one does privately, inside his or her own head. While there's a good deal of common sense to that, another question arises, "What *other* factors influence the learning going on inside the head?" Social cognition is the processing of information, which leads to the accurate processing of the dispositions and intentions of others. It is quite plausible that it was the development of complex social hierarchies, not our intellect that contributed to the rapid increase in the size of the human brain. As humans must learn to survive, it is likely the social brain is designed to handle some kind of social learning. A burgeoning new field, social neuroscience, has revealed an astonishing array of multilevel influences that social contact has on the brain. Areas of the brain dedicated to social structure are extensive and have been identified as the anterior prefrontal lobe, anterior cingulate, frontal gyrus, amygdala, fusiform gyrus, and posterior temporal lobe. To process social information, we use areas of the prefrontal cortex, somasensory cortex and amygdaloid complex.

Social Experience is Powerful

Many believe that the process begins at birth. Studies have shown that newborns, even as early as the first hours and days of life, preferentially look toward simple face-like patterns. This early tendency to fixate on faces might be to establish bonding with adult caregivers and to bias the visual input toward likely support. But the social systems that develop are much more complex than "eye contact with mom." A systems analysis suggests events at one level of an organism (molecular, DNA, cellular, nervous system, organs, immune, behavioral, social, etc.) can profoundly influence events at other levels. A social event is not isolated from the rest of our mind and body—and we ought to pay closer attention to the nature of social contacts at school.

We cannot think of ourselves and our social contacts as fragmented. Social events at one level of an organism (molecular, DNA, cellular, nervous system, organs, immune, behavioral, social, etc.) can profoundly influence events at other levels. If you fall in love one afternoon, you can be assured that you have a different biological makeup by evening! Naturally, if your sweetheart dumps you, your whole mind, body, and emotions are affected. This suggests that social contact at school may have a much more widespread influence than researchers earlier thought. We are strongly influenced by others in the social learning process through many ways including, but not limited to:

- explicit reinforcers given by others
- peer acceptance
- influences on decision-making
- risk of social disapproval
- role of emotions in decisions
- peer cognitive support.

If students do not feel socially accepted, comfortable, safe, or included, they run serious health and academic risks. Healthy social contact improves immune activity and social stress weakens immune systems. As the classroom and the school experiences take in over 13,000 hours in a child's K-12 schooling, the brain of students will be altered by those experiences. There are many types of social structures for learning including the school campus itself, lunch areas, clubs, teams, and cooperative learning in the classroom. Each elicits a different set of responses from us socially.

Learning with Many or Few?

Student class size changes how we behave. In bigger groups, the students may feel more lost, but there is less accountability. In smaller groups, the reverse is true. Class size matters to teachers, administrators, taxpayers, and students. More numbers create greater social opportunities (friends, potential mates, etc.) but also may expose greater risks (cliques, gangs, less attention, etc.). The evidence is somewhat mixed on this matter, but there is a general positive correlation between smaller class size and student learning but only at the primary level. This means the actual class size effect is negative on student achievement. To make any kind of an impact on student learning, class size has got to be at about a fifteen to one ratio. Children in smaller classes often perform better on literacy skills. The exceptions are where students are in ESL, special needs classes, or English composition. This may be a result of the type of teaching that is done or needs to be done as much as any other factor. For example, greater use of cooperative learning and other engaging strategies can mitigate the negative achievement effects of a larger class size.

Learning with Peers – Or Not?

Understandably, parents want their own children in groups that are either equal to or above the ability *level of the other students*. In general, this notion is supported by a decade of research. Ability grouping is highly controversial because of the potential implications for academic and life status. One study found that students of all ability levels could benefit from ability grouping when contrasted with a heterogeneous grouping. The student groups that benefit the most are those with low ability—they do better when placed in multi-ability groups.

Yet tracking, as you might suspect, can reduce the positive peer effect, says a Rand Corporation study. After all, students often, but not always, live up to the class norms. But mixed ability groups often learn other skills that may have more lasting value than a slightly higher grade. Many researchers have found positive social skills to be part of the results. The take-home message here is that ability grouping by itself may be helpful if done well. The greater issue is *how* grouping is done and the corresponding teacher affect. Some effective teaching strategies may ameliorate the negative social impact tracking may have on self-esteem.

To Cooperate or Compete?

Some social structures are less structured, such as context-dependent friendships or a temporary class partner for an activity. Others are more structured, such as ability grouping or cooperative learning groups. Cooperative learning pioneers Roger and David Johnson, have a distinct model for cooperative learning, which defines one of the key elements as positive interdependency. Putting students together in a relevant social structure can be highly effective. In fact, the evidence suggests that if you compare students who are in cooperative groups against those doing the tasks individually and competing individually, the collaborative social strategy works better. That is a key factor because positive time with peers can reduce **stress**. Excess cortisol can be a highly negative factor in learning. In rodents, after peer separation, cortisol levels for both males and females soar 18–87 percent higher than those housed with friendly established social groups.

Research on cooperative learning suggests that it produces better learning when compared to students competing against each other individually. Other studies corroborate this effect, showing that a quality cooperative learning strategy will outperform random grouping or individual learning. The perception among those interviewed, who are using cooperative social support, is that the academic challenges are more achievable. In fact, students do achieve more; even if the increase is not always robust, other social values are typically improved. The effects of social variables cannot be either isolated or underestimated. Part of the value of positive social experiences is that it generates peer acceptance and approval. That boost in self-esteem creates hope and optimism that influences brain chemistry and capability assessments.

Learning without Peers

Is there a negative side to social grouping? Students who dislike working with others cooperatively should be listened to, but not catered to exclusively. Provide some variety and some choice and ultimately students will feel included. This is not a case of saying that "All increased social contact is better!" The fact is, some students like working by themselves and may do better solo than with forced social contact. Their dislike or underperformance may actually skew the overall statistics, meaning that the rest of the *students may be doing even better* than earlier reported. Many students find intense or prolonged social contact to be more, not less, stressful. To those students, you have a message: "School is not always a democracy and you don't have to like everything, all the time."

Keep in mind, some students don't like technology, others don't like visual arts or physical education, and still others eschew music. We should respect, but not necessarily cave in to their wishes. It is still important to (1) explain WHY we are asking them to do something they don't wish to and (2) provide some variety so that no student has to spend 100 percent of their time in an uncomfortable, stressed social structure. But they ought to try it, even if they are not comfortable with it. One study among sixth graders randomly assigned them to work in either triads or individually on computer-based problems. After the initial assignment was over, the ones who had worked in triads outperformed (as individuals) the other individuals who had no exposure to the cooperative group. While some students may not be comfortable working with others, some cognitive and social benefits may persist.

Why Status Matters to Students

Sometimes adults are amused that schoolage students seem so obsessed with status in the classroom. But there may be a biological reason for the concern. Changes in social status influence an important neurotransmitter in our brain. Moderate levels are highly implicated with attention, mood, and memory, all factors that can drive achievement. In addition, lower serotonin levels are also correlated inflexible behaviors. Given these effects, it should come as little surprise that social status, serotonin, and academic achievement are all correlated. In another study of 345 children over two years, peer rejection assessed as early as kindergarten and social rejection that is stable across the two years are highly correlated with deficits in first and second-grade academic achievement and work habits. But for those who received stable social acceptance, their achievement was higher and this pattern remains significant even after the study authors controlled for initial kindergarten academic competence. Social status matters; and there is little doubt in the researchers' minds.

Part of the role of schools is to create a citizenry for tomorrow that has the ability to cooperate as well as compete. Some of our students may end up being better at competition and others better at cooperation. But all of them ought to be able to get along with others.

We can say there are significant and broad-based effects of positive social contact. It should not be left to random forces, but rather orchestrated and nurtured. The new field of social neuroscience suggests that educators be very purposeful in fostering positive, interdependent social contact. This does not mean that every single social grouping in school must be meaningfully engineered to nurture lasting emotional and social skills. But it does mean that every social contact a student has will either reinforce their positive capabilities, mood and self-concept, or undermine them. Consider every school contact we orchestrate as an opportunity to do just that.

See also: **Adolescent Social and Emotional Development; Emotions; Motivation.**

Further Readings

Feinstein, S. (2004). *Secrets of the Teenage Brain*. Thousand Oaks, CA: Corwin Press.

Jensen, E. (2003). *Tools for Engagement*. San Diego, CA: The Brain Store.

Johnson, D., Johnson, R. (1999). *Learning Together and Alone: Cooperative, Competitive and Individualistic Learning*. Boston, MA: Allyn & Bacon.

Lupien, S.J., Lepage, M. (2001, December). Stress, memory, and the hippocampus: Can't live with it, can't live without it. *Behavioural Brain Research* 127(1–2):137–158.

ERIC JENSEN

Spirituality

The concept of spirituality is defined differently among cultural groups. The common characteristics of spirituality across cultures, however, include a sense of transcendence and connection to something greater than the self, forming a framework from which to make sense of potentially chaotic experiences. Religion is a codified expression of spirituality shared by a particular people group. The observation of religious expression in rituals related to life and death practices throughout history and across cultures has led researchers to search for underlying structural and functional characteristics of the brain to help explain the similarity and universality of such behaviors.

This study is controversial because it touches on some of our most cherished ideas and beliefs. Some researchers approach the data from a reductionist perspective, defining spiritual experience as merely a chemical-electrical brain-based event, non-dependent on any cosmic force. Others point to the fact that all human experiences elicit chemical-electrical responses. Thus, the human brain would register and record an encounter with a "cosmic other" in the same manner it records an encounter with any other, neither proving nor disproving the reality of a divine source of spiritual experience. The emerging science attempting to bring neurological research, psychology, philosophy, and religion into dialog is called neurotheology. Neurotheology does not seek to prove the existence of God or to evaluate a particular religion, but rather to understand how humans perceive and relate to the concept of God or supernatural forces.

There are four primary arenas in which the relationship between spirituality and the brain has been studied: through experiments that attempt to cause a spiritual perception through brain stimulation; through fMRI scans of those who are willing to use meditative practices to induce perceptions of a mystical experience; through reports of those who have had near-death experiences they define as spiritual; and through correlative studies of spiritual temperament inventories with measures of serotonin uptake activity in the brain.

Through these studies researchers have identified sites in the prefrontal cortex that correlate with a sense of an unseen presence, a sense of being aware yet detached from physical limits or boundaries, and even sensory perceptions such as voices or visions. Other studies indicate that a meditative state activates the limbic system, forming powerful emotional connections to perceived spiritual experiences that can often be paradigm-shifting and thus life-changing. D'Aquilli and Newberg have specifically postulated a chemically based explanation for the sense of being at one with the universe that occurs when both the sympathetic and parasympathetic systems are operating at maximum levels simultaneously, and at least one study indicates that individuals with a spiritually sensitive temperament have a particular way of processing serotonin.

These kinds of spiritual experiences, though they can be physiologically documented, are often described as mystical and "beyond expression." Mystical experience is not the only understanding of spirituality, however. Non-mystical spiritual experiences are harder to study, though, because they cannot be predicted or induced on command. They are often linked to practices of a particular spiritual or cultural tradition, but engagement in the practice may produce inconsistent outcomes. When the practice does yield an identified non-mystical outcome, it generally results in a sense of personal or ultimate meaning, well-being, or purposefulness and can be expressed through language or by means of a story communicable through words or another art form. Such spiritual practices are usually intentionally engaged, cognitively mediated, and involve all components of learning including **motivation**, rehearsal, social reinforcement, memory, and transference. As such, these practices are usually passed from generation to generation through some form of religious or cultural education or indoctrination.

Some of the most commonly cited expressions of spirituality in practice include prayer; creativity; aesthetic appreciation or expression through design and music; ethical reasoning; virtuous behavior; ritualistic practice that is either deeply personal or highly traditional; altruistic service; philanthropic giving; caring for the weak or less fortunate; investing in intimate relationships; community-building; conscious suffering, birthing and/or dying; caring for the natural world and ecological system; generativity (leaving a legacy); and "mindfulness" (attending to both physical and emotional details of everyday experiences). Ultimately, the pursuit of any of these spiritual expressions flow from individual values and preferences that may be expressions of **multiple intelligences**, developmental levels, personality traits, or physiological states in an intricate web of cause and effect.

Each expression of spirituality is subjectively based, even though many people who practice particular forms of spiritual expression believe that they are operating in harmony with objective truths. The key to addressing spirituality in the classroom is to plan opportunities to allow for activities based on subjective engagement. Teachers can ask questions that require affective answers and structure assignments so that students can choose alternate modes of expression as well as draw from alternate sources of authority. The wise teacher recognizes that not all aspects of learning can be quantified or measured, but some learning can instead be observed along a continuum of growth. Children who fear or are intimidated by a measurement system lose their natural ability to wonder freely.

Opportunities for cooperative, collaborative, non-competitive, community-based service learning appeal to students who value corporate or social expressions of spirituality. Times of directive and non-directive silence, opportunities to discuss ethical implications of curricular material, and space to explore both materials and concepts independently will all help the intuitive child to pursue common ground between the spiritual and the intellectual agenda of the classroom. While all classrooms should allow for **creativity**, introducing elements of daily or weekly ritual can also help to anchor the spiritually sensitive child to the learning environment. In general, the younger the child, the stronger the need for ritualized practices in the classroom; yet students of all ages can be powerfully impacted by the establishment of unique classroom traditions.

Respect for differences and appreciation of cultural and religious diversity are important to the developing child because spirituality is interwoven with both family practices and personal experiences. An anti-bias curriculum can help to develop a classroom climate in which children of varying spiritual and/or religious traditions can flourish. A simple way of keeping students open to differences in perspective is periodically to invite them to spend three to five minutes writing down everything they observe in the classroom. At the end of that time, students can compare lists to take note of the differences of perspective represented by their observations. While each thing on both lists can be concretely identified, it is unlikely that students will have noticed exactly the same things as anyone else in the classroom.

If spirituality is about noticing and meaning-making, adequate time and opportunity for reflection and open dialog in a context of respect are essential to student processing. A playful, exploratory environment and attention to the aesthetic sensitivities of individual children can also contribute to the learning climate of the classroom.

Spiritually sensitive teaching techniques are educationally sound because they open opportunities for depth of knowledge rooted in self-awareness and personal application. A spiritually sensitive framework need not be religious in nature and does not violate any principles of separation of church and state.

There is very little doubt from the research perspective that the brain can and does become "spiritually activated." The source of that activation, its interpretation, and the effective outcome of it remain for the study of the theologian, the sociologist, and the philosopher. Still, the classroom practitioner can focus on utilizing teaching practices and encouraging a classroom culture that do not hinder a child's ability to engage in personal meaning-making and ongoing spiritual formation in the context of a content-driven curriculum.

See also: **Emotion and Self-Esteem.**

Further Readings

D'Aquili, E., Newberg, A., Rause, V. (2001). *Why God Won't Go Away: Science and the Biology of Belief.* New York: Ballentine.

Joseph, R. (2002). *Neurotheology: Brain, Science, Spirituality, Religious Experience.* San Jose, CA: University Press.

Lantieri, L. (2001). *Schools with Spirit: Nurturing the Inner Lives of Children and Teachers.* Boston: Beacon Press.

LORI NILES, M.A.

Stress

A salesman, stressed about being late for work, can't remember where he left his car keys. A student, worried that she just failed her final exam, forgets to stop at the store for groceries on her way home from school.

A doctor, troubled about a sick patient, forgets to drop off his infant son at daycare on his way to the office. Later that day, the boy, still in the backseat of his father's car, dies of heat exposure as his father is immersed in his work. These examples illustrate stress-related memory impairments and some of their consequences. In most cases, episodes of failed memory are relatively benign and may even be amusing, as when a harried commuter drives off to fight the morning traffic, oblivious to the coffee mug he left on the roof of his car. In other cases, stress-related memory failures can have tragic outcomes, such as when children are left in cars by otherwise loving and attentive parents; the death of a child forgotten in an overheated car is a memory lapse these parents will never forget. Stress-induced forgetting, which in it's most intense form is referred to as *traumatic amnesia*, is an important area of research by neuroscientists who are interested in studying how strong emotions can cause the brain's memory systems to go awry.

Neuroscientists think of the neurobiology of memory in terms of the interactions of brain structures, with each structure providing a different contribution to how information is processed. The entire limbic system, which includes the hypothalamus, amygdala, and the hippocampus, is involved in stress. This chapter will focus on one of the primary structures involved in memory–stress interactions, the hypothalamus which is also one of the most primitive of all brain structures. The hypothalamus controls the expression of our primal emotions, such as fear, anger, and our craving for food and sex. The hypothalamus is also the interface through which the brain communicates our feelings of being stressed to the rest of the body. When the hypothalamus is activated in times of fear, anger, frustration, or more generally, being stressed out, it responds as if your very survival is in doubt. To help you deal with a real or perceived threat the hypothalamus releases a chemical known as corticotropin releasing factor (CRF). CRF, in conjunction with epinephrine and cortisol (two stress hormones released from the adrenal glands), activate physiological responses that enhance the likelihood of survival in the event of an attack. For example, CRF, epinephrine, and cortisol increase blood glucose levels to enable you to have sufficient energy to escape or fight an aggressor. These hormones also stimulate the immune system to help you to ward off infections that could be caused by wounds inflicted by a predator.

The hypothalamus, in a primitive manner, takes a sledge-hammer approach to ensure that we pay attention to what is causing us to feel stressed. Hypothalamic CRF, in conjunction with epinephrine, cortisol and other neurochemicals, all intensify our attentional faculties to focus on the arousing stimulus. However, the hypothalamus has difficulty distinguishing between a real threat, such as the fear you feel if someone threatens you with a knife, from stressful experiences that are aggravating, but not life threatening, such as being afraid of failing an exam or when you get angry at someone for cutting you off in traffic. This intensification and focusing of attention at times of strong emotionality is called "perceptual narrowing." A common example of perceptual narrowing is when people experience an actual threat to their lives, such as being caught in the middle of a bank robbery. People tend to report that they have little or no recollection of the details of this kind of terrifying experience except that the image of the robber's weapon is forever "burned" into their memory. This phenomenon, called "weapon focus," is the bane of the prosecutor trying to convict a bank robber because witnesses may have accurate and vivid memories of the gun pointed at their faces, but only vague and flawed memories of the details of the criminal's face.

How does hypothalamic activation induced by stressful experiences get transformed into forgetfulness? The hypothalamus, itself, is the engine that drives emotions and helps to intensify attention. It is essential for the expression of emotions, but it doesn't have the internal circuitry to process specific memories. The actual memory storage and retrieval machinery is in other structures deep within the brain. One of these structures is the hippocampus, which enables us to store facts, details, and the events of our lives. Neuroscientists unintentionally learned about how the hippocampus has an essential role in memory in 1953, after a surgery was performed on a twenty-three year-old man suffering from uncontrollable epileptic seizures. This patient, referred to in the literature as "HM," had his hippocampus surgically removed because the neurosurgeons believed that his hippocampus was the source of his seizure activity. Indeed, the surgery was successful in that regard because it resulted in a reduction of his seizure activity. However, the negative side effects were so damaging to HM's ability to function that the surgery has not been conducted again on any other patient. HM is now seventy-four years of age, is fully capable of carrying on a conversation, and he can reminisce about the first twenty-three years of his life. The last five decades, however, are only a hazy fog of lost memories. Since 1953, all of the new experiences of HM's life, the mundane and the significant, have been forgotten almost immediately. For example, each time he is told of the death of his mother he expresses sadness and grief, as if he had never learned of her death before. He forgets that his mother died years ago and that he has expressed the same feelings of grief upon learning of the loss of his mother on dozens of previous occasions. Each time he is told of her death his awareness of her passing fades and is lost in a matter of minutes. The Vietnam War, Watergate, the destruction of the Berlin Wall and the terrorist attacks on 9/11/2001 all trigger strong memories in those who experienced these events; HM has no recollection of these events because they all occurred after he lost the ability to form new memories. As a result of work with HM and similar findings in other people and animals with brain damage, we have learned that the hippocampus is required for the storage and retrieval of new information, but is not necessary for the retrieval of remote (old) memories.

The connection between the hippocampus and memory is revealed by manipulations far more subtle than brain surgery. Neurochemical studies have shown that of all the structures in the brain, the hippocampus is the primary target of stress hormones. These hormones, including CRF, cortisol, and norepinephrine (a form of epinephrine), produce a profound disturbance of hippocampal electrical and chemical activity. Moreover, chronic stress, the kind that produces cardiovascular disorders and gastric ulcers, has a detrimental effect on the physical structure of the hippocampus. Prolonged periods of stress can cause parts of hippocampal neurons (another term for brain cells) to wither, in a manner similar to the way a tree loses its leaves in the winter. As a tree may die as a result of an extremely cold winter, the constant bathing of the hippocampus in stress hormones can bring about the death of its neurons. The debilitating effects of stress on the hippocampus have been documented in people with extreme stress and anxiety, such as in those who develop post-traumatic stress disorder (PTSD) as a result of suffering through a traumatic experience, and in people with Major Depressive Disorder. Brain imaging studies have shown that people with these types of anxiety disorders have a shrinkage (atrophy) of their hippocampus and profound memory deficits.

As gloomy as this story is about how a hyperactive hypothalamus in stressed people can lead to cell death and damage to the hippocampus, there is cause for optimism. The hippocampus shows great resiliency in response to stress. Animal and human studies have shown that with the termination of either chronic stress or with drug therapy, hippocampal neurons can regrow their withered connections, much as a tree recovers its foliage in the spring. Even more dramatic findings of growth and recovery come from work showing that the hippocampus, unlike virtually all other brain structures, can grow new neurons that help the hippocampus in its learning and memory functions, even in elderly individuals.

The latest research has led to a new generation of antidepressants and anxiety reduction drugs that help to improve memory performance in individuals under stress by blocking the stress-related chemical reactions that interfere with hippocampal functioning.

Neuroscience research over the past five decades has given us a good understanding of how and why stress exerts such a profound influence on our memory. Stress activates primitive brain structures, such as the hypothalamus, which increases production of stress hormones and shifts the brain into survival mode. This strategy is effective for animals attempting to escape from a predator, but is not an effective strategy in our highly technological society where a stressor is more likely to be a bill collector than a predator. Excessive production of stress hormones impairs memory and can trigger the development of anxiety disorders, all of which involve damage to the hippocampus. The next stage of progress is the application of our knowledge of how stress damages the brain to develop medication that will improve memory and provide life-long protection of the hippocampus from damage by stress.

The following strategies can reduce stress in the classroom:

1. Provide academic scaffolding. Students need the background knowledge necessary to accomplish assignments, along with clear expectations and fair consequences.

2. Offer homework helpers and tutoring.

3. Use competition carefully. Every student should have a chance for success.

4. Allow some choice in content, instructional strategies, or assessment.

5. Teach time management, study skills, and test-taking strategies to students that need the support.

6. Schedule special student–teacher meetings to enhance communication and convey that you care about them.

7. Have students rate and chart their stress on a scale of one to ten. This puts the stress level in perspective and is often preferred by students that enjoy logical/mathematical thinking. If the stress level is too high, refer them to a professional counselor.

8. Provide opportunities for students to journal or talk about stress in their lives.

9. Show role models of individuals that handled stress well.

10. Set a calm soothing tone through music.

See also: Animal Studies; Classroom Environment; Depression; Music Teaching Model for the Brain.

Further Readings

Bremner, J.D. (2002). *Does Stress Damage the Brain?: Understanding Trauma-Related Disorders From a Neurological Perspective*. New York N.Y.: W. W. Norton & Company.

Kim, J., Diamond, D. (2002). The stressed hippocampus, synaptic plasticity and lost memories. *Nature Reviews Neuroscience* 3(6): 453–462.

LeDoux, J. (1998). *The Emotional Brain: The Mysterious Underpinnings of Emotional Life*. New York, NY: Simon & Schuster.

McEwen, B., Lasley, E.N., Lasley, E. (2002). *The End of Stress As We Know It*. Washington, D.C.: National Academies Press.

DAVID M. DIAMOND, PH.D.;
COLLIN R. PARK, PH.D.;
ADAM M. CAMPBELL PH.D., AND
JAMES C. WOODSON, PH.D.

Suggestopedia (Accelerated Learning)

Researchers, teachers, and students are looking for ways to accelerate the learning process. Accelerated Learning integrates current research on how people learn into a teaching process and a curriculum design template. The goal of Accelerated Learning is to empower students to tap into their potential, overcome the often unconscious limiting beliefs they have, and apply knowledge and skills effectively in their lives.

Accelerated Learning developed from *Suggestopedia*, a methodology tested in Bulgaria in the 1960s by Dr. Georgi Lozanov. The name *Suggestopedia* derives from two words—*Suggestion* and *Pedagogy*. The method's main concern is the influence of *Suggestion* in teaching/facilitating. Lozanov describes *Suggestion* as the underlying messages people take in on both a conscious and unconscious level. The interpretation of those messages lead to both limiting and empowering beliefs. Neuroscience now confirms the power of our beliefs. Students who perceive themselves and their possibilities negatively do so because of their embedded memories of negative and significant emotional events that have now become part of their cognitive belief system and self-concept. The emotionality sets a process in motion that imprints the memory with all its related stimuli into the brain. Any of those stimuli can trigger the memory and the resulting stress. Accelerated Learning asks several questions in preparation for teaching: What will the classroom, the seating arrangement, the teaching methods, and the verbal and nonverbal communication suggest to, or trigger in, the student? What are the *Suggestions* that students bring into the learning environment about themselves and about learning? How can teachers help students move beyond their limiting beliefs and tap into their potential? The answers guide teachers in planning their lessons, in designing the classroom, and in preparing themselves mentally, emotionally, and physically to teach.

Neuroscience research shows the importance of positive emotions to both memory and learning. In fact, many researchers and educators say *there is no learning without* **emotion**. Positive emotional experiences reinforce learning by promoting the likelihood that memory will be stored immediately in the locale, spatial memory involving multiple regions of the brain. If the learning experience is stimulus rich, and the student is actively engaged in the process, there will also be many potential triggers to support retrieval when needed. Any stimulus can act as an anchor to recall the entire experience. Anchoring is sometimes called state dependence. It is the theory that recall of learning can depend on the state or other situations that existed when the learning took place. Neural networks connect the two, the content learned with the place, mood, smell, and physical condition. The richer the learning experience, the more possible connections can be made and used to retrieve information. Accelerated Learning creates multiple opportunities for students to experience positive emotional experiences that can significantly change how they see themselves. Classroom spaces, tone of voice, music, and certain ritualized events in the classroom act as anchors to support learning and a shift in perspective. The teacher also provides learning activities that are multi-sensory to both appeal to various learning styles and provide stimuli-rich learning to act as an anchor for later retrieval.

Extensive research also demonstrates the negative effects of **stress** on learning. The brain produces cortisol and other stress hormones, and activity in the neo-cortex slows down or stops completely. There is a downshifting to the lower regions of the brain, the so-called R-Complex or reptilian brain consisting of the brain stem and cerebellum. Accelerated Learning creates a safe environment for students. The teacher supports cooperation and team learning. When the students play learning games, there are only winners. No one is singled out as a loser. Mistakes are applauded as steps to mastering the material. Accelerated Learning also uses various relaxation techniques, guided imageries, and focusing activities to support students in their learning. Neuroscience research shows that relaxation response produces serotonin, a chemical in the brain that promotes sleep, relaxation, and positive self-concept.

Accelerated Learning orchestrates learning to appeal to both the conscious mind and the para-conscious, or things outside of consciousness at the moment. Research shows the ability of the brain to take in information at a conscious and unconscious level and store it for later retrieval. The brain also automatically registers the familiar and constantly searches for novel stimuli as part of the survival instinct. As the brain responds to everything within the sensory context of the classroom, everything in the classroom teaches and becomes part of the student's learning. Lozanov looked closely at the role of the environment in learning. The Accelerated Learning classroom uses peripherals to teach, to inspire, and to create a positive and engaging learning environment. Teachers learn the importance of voice, language, nonverbal communication and their attitudes to the success of their students. Everything in the classroom is orchestrated to support learning. The physical environment provides the needed light, oxygen, water, as well as the variety of stimuli the brain needs. The emotional environment supports students in moving beyond their limiting beliefs and opening up to possibilities. The design of the lesson facilitates students' meaningful interaction with the material, with one another, and with the teacher.

The brain is constantly searching for meaning. To make sense of an experience, the brain perceives and generates patterns. It resists meaningless patterns such as isolated and irrelevant bits of information. In Accelerated Learning, carefully designed learning activities offer opportunities for significant and positive emotional experiences that can shift students' perspectives. The lesson plan provides variety and novelty within enough structure to provide a roadmap for learners while they navigate through the learning materials creatively. Accelerated Learning encourages students to experience learning with the mind, body, and emotions. Students find personal meaning and importance in the subject matter and stay actively involved throughout the process. They create their own patterns and personal meaning in what they learn. Both interaction with others and self-reflection play a role in helping students connect the content with their lives in a profound way. The pace moves from more active phases to more reflective ones. The change in methods and pace reinforce the brain's need for rest and change to function optimally.

Accelerated Learning offers a philosophy, a teaching process, and a design template for lesson plans and the curriculum. The philosophy is based on the research of Lozanov into the effect of *suggestion* on learning and his theories on how teachers can help students *de-suggest* their limiting beliefs through carefully designed classroom activities. The teaching process integrates current thinking on the brain and learning and human development. The Accelerated Learning Cycle provides a template to create successful lesson plans and guide teachers in creating an optimal learning environment.

The Accelerated Learning Philosophy

Accelerated Learning operates on the theory that each person has innate but hidden capacity and talent that Lozanov calls the reserve capacities of the mind. Neuroscience today shows the enormous capacity of the human brain for learning and retention. As each student has untapped reserve capacities of the mind, the teacher's main task is to create opportunities for each person to tap into their potential. The task of a teacher is to support students in developing more empowering beliefs about themselves and their world. Robert Rosenthal's, of Harvard University, work on the Pygmalian Effect shows that what a teacher thinks of students translates into what a student achieves. Lozanov's research into the effects of *suggestion,* or the underlying messages in every type of communication, supports Rosenthal's research. The teacher's role becomes more important in light of their research. Accelerated Learning teachers carefully monitor their thoughts about students to make sure they are supporting and not hindering someone's learning. They pay attention to their verbal and nonverbal communication because they both contribute greatly to student success or failure. Teachers develop their sensory acuity or ability to recognize subtle cues from learners. Based on their observations, an Accelerated Learning teacher uses language, story, and ritual to help students widen their perspective and embrace possibilities. Teachers frame learning positively at all times. They help students reframe negatively perceived experiences to emphasize the positive.

The Accelerated Learning Process

Much of what Lozanov proposed in the 1960s has been confirmed by researchers today who have access to sophisticated equipment to study the brain—the importance of emotions to learning, the need for a wide variety of interaction with the learning materials, with other students, and with the teacher to support learning, the importance of both the physical and the emotional environment to learning, and the ability of the brain to process and create patterns in parallel. His emphasis on the learning environment, his belief in sensory overload to bypass the conscious brain, and his use of music, the arts and game-like activities to engage the student are in keeping with what we know about the brain and learning.

The Accelerated Learning process provides students with a variety of multi-sensory input based on the premise that the more senses involved in learning, the more neural pathways will be developed and strengthened. The more stimuli used in the initial learning phase, the easier it will be to recall the information later. Teachers include learning activities to appeal to all learning styles and build strengths in areas that are less developed in students. Accelerated Learning emphasizes the role of the learning environment. Add artwork and other peripherals that support learning and *de-suggest,* or enable a shift of perspective, in the student to your classroom. Use the space intentionally to create powerful visuals. Include posters with key learning concepts, positive suggestions in the form of sayings or proverbs, and graphics and colors that reinforce the key concepts. Provide a seating arrangement to support interaction, either using a circle of chairs and tables behind the circle for group activities for a small group or if the room is large enough, several round tables for groups of five to six students scattered around the room for groups of any size. Ensure full spectrum lighting if at all possible, and provide plenty of water to drink and fruit to eat. Place green plants around the room. The lecture-style seating, gray bare walls, and sterile atmosphere that act as negative anchors from the traditional school classroom suggest that learning is sterile, the teacher is the knower, and the students are passive receivers of knowledge. The pleasant physical environment replaces those underlying negative suggestions with more empowering ones. Learning becomes an interactive process involving all the senses. The seating arrangement places the student at the center and not the teacher. The interaction with the environment, the content, and the other students become equally important to the teacher–student interaction. The physical environment becomes a positive suggestive factor and not one that inhibits on both the conscious and unconscious level. Play **music** to support a positive internal state and to reinforce learning.

Neuroscience has looked at the impact of music on learning and retention. The right music creates and maintains an optimal state for learning. Lozanov also describes music as one of the most powerful suggestive factors in learning. Accelerated Learning uses music in a multitude of ways, to help students focus and center themselves, to add drama to the presentation of materials. Use music to support group work, facilitate creativity, and as an anchor to signal certain events. Play one type of music when it is time to change groups, another type to end the break, and a different piece of music to help students focus. Choose instrumental music to support learning. For breaks and energizers or to change groups or activities, select songs with a positive message and one that supports the learning or the activity. Use pop music to celebrate certain events. Play *One Moment in Time* by Whitney Houston when students are preparing for an important test or event. Choose *We are the Champions* to celebrate student success. Use the theme for *Mission Impossible* or *Pink Panther* to signal a detective-type activity. Play Baroque largos and adagios to review material or while students are doing individual work or reading.

Ritual also plays a key role in Accelerated Learning. The oldest part of our brain, the reptilian brain or R-complex thrives on ritual. You can use certain spaces in the room for certain types of learning or teaching. Use one part of the classroom for questions and answers. Designate other parts of the room as a creativity space, a reflection space, or a place to present new materials. Ritualize the beginning and ending of each day by playing a certain piece of music to begin and another to end the day. Create a special process to begin the day. Ask students to reflect on a quote, tell a story, or do a series of brain-gym exercises. Use music as part of the ritual when appropriate.

Accelerated Learning Design Template and Strategies

The Accelerated Learning cycle provides teachers with a foolproof design template. The cycle consists of a Learner Preparation Phase, a Connection Phase, a Creative Presentation Phase, an Activation Phase consisting of three parts, and an Integration Phase.

The Learner Preparation Phase includes an overview of the learning content and desired outcomes that answer the questions why, what, how, and what if. It also prepares the student emotionally, mentally, and physically to learn. In the overview, the *why* addresses the bigger picture of how the learning will impact the students' lives. It may include solutions to their perceived problems or ways to achieve their personal goals. The *what* offers a short description of the basis of the work to be done, gives an overview of the process, the timing, and the steps to achieve success. The *how* informs students of the ways in which they will learn and lets them see that the diverse methods will support each of them. Finally, *what if* demonstrates the potential impact of learning the content or process for them, and invites them to imagine their success, to experiment with possibilities, and discover for themselves how they will use the learning.

The second stage of the Learner Preparation Phase allows students to focus on the here and now, center themselves, and calm their minds. The process of *centering* or focusing their thoughts, relaxing their bodies, and freeing themselves of self-talk or distracting images prepares the student for the learning experience. To help students center and focus, allow them to listen to a few minutes of reflective music and think about a saying that relates to the day. Guide them through a short guided imagery that encourages them to remember a positive learning experience, and then connect the experience to the present. Walk students through a short relaxation exercise to prepare them for learning. Do brain-gym activities to coordinate and balance their bodies, minds, and emotions.

The Connection Phase provides activities that help students connect emotionally to the subject matter. They may include experiments, mini-simulations, guided-imageries, personal "burning" questions on the subject, drawing, or metaphorical activities. The activities allow students to find meaning in what they are learning and engage their minds, emotions, bodies, and spirit. Have students collect everything they know about a given subject on large pieces of paper using words or symbols. Lead a guided imagery that takes students to a period of history, through the process of photosynthesis, or on a tour of the digestive track or circulatory system. Involve students in an experiment that simulates reality and invite them to offer their hypothesis about what happened and why. Show a part of a movie that dramatizes something you will be teaching, and then elicit their feelings and thoughts.

The Creative Presentation Phase "teaches" the subject matter or process. Depending on the content, the needs of the learning group, and the timeframe, this phase may include any of the following: a simulation in which students experience all the key concepts, an experiment in which the students formulate questions, experiment to find the answers, then teach the concepts back to the rest of the class, a creative presentation that involves three-dimensional mindmaps, skits, panel discussions, game show formats, or interactive lectures. Foreign language teachers present the new dialogues in the form of *concert readings*. The dialogues are written in the form of a movie script. They are rich in imagery and natural language without the artificial grammar progression found in traditional foreign language texts. The story is dramatic and contains plot points, twists and turns and a dramatic and positive ending. The *Active Concert* is a dramatic reading of the foreign language text to music of the pre-romantic phase of classical music (Beethoven, Mozart, Haydn, Tchaikovsky). While the students listen, they repeat the sentences in the foreign language silently and read along. The *Active Concert* is followed by a *Passive Concert*. The *Passive Concert* begins with a short guided imagery to induce a relaxed state in the students. The students then listen to the dialogue to slow movements of Baroque music (largos and adagios, by composers like Vivaldi, Telemann, Albinoni, and others) and imagine they are in the scene.

The Creative Presentation Phase involves students in the process of teaching, allowing them to discover the key concepts, problem-solve, create, and interact with the material and one another. The students become familiar with the material at a basic level and their involvement in the teaching process creates a sense of ownership for the learning. Get students' bodies involved and use body, muscle memory to support the retention of the concepts. Personify parts of the body, parts of a sentence, and the like. Give them characteristics similar to their "role" in reality and tell a story to introduce key concepts. Have students play the parts of a process, use themselves to model it, move around, and make connections. Give students texts and other resources on a given subject. In groups, have them create a newspaper with a special section on the topic as if it had just happened. Ask students to create a boardgame that includes all relevant information from their textbooks on a certain subject, then let everyone play the various games in class. By deciding on the pertinent information, creating the game themselves, then playing it, they will master the material better than when someone teaches it. Have each person "become" a famous person from an area you are teaching. After studying their character and the role they have in history, science, economics, or any other subject area, invite everyone to a party and allow them to mingle and get to know one another in character. Keep the communication going by asking important questions and generating rich discussion. By identifying with key figures, students will retain more of the important information.

The Activation Phase consists of three parts and moves from more teacher-guided activities to more student-directed ones. The *Elaboration Phase* offers a series of structured game-like activities that allow students to practice the material enough to begin to master it. The activities promote the self-concept of the students by promoting win-win situations in which cooperation instead of competition is emphasized. Potentially difficult concepts and ideas are embedded in activities that engage the whole person and make it easier to learn concepts that, on their own, might seem daunting. Board games, card games, memory, dominoes, and other adaptations of children's games, as well as rhythm and movement, story and song can be used in this first activation phase. Create a board game and include a variety of question types—closed, one answer questions, open-ended ones that may have multiple right answers, and thought provoking questions that stimulate higher thinking skills. Add various surprise cards to spice up the game. Include sayings and proverbs to de-suggest or contribute ideas related to the subject. Create prize or activity cards to add variety to the game. Include cards to keep the game interesting like ones that read, *If you were born in the Spring, move two spaces forward.* Toy stores and game shows are a great resource for ideas on how you can make content fun and easy to master.

The Assimilation Phase uses many of the same generic types of activities, but encourages students to synthesize, use the material in new and novel ways and tap into their own creativity. The teacher's role is to observe, offer support when needed, maintain a positive environment, and encourage the involvement of each person. Have students develop a skit or role-play that includes the relevant information. Play game shows that require students to answer questions, give their opinions, and explain processes randomly.

The Implementation Phase provides an opportunity for students to demonstrate what they know. It can be a group skit, a collage, a story, or role-plays to demonstrate competency in a real-life situation. The Implementation Phase gives students an opportunity to experience how much they have learned and demonstrate their expertise in novel and creative ways. Ask groups to think about all the key concepts they have been practicing and create a documentary for younger students. Have them perform, and then allow the other students to ask the performers questions as if they were the actual audience for the documentary. Allow students to participate in a panel discussion as experts on the subject. Give students a complex task to solve that encourages them to manipulate the material and make connections between the various elements they have mastered.

The Integration Phase completes the Accelerated Learning Cycle by providing an opportunity for reflection. It brings closure to a learning module or class period. Conduct a guided-imagery that walks students through the day or module. Play music and give students time to journal or answer some key questions. Show a PowerPoint presentation that includes photos, images, the key concepts of the content, and some motivational phrases to close. Give students time to synthesize their learning in the form of a poem, a story, a work of art, or by creating a commercial, giving a speech, or writing an article. By taking time at the end the day or a learning module to reflect on what they've learned and experienced, students realize how far they have come, how much they have been able to master in a short period of time.

Even if time is short, take a few minutes and walk through the key concepts and invite students to reflect on what was important to them and how it will support them. Pause after each concept for students to contemplate its relevance. Play reflective music as you speak and match your voice to the music. Keep eye contact with everyone and point to relevant posters and other anchors for the group's shared learning experience. Mention any humorous or meaningful moments the students have shared in addition to simply summarizing content or process.

See also: **Aroma and Learning; Classroom Environment; Emotion; Multiple Intelligences; Music; Self-Esteem.**

Further Readings

Heidenhain, G. (Ed.) (2003). *Learning Beyond Boundaries. Fundamental Experiences Using Accelerated Learning.* Lawrenceville, Georgia: International Alliance for Learning Publication.

LeHecka, C. (2003). *Historical Review of Accelerated Learning Research: A Monograph.* Theoretical Implications and Practical Applications. Lawrenceville, Georgia: International Alliance for Learning Publication. www.IALearn.org, professional organization for Accelerated Learning. www.accelerated-learning.info

GAIL HEIDENHAIN

T

Teaching Model for the Brain

During the past decade the neurological and cognitive sciences have produced a vast frontier of knowledge on how the brain processes, stores, and retrieves information. As educators have increasingly recognized their role as consumers of this emerging knowledge, translating brain research into classroom instruction often becomes a challenge for the typical educational practitioner.

In an era of high-stakes accountability for student performance, many teachers feel pressured to prepare students to meet proficiency levels on standardized tests. At the same time, they are often required to implement a plethora of ever-changing educational initiatives and reforms handed to them by well-meaning school district supervisors. In this climate, it would not be surprising for new teachers to feel overwhelmed and seasoned teachers to view any educational initiative, including research in the neurosciences, as merely a fad that will soon be replaced by yet another new initiative. Perhaps this thinking accounts for the fact that educational research is largely ignored by practitioners; as a result little actual change has occurred in our nation's classrooms during the last several decades.

For any research, especially current brain research, to become readily accessible to teachers, fragmented initiatives must be integrated into a cohesive model of instruction. The brain-targeted teaching model described in this chapter is designed to meet this need. It provides teachers with a format for using research in the neurosciences as well as research-based effective instructional practices to guide them in planning, implementing, and assessing a sound program of instruction. The model also assists administrators, supervisors, and professionals supporting instruction as they guide teachers in implementing research-based effective teaching strategies.

First, it might be wise to address those critics who scoff at the term *brain-based learning*. Some, for example, might contend that the term has no meaning since all learning is brain-based. "After all," they may say, "we don't think with our feet!" We know, of course, that all learning involves the brain. Yet, we also know that not all teaching results in learning. Thus, while all *learning* is "brain-based," all *teaching* is not. Unfortunately, many teaching practices that regularly occur in our schools defy what neuroscience tells us about the brain's natural learning systems. The model presented here, therefore, does not refer to *brain-based learning* but rather to *brain-targeted teaching*.

BRAIN-TARGETED TEACHING
LEARING UNIT

Teacher: Dates:

Unit Topic:/Title   Grand Level:

Standard(s):

Brain Target #1
Emotional Connection:

Brain Target #2
Physical Environment:

Brain Target #3
Concept Map/
Advanced Organizer:

Learing Goals:

Introductory "Big Picture" Activity/Assessment of Prior Knowledge

---

The Brain-Targeted Teaching Model © Mariale M. Hardiman

Brain Target #4
Activities for Teaching Declarative/Procedural Knowledge

Brain Target #5
Activities for Extension and Application of Knowledge

Brain Target #6
Evaluating Learning

Materials:

The Brain-Targeted Teaching Model © Mariale M. Hardiman

The brain-targeted teaching model presents six stages, or "brain targets" of the teaching and learning process and describes brain research that supports each stage. While each brain target is presented separately, the components are interrelated. For example, Brain-Target One describes the importance of establishing a positive emotional climate to foster high levels of learning; these strategies are applied throughout the entire model. At the same time, evaluating learning, Brain-Target Six, is an integral part of each component of the model.

Brain-Target One: Setting the Emotional Climate for Learning

Neuroscientists have recently described the intricate interactions between the **emotional** and cognitive brain systems. Research has shown that the brain's limbic system, located just above the brain stem at the base of the brain, is responsible for our emotional responses. This system, which includes the thalamus, hypothalamus, hippocampus, and amygdala, is also the first to process sensory stimuli. Visual signals travel from the retina to the thalamus, which sorts the information and sends it to the neocortex, the thinking center, to be processed for meaning. The thalamus also sends the information to a small almond-shaped structure, the amygdala, which determines the emotional relevance of the information. This signal, sent simultaneously to both the cognitive and emotional centers, travels first through a "quick and dirty" route to the amygdala, arriving there about fourty milliseconds before it reaches the neocortex. If the amygdala senses threat, it triggers the hypothalamus to activate hormones, mainly cortisol, which elevates blood pressure, increases heart rate, and contracts muscles—all in preparation for an immediate emotional reaction. As the heart rate elevates, blood is directed away from the cortex to the muscles for quick movement, thus diminishing cognitive processing. This "downshifting" prepares the organism for fight or flight, allowing the limbic system to activate and process information before it is analyzed in our cognitive system. As a result, information is processed first in the emotional center before being processed in the thinking center.

Once released into the bloodstream, cortisol can remain in the system for hours. While cortisol levels are high, we may become more easily distracted and lose efficiency of working memory. Unfortunately, chronic high levels of cortisol can have troubling effects. Studies have shown a shrinkage of the hippocampus, a center for memory, when an organism is exposed to long-term stress.

The effects of stress and threat on learning have clear implications for educators. While we may be unable to control all the factors of stress in the lives of our students, the adept teacher can minimize threat-causing practices within the classroom. For example, teachers should liberally praise positive student performance and eliminate practices that cause a child to become embarrassed or disenfranchised within the classroom. At the same time, the teacher should maximize strategies that promote positive emotion. Research has shown that while threats impede learning, positive emotional experiences, during which the brain produces the neurotransmitter serotonin, can contribute to long-term memory. The more intense the arousal of our amygdala the stronger the memory imprint, which, in turn, enhances long-term learning.

Teachers are encouraged to deliberately plan for positive emotional connections within the framework of a specific unit of study. Such connections include specific activities that will connect the students emotionally to the content. For example, within a history lesson students could assume the role of a historical figure and describe feelings and attitudes associated with a particular historic event. When studying literature, students' creative thinking could be encouraged by having them engage in activities to role play various characters in a story or rewrite the story's ending. The infusion of the visual and performing arts is an effective way to tap into children's emotional response systems to enhance learning and should be included within the activities of every learning unit.

Brain-Target Two: Creating the Physical Learning Environment

While the first strategy focused on establishing a positive emotional climate and using emotional responses to enhance learning, Brain-Target Two fosters the careful planning of the physical learning environment. We know that our eyes register about 36,000 visual images per hour, with about 90 percent of the brain's sensory input coming from visual stimuli. The retina supplies about 40 percent of all nerve fibers that are connected to the brain. With this vast visual capacity, the active brain constantly scans the environment seeking visual stimuli.

Researchers tell us that the brain's visual attending mechanism is strongly influenced by *novelty* in the environment. Studies by Sydney Zentall (1983) compared the effects of bland, unchanging environments on the learning habits of children. Such environments were compared with classrooms that provided students with stimulation through frequently adjusting and changing classroom displays. Findings revealed that children were off task more often in settings that lacked novelty. In bland environments, students tended to seek out their own stimulation through movement, off-task talking, or disruptive behaviors.

Sound, lighting, and scent also appear to have an effect on learning. Soft background music can help to relax students although, while performing tasks that demand high levels of concentration, a quiet environment appears to be most effective. Lighting also seems to have an effect on student performance. Researchers have demonstrated up to an 18 percent increase in achievement levels of students who were taught in classrooms with the most natural and full spectrum lighting compared to classrooms with cool-white fluorescent lights. Scent can also be used to enhance the memory system. As we have learned, most stimuli is sorted first by the thalamus, then sent to various structures within the brain for processing. Olfactory input, however, is the exception as it bypasses the thalamus and moves directly into the brain's limbic and memory systems. This may account for the vivid memories that certain scents seem to produce such as the smell of our mother's favorite recipe or the cologne of a friend.

Carefully plan the physical learning environment by providing novelty within each learning unit. In preparation for a new learning unit, teachers are encouraged to create flexible seating arrangements, recreate bulletin boards and other classroom displays, add content-specific artifacts, soften harsh lights with lamps, use natural lighting when possible, organize horizontal and vertical spaces to add color and beauty, and use scents such as peppermint to promote alertness or lavender for calm.

Brain-Target Three: Designing the Learning Experience

Brain-Target Three encourages teachers to design the learning experience in a way that is compatible with the brain's natural learning systems. While it may seem natural for teachers to write lesson plans that present information to students in sequential order until all of the content has been covered, this approach may in fact impede learning. Neuroscientists tell us that the brain categorizes new stimuli into concepts that are either familiar or novel, then combines these concepts to create new patterns of thinking and understanding—a concept referred to as *patterning*. The brain filters new information through the lens of prior experience and prior knowledge to create new meaning. New information, then, becomes integrated into a holistic pattern of cognition.

Imagine completing a jigsaw puzzle without ever having seen the overall image that the puzzle displays. Without giving students "big picture concepts" of the content that they will learn in a unit of study, students are often learning disconnected bits of information that too often never come together into an overarching concept or pattern. Lack of conceptual understanding typically results in loss of retention of the disjointed facts and details.

Use content standards and curriculum guidelines to design overarching goals and concepts, then display these learning goals in non-linguistic representations such as concept maps or graphic organizers. Activities are then designed to allow students to understand how the objectives they will learn during the unit relate to the big picture concept. As they continue through the content, students are referred back to the concept map to reinforce the relevance of each learning activity.

Brain-Target Four: Teaching for Declarative and Procedural Knowledge

The next stage of the Brain-Targeted Teaching Model is to engage students in activities that will enable them to demonstrate mastery of skills, content, and concepts. Brain-Target Four promotes mastery of learning goals and objectives by planning multiple activities to activate the brain's memory systems.

In teaching for declarative and procedural knowledge, teachers must provide students with learning activities to create and sustain new *engrams,* or memory patterns. Cognitive scientists have identified three types of memory systems: short-term, working, and long-term memory. Short-term and working memory systems provide a form of temporary storage; short-term memory allows us to retain information for a few seconds or minutes, while working memory serves as a "desk top" for retrieval of information when it is in immediate use. Once the brain determines that the information in our working memories is no longer needed, it is partially or totally forgotten. Unfortunately, too often what is presented in our classrooms is designed for students' working memories—students learn information so they can retrieve it on a test or quiz then quickly forget much of it as they move on to the next topic.

Clearly the goal of teaching and learning is for students to acquire knowledge, processes, and skills that they can use to build new knowledge, a process that requires the use of long-term memory systems. Leading researcher on memory, Larry Squire (Squire and Kandel, 2000), tells us that the most important factor in determining how well we remember information is the degree to which we rehearse and repeat that information. Based on the method and frequency of presentation, memories consolidate as the brain reorganizes, modifies, and strengthens synaptic connections among neurons. During tasks that involve only working memory, the brain uses proteins that currently exist in brain synapses. When information moves, however, from working to long-term memory systems, new proteins are created. Effective teaching can result in biochemical changes in the brain!

Planning for repeated rehearsals of content, skills, and concepts ensures that the information becomes part of students' long-term memory systems. Such repetition would be terribly boring for students (and teachers too) if the same activities were presented multiple times in the same way. Instead, teachers are encouraged to plan varied experiences so that students can manipulate information within a variety of modalities. For example, students could demonstrate understanding of a concept by designing a graphic organizer, preparing a power-point summary, designing a lesson to be taught to students in a lower grade, preparing an oral debate depicting multiple points of view, preparing a dramatization, or representing the concept in a visual display. By providing students with multiple ways to manipulate content, skills, and concepts, teachers are not only promoting long-term memory but are providing the opportunity to differentiate instruction based on students' needs, abilities, and learning styles.

Brain-Target Five: Teaching for Extension and Application of Knowledge

The acquisition of knowledge is only the beginning of a sound instructional program. Brain research supports what educators know to be the hallmark of effective instruction—lifelong learning best occurs when students are able to apply content, skills, and processes to tasks that require them to engage in higher-order thinking and problem-solving skills. Using knowledge meaningfully requires students to extend thinking by examining concepts in deeper, more analytical ways, thus requiring the brain to use multiple and complex systems of retrieval and integration. Brain researchers have used the concept of the *modular brain* to describe differentiated functions of brain regions. Modules from one part of the brain connect to other modules when we perform complex tasks. Research has demonstrated, for example, that the motor cortex, originally thought only to control motor functions, becomes activated when the brain engages in problem-solving that includes such cognitive components as memory, language, emotion, and active learning.

Utilize performance-based instructional activities within each learning unit. Such activities require students to engage in inductive and deductive thinking, analysis, and problem-solving skills. It allows students to apply what they have learned in tasks that have real-world application. Activities include conducting investigations, designing experiments, creating metaphors and analogies, examining cause and effect patterns, analyzing perspective, and engaging in creative thinking through the visual and performing arts. For example, a third-grade teacher integrates science and mathematic objectives by having students measure a plot of ground, then design and plant a flower and vegetable garden. Sixth-grade students study immigration patterns by researching archives at Ellis Island, then designing a map that depicts the settlement of various ethnic groups throughout the United States. Seventh graders build a model of a human cell and write a skit in which each character assumes the role of a different cell structure. Eighth graders rewrite a novel into a children's book including illustrations and present the book to a younger child.

Brain-Target Six: Evaluating Learning

While Brain-Target Six is the last stage, each stage of the model includes evaluation activities. The goal of evaluation is to provide students with relevant **feedback** about their performance so that the student can adjust learning habits and the teacher can make sound instructional decisions. Cognitive science supports what teachers know by experience: Immediate feedback strengthens learning and memory patterns. In addition to traditional grading methods (quizzes, tests, essays, etc.) evaluation measures should also employ a combination of tools including scoring rubrics, grading keys, and self-grading tools (e.g., the KWL chart

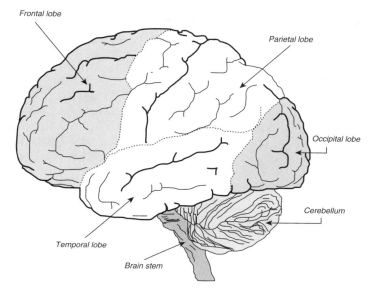

Frontal lobe

Parietal lobe

Occipital lobe

Cerebellum

Temporal lobe

Brain stem

The structure of the brain

in which students indicate what they know in the K column, what they want to learn in the W column, and what they learned in the L column).

By using the following format teachers can be assured that they are implementing research-based effective teaching strategies as well as implementing what the neurological and cognitive sciences tell us about how the brain thinks and learns. Teaching and learning not only becomes more effective, it becomes more fun!

See also: **Aroma and Learning; Drama; Music; Physcial Environment; Visuals and Classroom Management.**

Further Readings

Hardiman, M. (2001). Connecting brain research with dimensions of learning. *Educational Leadership* 59(3):52–55.

Hardiman, M. (2003). *Connecting Brain Research with Effective Teaching: The Brain-Targeted Teaching Model.* Landam, MD: Scarecrow Press, Inc.

LeDoux, J. (1996). *The Emotional Brain: The Mysterious Underpinnings of Emotional Life.* New York: Touchtone Books.

Marzano, R.J., Pinkering, D.J., Pollock, J.E. (2001). *Classroom Instruction That Works.* Alexandria, VA: Association for Supervision and Curriculum Development.

Sylwester, R. (1994). How emotions affect learning. *Educational Leadership* 52(2):28–32.

BrainConnection: The Brain and Learning, http://www.brainconnection.com

MARIALE M. HARDIMAN

Transfer

Transfer is the process of using knowledge from previous experiences in novel situations. Most formal education aspires to promote transfer, because the context of learning usually differs from the contexts in which the learning will be applied. However, research has shown that transfer does not inevitably occur. For example, a lack of transfer is evident when we see students get an "A" in math class, but are not able to apply their math skills to balance a checkbook. Why is it so difficult to take what we know and put it to purposeful use in a new context? To discover the key to answering that question, let's consider transfer in a bit more depth.

What are the neurobiological underpinnings of transfer? While the specific phenomenon of transfer has not been explicitly explored, research in three major areas—cognitive neuroscience, system-level neuroscience, and molecular neuroscience—has contributed to our understanding of some forms of learning and memory, which form the basis for transfer. At the molecular level, we know that biochemical changes accompany memory and learning. As long ago as the late 1800s, Santiago Ramon y Cajal proposed that increased connections between neurons resulted from learning and led to better communication and stronger memories. This proposal has been confirmed by extensive experiments in simple nervous systems like those of the marine snail Aplysia and the fruit fly Drosophila, enabling the modeling of both non-associative (habituation and sensitization) and associative (classical conditioning, operant conditioning, and extinction) learning at the cellular level.

Research at the molecular level continues to provide ever finer grained resolution of the state and condition of specific single neurons or subcellular components. For example, it has been found that RNA content is altered and new proteins are created and deposited at synapses involved in long-term potentiation (LTP). Additionally, researchers are now able to explore the genetic basis of learning and memory through gene knockout in mice.

While there is a certain delight and authority in being able to explain the basis for learning and memory at such fine levels of resolution, the degree to which this can or should inform our educational practice is uncertain and negligible. With the pervasive notion of brain-based education, we are unreasonably forced to justify what we do in our classrooms not in terms of what experience has shown works, but in terms of what is learned in the neuroscientist's laboratory. This is a worthy long-term goal but one that requires carefully balanced and honest collaboration between scientists, psychologists, and educators. At this point, it is feckless and counterproductive to elaborate an explanation of cognitive behavior in terms of subcellular components. In one instance, James Byrnes (2001) pointed out that some authors have erroneously indicated learning is more effective with increased synapse formation and that this can be accomplished via divergent thinking as part of a lesson. There is no sensible bridge that can span the enormous conceptual distance between the single synapse and human behavior, and there are currently no experimental paradigms available that would prove or disprove such an assertion.

Much more intuitively resonant, though perhaps not so seductively and fashionably "cutting edge," are the findings generated from the fields of cognitive neuroscience (which incorporates cognitive psychology and overtly recognizes that the brain is the seat of all behavior), and systems level neuroscience. From these fields, which generally study human or higher primate learning and memory in conditions that come to some degree closer to what we do as educators, have come increasingly useful constructs of learning and especially memory. These are the fields from which the techniques outlined above have emerged. We expect that these fields are the ones that will come closest to providing guidance to educational practice, if educators continue to hold researchers to such a goal.

Most of what is known about memory at the systems and cognitive neuroscience levels can be summarized in three principles: (1) Storage of memory occurs in stages and is constantly changing; (2) the hippocampus, responsible for short-term memory, plays a unique role in memory processing; and (3) memory traces—chemical or structural changes encoding memory—are found throughout the brain. We know different structures of the brain are critical in short-term vs long-term memory, and there are multiple memory systems distributed throughout the central nervous system. Important structures for declarative memory (e.g., of facts, dates, etc.) are the hippocampus (part of the limbic system), diencephalon (including parts of the thalamus and hypothalamus), ventromedial prefrontal cortex, and the basal forebrain. The prefrontal cortex appears to function as the structure that excites or inhibits other brain regions, the hippocampus is essential for the learning and memory of spatial relationships, and the amygdala has a special role in memory of emotional content. The basal ganglia and cerebellum have roles in motor skill learning and habit formation, and much of the cerebral cortex is important in long-term storage of memory. It is likely that in the foreseeable future, research at the systems and cognitive levels, using powerful imaging techniques and with enhanced collaboration between scientists and educators, will provide answers to questions about the parts of the brain that are important in transfer and how educators can structure learning environments to efficiently activate those parts to ensure that transfer occurs. Given the high cognitive demands of transfer it would not be surprising if all the known areas participate to a greater or lesser degree when transfer occurs.

Transfer encompasses many subtleties. Transfer can be positive when the application of knowledge to a new problem results in new and strengthened learning, or it can be negative, interfering with new learning. Negative transfer is a short-term condition. When learning a new language, for example, the learner's native tongue may encourage use of grammar rules not applicable in the new language. With appropriate feedback, the learner adjusts to rules of the new language, rendering negative transfer harmless in the long term.

When positive transfer occurs, the benefits of learning are fully realized: one's knowledge is successfully leveraged. Some authors distinguish between "high-road" and "low-road" transfer. "Low-road transfer," or "near transfer," occurs when the new learning situation closely resembles the original situation. This kind of transfer holds for situations where the learning is task specific, or routine and consistent, and for mastery of procedural objectives, those that involve a series of steps. If in the original learning context there is ample practice, such that the learning becomes almost "reflexive," near transfer occurs when a new stimulus evokes almost automatic application of the previously learned strategy. For example, in a health education class, high school students learn steps in the process of negotiation. They practice these steps repeatedly. In a similar situation, at home or on the job, if students use the steps of negotiation successfully, they have experienced "low-road" or "near" transfer.

At the other end of the continuum, "high-road" or "far" transfer occurs when one's existing knowledge is applied to situations that vary from the initial learning situation. The variation can be relatively benign or quite profound, but a key feature of far transfer is that it involves judgment about how the knowledge is to be applied. Consider a student who has learned how to write an essay, and now needs to create a policy paper for government officials responsible for determining the level of state funding for mental health needs. The essay writing skills need to be applied in a different context, one with much higher stakes and one requiring critical judgment skills, sensitive to the needs of a specialized audience in a particular situation. This specific "essay" had not been practiced previously.

Before we explore ways to encourage transfer, we need to clarify the relationships that link learning, knowledge, memory, and transfer. Learning means that we had an experience that left us with more knowledge than we had previously. Knowledge can be facts: an art teacher indicated the primary colors are red, yellow, and blue. It can be information perceived or inferred from the environment: it is a cloudy day, so there's a chance of rain. It can be confidence in content: knowing times tables from one through twelve. Or, it can be acquisition of a new skill: performing cardiopulmonary resuscitation (CPR). Memory refers to the storage of knowledge that can be retrieved at will. For transfer to occur, learning needs facilitation by strategies that support memory storage and retrieval.

Madeleine Hunter identified four factors that impact transfer: similarity, critical attributes, association, and the context and degree of first learning. The following example of driving a car illustrates these factors at work:

1. Similarity refers to the degree to which a new learning experience resembles a past one. Similarity from one vehicle to the next—location of ignition, brake, accelerator—increases the likelihood of skill transfer. There is some tension in the concept of similarity—negative transfer can occur when the new environment is too similar (or perhaps only superficially similar) to the past situation.

2. Critical attributes, the unique characteristics that distinguish a task or situation from others like it, impact transfer because identifying them allows for appropriate allocation of attention to the novelty. If you drive a car with automatic transmission, and subsequently need to drive a car with manual transmission, identifying the presence of a clutch allows you to devote most of your attention to training the previously uninvolved left foot in a new motor pattern. Critical attributes and similarity are two sides of one coin.

3. Association is demonstrated as follows: If you learned to drive while listening to Beethoven's Moonlight Sonata, hearing the song while you attempt to drive a new car may help resurrect previously learned skills for tasks common to driving both cars. Things learned together are recalled together even if they are not similar. One evokes the other in the same way trademark logos and advertising jingles bring products to mind.

4. Finally, the context and degree of the original learning lead to transfer if the original learning emphasized the range of contexts where you use this information and provided you with ample practice (repetition, feedback, guided practice, etc.). The deep, thorough learning resulting from diverse practice before one is able to get one's license enhances the probability that even in a different car you will easily transfer motor skills and driving strategies.

To the extent that transfer is not inevitable because we tend to overlook it in instructional design and delivery, adopting these strategies should enhance transfer. The techniques relate to planning, delivery, and future instruction. At the planning level, teachers need to assess the degree to which a new topic or situation is similar to one just taught. If near transfer is desirable, one might plan to employ hugging, a technique that depends heavily on similarities, especially involving the use of skills, or a series of steps, and builds on them. Examples are: simulation games for practice in diverse situations, mental practice to review applications of new knowledge, and contingency learning for challenging students to seek out additional information needed to solve problems. If there is a risk of the similarity interfering with transfer, or causing negative transfer it is desirable to teach similar concepts at different times, or at least take special care to emphasize and teach the differences before addressing the similarities.

In the delivery stage of instruction it is essential to (1) identify what students already know and (2) "bridge" or help them to see the differences and similarities between what they already know and the new material. Asking students to write short stories or songs, to interview other students, use graphic organizers, or make murals, collages or models are all strategies that serve the dual purposes of helping a teacher assess current knowledge and of helping students retrieve and activate their past learning, a first step in transfer. Bridging can be achieved with activities like brainstorming (identification of other ways to apply new learning), analogies (comparisons of the new learning to something else, allowing for identification of critical attributes), and metacognition (thinking about solving problems, and evaluating the success of the solution as well as alternative strategies for the future).

Emphasis on critical attributes throughout all stages is a key technique in facilitating transfer. The teacher identifies critical attributes, illustrates them with simple examples, further illustrates with conceptually richer examples, provides students with opportunities to create their own examples and finally, teaches the student the limits of the critical attributes; helping them to recognize the times the rules don't apply. In a parallel fashion, West, Farmer and Wolff recommend the use of metaphors to enhance transfer, proposing a sequence that runs like this: select a metaphor that fits, emphasize it consistently through the lessons, establish a context for its use, provide instructions to benefit from the imagery, emphasize similarities and differences, and provide opportunities for rehearsal.

To ensure that the *new* learning transfers well to *future* learning, teachers need to foster deep learning. Ample practice of a new skill in different contexts, engaging in abstraction highlighting the importance of principles underlying the new learning, active self-monitoring, and arousing the level of mindfulness to the environment rather than simply being passive participants in it, are all techniques that set the stage for positive transfer in future learning situations. Use journal writing as a reflective tool at the end of a lesson to help students identify what they learned, how it relates to what they already know, and how it can be used in the future.

Over the last few years the traditional construct of transfer has been criticized as limited, and a new focus on the role of attentional processes in explaining how transfer occurs is emerging. The bottom line though, is that to facilitate transfer, teachers need to be ever mindful of design and delivery of instruction, and learners need to be provided with the tools that will allow them to reap benefits.

This brief introduction gives a sampling of the ways transfer can be enhanced based on psychological models and a summary of what is known about the neurobiological basis for learning and memory. With an understanding of the strategies and conditions that facilitate transfer, educators as well as learners can capitalize on this knowledge, ensuring that learning will be a productive venture. Further exploration through additional reading of historical and contemporary research, and careful application of the principles and concepts discovered, will yield satisfying and efficient learning experiences.

See also: **Constructivism, Mastery, Nature of Knowledge.**

Further Readings

Bransford, J.D., Schwartz, D.L. (1999). Rethinking transfer: a simple proposal with multiple implications. *Review of Research in Education* 24:61–100.
Shank, P. (2004). Can they do it in the real world? Designing for transfer of learning. *The eLearning Developers' Journal, September 7, 2004.* Retrieved August 15, 2005, from http://www.learningpeaks.com/pshank_Transfer.pdf
Sousa, D. (2001). *How the Brain Learns: A Classroom Teacher's Guide* (2nd ed.). California: Corwin Press, Inc.
Squire, L.R., Kandel, E.R. (2000). *Memory: From Mind to Molecules.* New York: Scientific American Library.
Dana Foundation www.dana.org

TREZ BUCKLAND, M.A. AND
KATHLEEN A. MULLIGAN, PH.D.

Trauma

The effects of trauma are linked to such far-reaching and long-term consequences as difficulty thinking and concentrating, persistent and recurring memories of the traumatic event, and social detachment. When traumatic experiences invade the landscape of the developing child, the effects form patterns of adaptation that predispose a child to live in a heightened state of **stress** and fear, undermining the child's normal developmental processes. Both the structural and the neurochemical systems of the brain can be permanently altered by trauma. In the classroom, this can affect a child's attention, behavior, emotions, social function, and ultimately the ability to learn.

In general, the earlier trauma is experienced, the greater the effect on the developing brain. As the brain grows from the brainstem to the neocortex in an orderly manner beginning before birth, the least conscious areas of the brain are organized earliest. When those areas of the brain are organized in response to the chemical flood engendered by fear, chaos, or threat, the unconscious functions of the brain come to "expect" danger and are set up to function accordingly. This may cause the traumatized child to experience altered and poorly regulated neurological functioning with increased levels of stress hormones and associated physical responses such as anxiety, impulsivity, sleep problems, and hyperactivity. In short, the traumatized child may be in a perpetual state of "fight or flight" and this state is not subject to the logic or reason of later developing areas of the brain. A traumatized child does not know why he or she experiences the physiological responses of this state, nor does the child perceive the state as abnormal.

Studies of adult survivors of childhood abuse show a statistically significantly smaller hippocampus than that of non-traumatized adults. Decreased functioning of the hippocampus may result in dysfunctions of remembering and forgetting and in hyper-responsiveness to environmental conditions.

Not all children who experience a traumatic experience suffer lasting effects, but specialists estimate that of the four million who experience trauma in the U.S. each year, half will exhibit symptoms related to the event in the form of behavior disorders, anxiety, **depression**, or phobias.

Some researchers have indicated that the predictability of persistent low-level stress can be less damaging than chaotic, unpredictable trauma because in some way the dysfunction creates its own normative pattern. When a child never knows what to expect, he or she maintains a hypervigilance in case there is a need for a defensive response. While this may be a useful state in a high-threat environment, it undermines the child's ability to function successfully in a safe environment. Children who are wired to "survive" have a difficult time responding to situations in which there is potential to thrive, because their energy is being sucked up at a level of brain function beneath that of conscious thought and reasoning. For example, these children often have a deep sensitivity to the environment and to nonverbal cues that interfere with their ability to attend to language. In the classroom, traumatized children may be waiting anxiously for signs that a threat is about to appear and have little attention left over to engage in planning for the accomplishment of a learning task that requires a state of relaxed alertness.

Different children respond differently to the same stressor based on a number of factors including age, family history, and previous experience with trauma. Bruce Perry and his colleagues have linked specific stress responses to gender. Young males are likely to respond to perceived threat with aggression, while females are more likely to have an internalized response, indicated by physical signs such as a lowered heart rate during questioning about a traumatic experience. Thus, females, as well as very young children, may be more prone to dissociative symptoms such as avoidance, compliance, and physical illness, than to active aggression in response to perceived danger. While males are likely to pick a fight with a peer, be resistant or defiant of authority, females are more likely to suppress aggression unless it can be expressed against someone they consider weaker. However, impulsivity, cognitive distortion, hyper-reactivity, and intimacy avoidance are common characteristics of any traumatized child and may be expressed in either a hyper-aroused or dissociated manner. For example, rugged individualism and intense loneliness are both expressions of intimacy avoidance.

Some researchers have postulated that both experienced violence and images of violence can have an impact on the developing brain. Violence and threat need not be physical to cause a fear response. However, intensity and frequency of the occurrence of threat, as well as the developmental stage at which the threat occurs, influence the degree to which a child's brain functioning will be affected by trauma. Supportive individuals and systems can mitigate the impact of trauma upon the child, and the sooner a fear-reducing intervention is introduced, the lesser the degree of impact on the child's brain organization.

Children who are traumatized by sudden unpredictable events such as sexual abuse or irrational physical violence may pursue behaviors that help them to establish a sense of control over the abuse. This is the mechanism behind provocative or seductive behavior in the victimized child, as well what motivates a victim of violence to become a perpetrator.

Children who experience trauma may be subject to later disease in adulthood. These include increased incidence of high blood pressure and other cardiovascular conditions, neuroimmunological, gastrointestinal, and psychiatric conditions for which they have familial or genetic predisposition. Children who experience violence are more likely to exhibit violent behavior in adulthood.

The classroom teacher's goal must be to provide a learning environment that is safe and comfortable for the traumatized child. Just as experiences formed the traumatized child's view of the world, new experiences can help to alter the child's view of the world. Repetitive and patterned activities that emphasize respect and healthy boundaries can be helpful. Even such simple classroom rituals as observing manners (saying "please," "thank you," and "may I?") can contribute to learning appropriate social interactions. Don't expect a traumatized or maltreated child to engage in socially acceptable behavior without modeling, discussing, and practicing your expectations.

A child will not learn to react differently to threat situations simply by changing the environment or by taking an abstract thinking approach to behavior management. The traumatized child must build an experiential base of consistent responses that are different from those which initially influenced his or her inappropriate adaptation. As a child relates to an adult authority who does not overreact to him or her, the child will be able gradually to try out different responses. As a child role-plays a different way of reacting to stress with a peer, he or she builds a range of responses that can be used instead of relying on those that are instinctual.

A teacher can best help student performance by being a caring, non-anxious presence who gradually increases expectations as a child's fear-state subsides over time. If you know about a specific traumatic event in a child's life, don't be afraid to talk to the child about it, but don't force **conversation** about it either. Wait until a student creates an opening to talk and allow the student to decide how much to reveal through conversation, art, or writing opportunities.

Offer a classroom environment that is predictable through scheduling and clearly defined rules and policies. Make plenty of room for choice-making within reasonable limits. This will help create an external structure that focuses a chaotic internal state without demanding unreasonable rigidity. Be responsive to a child's need for physical reassurance rather than initiating physical contact that may be uncomfortable for a traumatized child.

Observe and record the student's reactions to specific activities and don't be afraid to modify expectations based on the child's emotional responses to activities or lesson content. Be especially careful to watch for withdrawal behaviors that are sometimes harder to spot than extroverted behaviors that can sometimes be obviously irritating.

Remember that a traumatized child's ability to cope with stressors will vary and learning new ways of approaching social and relational situations such as those required in school will take time to develop.

See also: **At-Risk Behavior.**

Further Readings

Perry, B.D. (August 1999). Post-traumatic stress disorders in children and adolescents. *Current Opinions in Pediatrics*, (11)4.

Soloman, M.F., Siegel, D.J. (Ed.). *Healing Trauma: Attachment, Mind, Body, and Brain.* New York, NY: W.W. Norton & Co.

Stein, P.T., Kendall, J.C. (2004). *Psychological Trauma and the Developing Brain: Neurologically Based Interventions for Troubled Children.* Binghamton, NY: Haworth Press, Inc.

The ChildTrauma Academy http://childtrauma.org

International Society for Traumatic Stress Study (ISTSS) http://www.istss.org

http://www.trauma-pages.com/vanderk4.htm

LORI NILES

Visual Brain

The visual sense is arguably the most powerful way that the brain gathers information about the environment, and the processing of visual data and its resulting images is intimately and essentially linked to learning and cognition. It seems impossible to discuss learning without reference to vision and images. We see, we imagine, we develop insight, and we "get the picture."

The following paragraphs, then, do not purport to be complete or profound. Rather they touch briefly on the key topics of the process of vision in the eye, the way the cortex maps and responds to signals from the eye, the use of visual information for cognition, and other important topics related to vision and learning such as **critical periods** and **learning styles**.

The Eye

To understand the role of vision and images in learning, it is helpful to first identify the nature of information about the environment that is gathered by the visual organ, the eye. Visual information can be divided into distinct categories such as contrast, color, and location. Contrast depends on the existence of different intensities of reflected light emanating from objects, and this information is first gathered by *rod* cells in the retina of the eye that respond *differently to lights of varying intensity. Cone* cells in the retina respond to light of different wave-length (colors,) and cellular networks in the retina are the first to analyze signals from rods and cones with regard to motion.

The physical structure of the eye also allows for faithful mapping of the *location* of objects in the visual field. Thus, light reflected from objects in the visual space to the left, impinges most directly on the right half of the retina for both eyes, and vice versa for light reflected from the right. This is a direct result of the fact that the retina follows the curvature of the back of the eyeball, so light entering the eye strikes the retina most directly (i.e., perpendicular to the retinal surface) on the opposite side of its origin, while only glancing off the retina on the same side as its origin. The reader can envision this phenomenon by holding up the index finger of the left hand off to the left of the visual field. Following the straight line from the finger to the eyes, it becomes apparent that the light impinges most directly on the retinal tissue to the right side of each eye. Likewise, light coming from above the height of the eye impinges most directly on the bottom half of the retina, and light from below the height of the eye impinges with the top half of the retina. Thus, the retina of the eye makes a faithful spatial map of the contrast, color, and location of objects in the visual field. The environment is mapped on the retina of the eye.

Visual Cortex

The eye itself thus records information about both the nature of objects and their location. This information is then passed on to the visual regions of the brain, where, remarkably, it is literally mapped on the brain surface layer of cells, the *visual cortex*. Thus signals from any particular part of the retina always send information to a specific and fixed region of the visual cortex.

The first region of the cortex to receive signals from the eyes is called the *primary* vision cortex, or V1. Located at the very back of the cerebral cortex, V1 then simply contains information about shapes, colors, movement, and location. However, this information is not yet in a form that identifies intact objects, or comprehension of relationships. It is still just bits of data.

The strength of firing of neurons in each specific subregion of the cortex depends on contrast generated by edges of objects and the color of these objects, while the physical location of the different active neurons over the surface of the V1 cortex maps their location in space. Thus, the brain begins to separate form and location.

The flow of information from V1 to deeper regions of the cortex is required for perception of intact objects and establishing spatial relationships. These processes occur in integrative regions of the cortex, which are still considered visual cortex, but are identified as V2, V3, V4, and so on. As bits of perceived information flow into these regions, the separation of form and location is preserved, with information about form taking a physically lower route toward the temporal lobe of the brain, and information about location taking an upper route toward the parietal lobe. These two pathways are often called the *what* (lower) pathway, and the *where* (upper) pathway.

Ultimately, information in the *what* regions of the cortex is used to establish categories of objects (e.g., tables, cars, faces) with similar features, and also images of individual objects in categories, such as individual faces, or specific tables or cars. Thus, in this region of the cortex we find the so-called "face" cells, where specific neurons fire only when an intact and specific face is seen.

Information in the *where* regions is used to establish spatial location, and by extension, relationships in general. Thus, it has also been found that this region is active when we are required to estimate significance (which is derived from relationship—things of less significance are in a smaller, or less important, space from those of great significance,) relative positions such as number lines, and even relative value of objects or experiences. Thus, a great deal of cognitive information relies on the spatial relationship analysis capability of the *where* visual pathway.

In addition to this integrative process, visual information is also sent directly from V1 to regions of the brain in the frontal lobes. This route often has been found to lead to a region called the anterior cingulate, which is central in decision-making. Thus, even as we analyze the nature and location of what we see, we are also making judgments about whether we should act on it, and what the nature of such actions should be. This route is fast and can bypass the integrative processes above. We may act on what we see before we fully understand it.

All these pathways are thought to be bi-directional. That is, signals can also flow from anterior cingulate back to the visual integrative cortical regions, or from the integrative regions back to V1. The direct receipt of visual data from the environment described thus far, is sometimes called the "bottom up" processing, whereas the internal activation of the visual regions initiated by the anterior cingulate through conscious choice, is called "top down" processing. We can get the same image either by directly experiencing it or by recalling it from memory. And the *what* and *where* regions of integrative cortex are activated though either route. Whether seen directly or recalled from memory, the same neurons fire in the same patters when we sense a particular image.

The Image

What, then, is an image? The neuroscience answer to this question is that an image is the firing of collections of neurons together in a pattern that depends on the physical form, color, and location of objects in the world. The image is the *primary* product of perception. This can be contrasted to language, which consists of symbols for images. That is, language is the *secondary* product of perception. Language is represented by patterns of neuron firing also, but those patterns are only meaningful if they trigger firing of the primary patterns for the image itself.

Given their primary nature, and the fact that large regions of back integrative cortex are dedicated to processing of visual information, it is perhaps not surprising that memory of images seems almost unlimited. Humans can recall having seen hundreds of pictures even days later, and can sort out pictures that they have not seen before with remarkable accuracy. We "picture" our lives through recall of meaningful images, and to the extent that we can recall what has occurred throughout our life, we can say that we remember literally millions of images. The *what* region of the visual cortex also surrounds the hippocampus, and interacts with other nearby cortical regions important in the formation of long-term memory (and short term, to some extent.) In part this may account for the great capacity for memory of images noted above.

The vast flexibility and variability of images most likely results from the repeated use of *parts* of firing patterns. Thus, the image of a window consists of parts that can be repeatedly used for images of non-window objects. For example, the corner in a window is part of the image, but there are countless objects that can use the "corner network." It seems very likely that recall of images is primarily triggered through cues that consist of such image fragments. That is, firing of the pattern for a cue triggers firing of a larger pattern for an object that includes the cue. The human brain seems to be particularly adept at picking up these cues, and reconstructing an image from bits and pieces.

Images and the Non-Visual Senses

The other senses (auditory, touch, olfactory, and gustatory) are variously limited with regard to sensing shapes, colors, distances, movement, and physical attributes of objects, but vision gives us detailed information about all these and others as well. Vision is generally more precise and faster than the other senses. Indeed, the other senses sometimes channel information into the visual cortex for analysis and perception, or alternatively, are modified and regulated by input from vision.

The primacy of the visual sense is also indicated by the fact that, the data from the other senses is subject to modification and interpretation by interaction with the visual system. Recent research has shown that the sense of touch enhances perception of visual images through neuron pathways that run from the primary somatosensory (touch) cortex to the visual cortex. Further, research with owls demonstrated that the visual pathways can gain entry to the auditory pathways, thus correcting or adjusting auditory spatial maps so they correspond to visual spatial maps. This influence of the visual on the auditory is normally inhibited, but that inhibition breaks down when the two sensory maps do not correspond, leading to learning and correction of the non-correspondence.

The senses of smell, taste, and sound do not generate images directly, but they do evoke neuronal pathways that are linked to images, thereby enhancing memory of images. For example, we cannot smell the shape of a rose, but we can visualize its shape when triggered by smell. We can also use these "non-image" senses to create maps of space, by remembering the intensity of smell, taste, or sound in different locations of the space around us. But again, the maps generated in this fashion only become meaningful when we visualize them—when we trigger firing of a primary pattern that is derived from or part of a visual image.

Images in Cognition and Learning

The neurological explanation of images provides insight into many aspects of cognition and learning including **creativity**, estimating, theorizing, and problem-solving. Some examples of this are found in the following paragraphs.

Creativity seems heavily dependent on front regions of the cortex that are responsible for working memory and decision-making. It is this region of the brain that initiates the "top-down" functions mentioned above. Through such top-down instructions, working memory space in the front cortex is loaded with a small number of images, or parts of images, to generate new combinations that represent potential solutions to problems, or novel arrangements—new images! For example, Salvador Dali's painting, *The Persistence of Memory*, shows images of clocks, home furniture, and desert assembled in novel ways that trigger many new ideas—new images—for the viewer. The clocks drooping over tree branches or table edges, and this image of melted time in a desert environment, may trigger thought about our own life in which we recall moments where time seemed warped, or the pressures were great. Thus assembly of new images from parts of others is the foundation of creativity. The number of images triggered by great **art** is virtually unlimited and varied between different individuals.

Estimation in **mathematics** engages the *where* region of the visual cortex. This is also a brain region activated when we judge the relative value of objects or experiences. These approximations and judgments seem to be based on the spatial information in a number line, which progresses from small to large numbers; things of high value are analogous to the large numbers, or the first number (the most important ones). We mentally place things in relationships relative to each other, which provide the basis for estimation. We may estimate the size of a dog by visualizing it between other dogs of larger and smaller size, or by mentally comparing it to a measuring instrument marked off in feet or inches. Value, then, seems to be judged in this same physical way, through physically estimating *where* on some value scale a particular object lies.

Theories, ideas, and hypotheses also heavily engage the visual brain. We imagine (note *image* root of imagine) the outcomes of a series of actions, by picturing the sequence and its natural results. For example, we develop strategies for games, business, or war by picturing a sequence of actions with predictable outcomes, and linking those outcomes to an image of goal achievement. We imagine overcoming an opponent by a "pincers" action of two objects or forces, leading to the image of entrapment, and overpowering.

The assembly of a collection of specific features of objects by the *what* pathway in visual integrative cortex leads to generalizations and categories, which in turn allow us to predict behaviors and results in future actions. We picture some objects as similar to others in their form, or their force, or other physical properties, and we put them together in categories. This allows us to predict the properties and behaviors of new objects, and to solve problems based on known behaviors of members of the group. For example, we characterize some mathematical equations as "quadratic" and that allows us to proceed in our analysis and methods appropriate for this type of equation. Or, we place new chemical structures in the category of "nucleophile" and thus we can visualize how this chemical will behave when it is combined with others of the same, or different, category. In all such cases, we "see" the nature of things, and then, we visualize the result of specific interactions between things of a different, or the same, category.

In sum, the visual brain gives us information about relationships and categories, which are the tools of cognition. This applies to objects, but also to stories, people, and principles, encompassing virtually all thought and creativity. Learning, then, is enhanced by paying attention to relationships and categories in *every* problem and challenge, rather than relying on the limited and specific information provided by recall of individual images and experiences.

Study of the details of specific images can, however, be of great value in developing deeper understanding. For example, in language, it is powerful to use the "image test" when choosing words or phrases. Asking, "is this the image I want?" will lead to greater clarity in language expression, which in turn leads to deeper learning. Creating and reproducing images with attention to details of form and spatial relationships, requires deeper and specific use of front parts of the cortex and the motor cortex. This engagement of more parts of the cortex in analysis, creation, and utilization of images in all steps of the **learning cycle** will produce exceptionally powerful learning experiences.

Emotion

The amygdala, an emotion center of the brain, also is heavily connected to the visual brain. The connections appear to be primarily to the *what* region and the primary visual cortex. The specific meaning of these connections for learning is a matter for speculation, but combined with the visual-anterior cingulate interactions mentioned above, they support the idea that visualization and interpretation of images depend on emotion. Thus, what we see and how we act on what we see is subjective, so that one learner may see danger in an image, and another learner may see opportunity. Thus, visual images are subjective, pointing to the centrality of emotion in learning and interpretation.

Laterality and Attention

There seems to be little difference between V1 in the right and left hemisphere. However, damage to the visual integrative regions, for example, the right spatial cortex (*where* region) can lead to what is called the "neglect syndrome," in which the left visual space may be ignored, literally remaining unperceived. Thus, the *where* region of visual cortex, then, is strongly implicated in attention. Commonly, this function is attributed to the right hemisphere, but some research also indicates a role for the left *where* region of attention is directed to objects by drawing a circle around them, or by otherwise delineating a limited region of space for visual examination. These results lend support to the belief that the right cortex functions in a more global manner, whereas the left cortex functions on the fine details within a limited space. This further suggests that learning may be enhanced by challenging learners to attend both to the detailed aspects, and the global aspects of visualized material.

Development and Critical Periods

The development of the V1 region in newborn animals and humans is strongly dependent on visual experience. If one eye is covered or otherwise closed immediately after birth, such as can occur in newborn humans who have cataracts, the wiring of the V1 region develops improperly, and if sensory input is not restored in a relatively short time period (weeks to a few months in humans) it can lead to permanent blindness in the covered eye. This is not due to malfunction of the eye itself but rather to inadequate or incorrect wiring in this region of the visual cortex. Experiments of this sort were the first to directly demonstrate the impact of experience on the physical structure of the brain, and have been central to the now accepted proposal that the process of learning depends on physical change in neuron networks. Also, the idea that certain experiences must occur within a limited timeframe for the brain to develop normal wiring, is the basis for the belief in "critical periods" for learning particular things. In the case of visual learning, this period can be quite short, but in a different sensory experience, the development of language, may be years.

Learning Styles

Finally, we briefly address the concept of learning style and images. It is common to identify different learners as having a visual or an auditory learning style. However, the way that images and language are produced in the brain suggests that these two learning styles are not equivalent, and that serious efforts should be made to assure that *all* learners develop visual images of the world and their experiences. The basis for this contention is that image is primary, and language secondary. We cannot create an image with all its rich content of category and relationship, based on auditory experience in isolation. We may remember a great deal of what we hear, but still have no image for it. The argument leads to the suggestion that learners who claim an auditory learning style already have good visual images, and are simply using auditory experience to recall them. Alternatively, they may actually believe that memory of the language is real learning. However, we contend that no amount of auditory input can substitute for lack of visual images.

See also: **Blindness; Visuals and Classroom Management.**

Further Readings

Gangwer, T. (2005). *Visual Impact, Visual Teaching.* San Diego, CA: The Brain Store, Inc.

Mathew, W., Zeki, S. (2005). The integration of colour and motion by the human visual brain. *Cerebral Cortex* 15:1270–1279.

Posner, M.J., Raichle, M.E. (1997). *Images of Mind.* New York, NY: Scientific American Library.
Silverman, L.K., Jones, B. (2002). *Upside-Down Brilliance: The Visual-Spatial Learner.* Glendale, CO: DeLeon Publishing, Inc.
Zeki, S. (1999). *Inner Vision: An Exploration of Art and the Brain,* New York, NY: Oxford University Press Inc.
Visual/spatial Learning Study Guides & Strategies http://www.studygs.net/visual.htm

JAMES E. ZULL, PH.D.

Visuals and Classroom Management

Many teachers complain that effective classroom management skills are primarily invisible—the teachers can't see what to do to get their students on track and focused. Indeed, unless one knows what to look for, it's often hard to see what works. And this can cause hardship for teachers trying to succeed at their craft. Without effective classroom management, content won't easily follow.

One way to make management more visible, to students and to teachers, is to increase the use of visuals, particularly when teaching classroom procedures to students. Recent brain research is corroborating what teachers already know intuitively—that visuals in the classroom help students learn.

The brain is built to do imagery quickly and efficiently. When a visual is presented the retina perceives the representation and launches it on its journey to the visual cortex. The visual cortex, located in the occipital lobe, or lower rear portion, of the brain's hemispheres, is continually adapting and interpreting information. It is highly specialized for processing information and pattern recognition. For instance, when one meets someone, one's brain first identifies "human" and then differentiates between friend and stranger.

A common belief is that vision is primarily deciphered in the right hemisphere, while language is located in the left hemisphere. Neuroimaging sheds light on this issue; vision and language are both too complex to be delegated to one hemisphere of the brain. The complex deciphering of images and language requires interaction between both hemispheres.

A study by the Institute for the Advancement of Research in Education found that graphic organizers improved student learning and retention across grade levels and content areas. A number of educational research studies support these findings, suggesting that using visuals in teaching results in a greater degree of learning. Indeed, many in the field suggest that over half of what we learn is from visual images. This increased focus on using visuals for classroom content ought to be mirrored in an increased use of visuals for classroom procedures.

Visual Rubrics for Procedures

Most teachers are familiar with rubrics for content, but very few are familiar with rubrics for procedures. For example, for many elementary teachers, one of the toughest procedures to teach is getting kids to line up. To use visual cues, teachers can have their students form five separate lines, and number them from one to five. A one is a poorly structured line, a five is a perfect line. Now the students have a common language, and they'll tend to self-correct: "C'mon guys we look like a three – let's go!" To close the deal, teachers can take pictures of their students in their five lines and number the pictures one through five. They can then be put above the door where the students exit the classroom. The teacher stands in the doorway, waiting for the kids to line up. Then she uses the fingers on one hand to signal what "caliber" line they have. When she holds up all five fingers, they can start to walk.

Another example centers on "classroom dismissal formation." Teachers often tell their students "I'm not dismissing the class until the desks are clean, lined up, organized, and everyone is seated." Unfortunately, students have different definitions of those words. Some are out of their seats in "sprinters position," ready to race out the door. In addition, many students put their packs on before the bell rings to end class. One solution is to have five pictures of "dismissal readiness" up on the wall above the board. In number four, the desks are clean and lined up and everyone is seated, but two students have their packs on. The teacher doesn't have to say a word. She simply holds up four fingers and waits. The kids see the fingers, look at the pictures, and look around the room. Within seconds they yell out to their neighbors "hey- your pack! Take your pack off!" The packs fly off, the teacher breaks into a big smile, raises a fifth finger, and points to the door, signaling that the students can leave.

Pictures for Procedures

Teachers don't need to use rubrics—just pictures. With a digital camera they can take a picture of the kids in their "dismissal formation." The photograph can then be run through a computer onto an overhead. The teacher simply places the picture on the overhead screen. The students will quickly get the desks clean and lined up and ready to go, using the overhead photo as their guide. No longer does the teacher need to say "okay class it's time to clean up and get ready to go." She can simply turn the overhead on with the picture, and watch the magic happen.

This works for just about every possible classroom procedure. Setting up labs in science provides a clear example. The teacher can take an aerial photo of the lab table with all the items where they are supposed to be. She then can put it onto an overhead and turn it on, announcing "Okay. You have thirty-nine seconds to form your teams around your lab tables, set up like this. Go."

This works as well for putting things away, such as books on the bookshelf, physical education supplies in the closet, and art supplies in their trays. Teachers take photos of what the supplies are supposed to look like, put the photos next to where the supplies live, and the students will tend to put things away according to the photographs.

This works for parents at home. A declaration parents often make to their kids is: "You're not going out until your room is clean." After the declaration, there is often a full-scale debate about characteristics of a clean room. The solution? Parents can take a photo of their child's clean room, and put the photo on the wall. The child will tend to clean the room according to the photo. Inside the child's sock drawer is a photograph of a clean sock drawer! One parent confesses that her three-year-old daughter can't read, but loves to clean: "Can we play clean up again mommy?" It's a game to her—and she plays it well!

There is no limit to how teachers can use pictures to communicate clarity of procedures. Photographs aren't necessary. Diagrams and drawings work just as well. The students can be put in small groups and each group given a procedure for which to generate an appropriate picture.

This works wonderfully for substitute teachers. The classroom teacher can take photographs of her class or classes while the students are sitting in their assigned seats. Then, the name of each student can be written next to his or her face. When the substitute teacher starts class, she will know the names of all the students and where they are supposed to sit. One substitute teacher claims: "Personally, I would never sub again, unless I brought my digital camera to class: "You two are making mischief'– Click!" One doesn't need batteries or film—just the camera. The kids see the camera and are suddenly transformed into angels.

Other classroom procedure examples include setting up centers, keyboarding posture, proper listening body language, desk cleanliness, headings on papers, test taking readiness, and what the computer desktop should look like when students log off. Pictures work for schoolwide issues and procedures such as school dress code, sitting during assemblies, and clean cafeteria tables.

Airplane safety direction cards no longer use words—just pictures and diagrams. Passengers see images of a seat belt being fastened, oxygen masks being used, people evacuating the plane. This is true as well for directions for how to put together a computer system or bookshelf. Companies have discovered that for safety and increased customer satisfaction, visuals communicate clearly and quickly. This same approach works wonderfully in our classrooms. Neuroscientists are echoing what teachers have known for a long time—visuals are highly brain-compatible. We need to translate this not only into teaching content, but also into teaching classroom procedures to our students.

Step-By-Step Visuals for Content

Additionally, visuals can also be used to teach content. I taught a woodshop class for several years. I took photographs of finished projects, laminated them, and put them on the wall to inspire kids' choices of projects. Then I learned to take a series of photos of the works in progress—five or seven photos. The students would then use the photos as a teaching tool to see what their next steps were in the process. Rather than ask me what the next step was, they would simply go over to the picture wall for a visual consultation. I was out of a job!

Students often do such great projects in class that they take them home and they're never seen again. Why not take pictures of the finished projects to use as inspiration for next year's students?

As teachers increase the use of visuals for procedures and content in their classrooms, they realize the profound benefits. Management is easier, students are more focused, and the learning environment is enhanced.

See also: **Classroom Management; Visual Brain.**

Further Readings

Hyerle, D. (2004). *Student Successes With Thinking Maps : School-Based Research, Results, and Models for Achievement Using Visual Tools.* Thousand Oaks, CA: Sage Publishing.

Smith, R. (2004). *Conscious Classroom Management: Unlocking the Secrets of Great Teaching.* Fairfax, CA: www.consciousteaching.com

Wolfe, P. (2001). *Brain Matters: Translating Research Into Classroom Practice.* Alexandria, VA: ASCD.

RICK SMITH

Writing

Mental activity occurs when the billions of tiny neurons of the brain communicate information using small electrical signals. The point of contact between neurons is called the synapse. Synaptic connections tend to be reinforced by repetition over time, thus reinforcing learning. As cognitive and sensorimotor skill connections develop, alphabetic letters become words, then sentences. Eventually, writing emerges as a skill that provides a virtual window into cognitive thought patterns. Writing documents the brains' sensory experiences, thoughts, ideas, beliefs, and opinions.

One of the first brain activity imaging studies conducted in 2001 examined how the brain processes information. It was discovered that listening to a sentence affects cortical activation pathways different from those affected by reading a sentence. As spoken language is fleeting, information must be immediately processed or stored to make sense of it. Writing acts like an external hard drive facsimile that provides permanent records.

With the stroke of a pencil, pen, or keystroke, writers express real or imagined sights, sounds, tastes, touches, and smells. Writing is a dynamic manifestation of **creative** and **critical thinking** skills. Both a sensorimotor and cognitive process, writing serves all of Howard Gardner's **multiple intelligences** not just verbal-linguistic. Writing serves the *music* intelligence when maestros share their genius through written composition. Writing serves *bodily-kinesthetic* intelligence when athletic coaches write strategic plays that athletes execute. It services *logical-mathematical* intelligence when scientists write proofs to theories and *interpersonal* and *intrapersonal* intelligences when people become everything from speechwriters to novelists and philosophers.

Writing is active, reflective, spontaneous, fluid, erratic, exhilarating, or frustrating. It can be a pleasant experience, the tool by which ideas and memories spill onto pages and computer screens. It can also be a painful experience that blocks and stalls ideas and memories, causing student writers to feel frustrated and ignorant, because the brain must feel safe to sustain the **motivation** necessary to master the writing process.

Brain translator Robert Slywester explains that neurons thrive in environments that are emotionally safe and intellectually stimulating. Learners must therefore experience emotional and physical safety to be fully engaged in learning, especially learning about writing, which easily intimidates students to believe they "can't do it." Help students remain motivated by creating writing process settings within safe, supportive environments that promote productive cognitive thinking.

Writing helps the brain organize and reflect. Writing enables students to make sense of complex, multifaceted pieces of information. Journaling and other note-taking forms provide written records for review and reflection that enhance both immediate and long-term recall ability. Reflective journaling can also help the emotional brain.

A two-part study on the effects of expressive writing on the working memory conducted by Klein and Boals revealed that individuals who wrote reflective narratives about negative experiences experienced a decline in dissonant, avoidance thinking related to the events. Such findings suggest that writing provides a healthy and productive way to improve memory and in fact, deal with trauma, offering tremendous opportunity as a life skill and also a life-coping skill.

Kinds of Writing

Writing can be expressive, descriptive, narrative, expository, or persuasive. It can involve untimed *process writing*, which includes brainstorming, drafting, conferencing, revising, editing, and finalizing. Writing can also be a timed process often called *demand writing*, whereby writing is timed and prompt-specific, that is, writing that answers an essay question. Writing that is completed within test environments is an example of demand writing, which, as a result, is more stress-laden than process writing. Grooming students to be proficient in both types of writing requires a safe and enriched learning environment.

Planning

To help the brain make connections that lead to writing mastery, a strategic plan must be in place that helps to develop the strengths of young writers. The plan must attend to the challenges inherent in each type of writing. Begin the school year with more expressive types of writing, description and narration, which readily tap into existing **episodic memories** and sensory experiences. Within the safety of their own memories and creative thoughts, students write with relative willingness.

Jean Piaget suggested that when introducing experiences that initially may produce some struggle, students need tools to resolve their cognitive difficulties. Provide students with examples of topics from which they might choose and help them remember episodes from their past by inviting students to recall experiences that made them happy, sad, embarrassed, and the like. Encourage them during the drafting stages. Use student writing to provide proof that students do indeed have something to write about. Empower and instill students with confidence to move on to the more challenging forms of writing, exposition and persuasion, which require higher order thinking skills. Provide them with writing activities that are both challenging and engaging. Ask them to argue a controversial topic using a "Letter to the Editor" format. Invite them to write cover letters that persuade employers to hire them. Allow them to express their feelings through poetry.

No matter what students are writing, allow them to compose freely. Unimpeded by analytical cognitive processes that monitor mechanical skills, for example, frees students' cognitive thought processes to more readily tap into memories, ideas, and opinions. Researcher and educator, Frank Smith describes a study conducted by two leaders in writing pedagogy, Donald Graves and Lucy Calkins whereby third grade students were encouraged to write using their own punctuation. By the year's end, the children who had no formal training demonstrated a greater command of punctuation and its function than those who had had typical skill and drill training.

Employ patience while observing student errors in early drafts. Holding students to high expectations regarding mechanical skills stifles the spirit to experiment and succeed that fledgling writers show when they are left free to write. This freedom helps students view writing, not as a laborious or boring school requirement, but a tool by which they can truly express themselves.

By emphasizing creative versus critical thinking during the early stages of writing instruction empowers students with the confidence that they can write. Learn how to use textbooks as resources and guides. Have faith in authentic writing processes whereby quantity, generated in safe yet rigorous environments, produces quality.

Modeling

Social cognitive theorist, Albert Bandura, has emphasized that learners are motivated to learn when their own levels of competence and self-efficacy are high, and when they perceive activities as meaningful. There is no better way to promote the self-efficacy levels of students and to make the writing process more meaningful than for teachers to act as coaches who take part in that process, sharing their abilities with their fledgling writers.

Writing becomes more meaningful and less threatening for students when they identify their teachers as fellow writers who brainstorm topics, compose drafts, discuss experiences, share frustrations and ultimately produce final products. Model for students how real writers write—and rewrite. Enhance writing environments with frequent feedback, peer and teacher interaction, and stimulating and meaningful writing opportunities.

Make sure that peer model samples are also plentiful to help students of all age levels and abilities learn from others in their own age groups. Samples of work of various qualities from weak to strong provide opportunities for students to strengthen their evaluation and **assessment** skills that they can apply to their own and their peers' writing.

Strategic Flexibility

An understanding of Piaget's stages of cognitive theory of development enables writing coaches to understand that moving from young child to adolescent stages means moving from concrete to more imaginative and abstract thought. For the youngest group of writers, help students by scribing for them when they may excitedly recount memories faster than they can write them down themselves. Prepare handouts containing a series of *I remember* blanks to help youngsters identify their memories. Prepare engaging writing assignments that invite students to incorporate their interests into editorials, screenplays, or commercials for their favorite products.

Encourage thinking and groom proficient writers by learning more about the differences in the behavioral and cognitive stages of various age groups. Even coaches of adult writers, senior citizens in a creative writing class at an adult center for example, must understand the nature of their learning audience. Encouraging memory writing for example would be particularly useful (and perhaps vital) for the senior age group not just because narration readily taps into episodic memories as with young children, rather, reflecting on the meaning of their lives in a safe learning environment can help seniors process through difficult memories they might otherwise keep private, causing cognitive or emotional discord or despair.

Cognitive Freedom

Just as real writers do not produce all kinds of writing, they also do not always follow rules, schedules, or stages of a writing process. When such rule-breaking writers are students, they are often labeled as problematic or weak writers. Provide writers the cognitive freedom to demonstrate ability in their own way. If students struggle with expository essays, encourage them to change their products (and consequently their audiences) to newspaper articles or letters. Provide writers flexibility and opportunity to demonstrate *their* ability, guiding them beyond what Piaget called *disequilibrium*, cognitive conflict, to self-confidence and discovery. Their tools: reassurance, encouragement, and empowerment.

Sequence each day's activities carefully. Move students through the writing process by following the lead of each writer's needs. Writing coaches must know their craft well to prepare effective lessons and activities for whole, group, and individual instructional settings, again dependent on student and process needs. Diagnoses of students' needs gathered from their writing, drives the direction of what Nancy Atwell calls *mini-lessons* that instruct students on, for example, topic choice, dialogue, paragraphing, correcting fragments or run ons, and the like.

Editing

While evidence like the Graves and Calkins study suggests that even the youngest students acquire mastery skills when left unfettered by *skill and drill* approaches, at some point, conventions and mechanics instruction becomes very important to students who ultimately must be able to effectively communicate in both oral and written modes.

Help students care about *how* they write what they write, that is, conventions and mechanics. Using student products that contain authentic mistakes to teach mechanical skills captures the enthusiasm of students who are typically bored by traditional grammar lessons. Student engagement is high when game-like, *solve the* (grammar) *problem* activities rely on genuine mechanical problems from student writing, not textbooks. Students routinely challenged to identify mechanical errors within anonymous peer models become proficient at identifying increasingly more subtle errors. Freed from meaningless textbook grammar activities, mechanical skills improve, because students, empowered by continuing successes, routinely attend more critically to their own mechanics.

Educator and researcher Frank Smith, reminiscent of Dewey, wisely argues that students can be trusted to learn as long as they are provided meaningful learning environments that encourage thinking. The brain-compatible editing process, which uses student work to illustrate examples of conventions and mechanical miscues, provides just such a personalized and meaningful environment in which students can learn.

Assessment

Students must learn to think critically about their writing so that they become literate and successful adults. Use of rubrics and criteria may be the single most effective way to empower students with a real understanding of what proficient and superior writing looks like. Ideally used as guiding, not grading tools, rubrics enable students to evaluate and assess their writing as well as their peers', leading them to mastery. It is important therefore that students learn the language of rubrics so that they can receive and offer worthwhile **feedback**. Research findings, for example, of D. A. Rogers suggest that verbal feedback during and after a learning task is critical in the error-connection process. Let students know what they are doing well and ask probing questions that stimulate them to challenge what they have written.

Never give students a grade without feedback. Learners always need to know if they are on track; using the language of rubrics is one way of ensuring their learning. Writing coaches will first need to learn their state's rubric and scoring system before they can help their students understand them.

Demand Writing

Writing exams—prime examples of demand writing—can produce anxiety and **stress**, which inhibit the cognitive processes essential to writing prowess. Some stress is beneficial, releasing adrenaline that makes students mentally alert. Harness *good* stress in ways similar to athletic coaches who pump their players up for the big game.

Demand writing requires a synthesis of the creative and analytical skills of student writers who must, within a specific amount of time, read and interpret an essay prompt, then apply and demonstrate their writing skills in finished products that demonstrate writing proficiency. Proficiency will not be obtained without first providing students the strategies that will keep cognitive thinking optimal and interfering stress signals minimal.

No matter what a prompt asks, students will succeed if they learn to follow their brain's natural inclination to organize. It was the organizational genius of the **pattern**-seeking brains of NASA engineers that transformed a seeming pile of junk into an air filter that safely returned the Apollo thirteen astronauts to Earth. Engineers saw beyond the random items strewn before them to their potential functionality, which they harnessed under an unimaginable amount of anxiety and stress to create a life-saving filter. How much less stressful to organize random thoughts into proficient essays!

Train students to analyze and organize carefully, but swiftly, the components of specific essay prompts. Train students to master the rubric of organization. Careful analysis of essay prompts produces word and phrase maps that establish their exact requirements. Entering stressful testing environments armed with organizational writing strategies and confidence is the gift that brain compatible writing coaches give their students.

A Celebration of Writing

To appreciate themselves as writers, students must celebrate themselves as writers. Without celebration, there is no evidence that working to become a stronger writer has value. Making time at the end of each quarter or at least each semester, for students to share their writing validates students as writers.

Brain researcher and educator, Robert Sylwester, suggested in the title of his book, *Celebration of Neurons*, that there is something worth celebrating in learning about the brain. Einstein believed that imagination is more important than knowledge. As writing miraculously transcribes imagination into words, perhaps learning about the brain's expression of itself is cause for the celebration of *writing*.

See also: **Classroom Environment.**

Further Readings

Alexandria, VA: Association for Supervision and Curriculum Development.

Hanson, A. (2001). *Visual Writing.* New York: Learning Express.

Hanson, A. (2002). *Write Brain Write.* San Diego: The Brain Store.

Michael, E., Keller, T., Carpenter, P., Just, M. (2001). FMRI investigation of sentence comprehension by eye and by ear: Modality fingerprints on cognitive processes. *Human Brain Mapping* 13(4):239–252.

Rogers, D.A. (1998). Computer-assisted learning versus a lecture and feedback seminar for teaching a basic surgical technical skill. *American Journal of Surgery* 175(6):508–510.

Slywester, R. (1995). *The Celebration of Neurons. An Educator's Guide to the Human Brain. Explorations in Learning & Instruction*: The Theory into Practice (TIP) Database. (2004). As stated at their site, "TIP is a tool intended to make learning and instructional theory more accessible to educators. The database contains brief summaries of 50 major theories of learning and instruction. Available at: http://tip.psychology.org/

North West Regional Educational Laboratory 6 + 1 Trait Writing – Training, http://www.nwrel.org/assessment/trainings

ANNE M. HANSON, M.A.

Glossary
of
Brain Terms

ACTH – Adrenocorticotropic hormone is secreted by the pituitary gland. It acts directly on the adrenal glands to increase the secretion of cortisol and other hormones.

Adrenal Glands – They are adjacent to the kidneys and responsible for the secretion of various hormones from the body; particularly cortisol and adrenaline.

Amygdala – The amygdala is an almond-shaped structure located in the base of the brain. It is involved in emotions such as anger, fear, and pleasure. It is part of what is sometimes referred to as the limbic system.

Androgens – The general class of male hormones, with the main one being testosterone. Testosterone is responsible for primary and secondary sex characteristics such as pubic hair and lowered voice.

Axon – A long extension of a nerve cell that takes information away from one neuron to another neuron.

Basal Ganglia – Loosely grouped collection of large neurons within each cerebral hemisphere. It plays an important role in motor control and learning.

Brain Cells – Neurons and glial cells are the two main types of cells found in the brain.

Brain Stem – The brain stem plays a vital role in basic attention, arousal, and consciousness. All information passes through the brain stem on its way to and from the brain.

Broca's Area – This area of the brain is located in the frontal lobes and controls speech production and language understanding. It is connected to Wernicke's area by a neural pathway.

Cerebellum – Located at the base of the brain, it is two peach-sized mounds. It is in charge of coordinating movement, balance, and posture. Mental activities are also coordinated in the cerebellum; it is involved in thinking and memory.

Cerebral Cortex – It is the outer layer of the cerebrum. It consists of deep folds of gray matter. It determines intelligence, personality, sensory impulses, motor function, planning, and organization.

Cerebral Hemispheres – They are the right and left portions of the brain.

Cerebrum – This area of the brain controls sensory interpretation, thinking, and memory. In the cerebrum, there are up to one hundred thousand neurons. The cerebrum is divided into two hemispheres, the right and left hemispheres.

Corpus Callosum – The corpus callosum is a network of fibers connecting the cerebral hemispheres. It facilitates communication between the two hemispheres.

Cortisol – This hormone is released from the adrenal glands when the body is under stress. It increases blood pressure and heart rate and lowers the immune system.

CT scan – Computerized tomography, formerly referred to as a CAT scan. This technology utilizes x-ray pictures to examine the structure of the brain.

Dendrite – A dendrite is part of a neuron, it brings information to the cell body. One neuron may have as many as 100,000 dendrites.

Dopamine – Dopamine is a chemical substance (neurotransmitter) manufactured in the brain involved in feeling pleasure and pleasure-seeking behavior.

Endorphins – Endorphins are naturally occurring painkillers in the brain.

Pleasurable activities cause the release of endorphins and a sense of well-being is created.

Estrogen – A female sex hormone produced primarily by the ovaries; and in smaller amounts by the adrenal cortex. In women, levels of estrogen fluctuate with their menstrual cycle. It is involved in the development of secondary sex characteristics, including breasts, menstruation, and preparation for pregnancy.

fMRI – Functional Magnetic Resonance Imaging (fMRI) is a brain imaging technology that shows the increased blood flow to areas activated in the brain. It is used to examine the functions of the brain.

Frontal Lobes – They are located in the front of the brain and are considered the higher-level thinking center, emotional control site, and locus of personality. The frontal lobes are involved in problem solving, memory, language, decision-making, and social and sexual behavior.

Glial Cells – They make up 90 percent of the brain's cells. Glial means glue, they are involved in digestion of dead neurons, manufacturing myelin, and provide physical and nutritional support for neurons.

Gray Matter – It consists of the neurons that make up the cerebral cortex. Gray matter consists of dendrites and synapse.

Hemispheres – The brain is often illustrated as being divided into two sections (hemispheres) that are connected by the corpus callosum. The two hemispheres are symmetrical in design and divided into four lobes: frontal, parietal, temporal, and occipital. See Left Brain Hemisphere and Right Brain Hemisphere.

Hippocampus – The hippocampus is a horseshoe shaped set of neurons located within the temporal lobes and adjacent to the amygdala. It is associated with working memory, emotions, and visual-spatial perception.

Hormones – Chemicals produced by glands in the body that circulate in the bloodstream. Hormones control the actions of certain cells and organs.

Hypothalamus – The hypothalamus is located below the thalamus. It controls the pituitary glad. Its functions include emotions, homeostasis, pain, pleasure, hunger and thirst, sleep wake cycle, and sexual desires.

Lateralization – Different functions are handled mainly by one hemisphere of the brain. For most people, speech primarily resides in the left hemisphere of the brain, and visual-spatial on the right.

Left Brain Hemisphere – Psychologists often associate the left hemisphere with language skills (both Broca and Wernicke's areas are located in the left hemisphere), logic, and sequential skills.

Leptin - A hormone synthesized by fat cells and thought to be involved in the regulation of hunger and eating.

Limbic System – The system of areas in the brain that control emotions, hormonal secretions, motivation, pain, and pleasure. The structures included in the Limbic System are: amygdala, cingulated gyrus, fornix, hippocampus, hypothalamus, olfactory cortex, and thalamus.

Medulla Oblangata – It is the lowest part of the brain stem, regulating involuntary behaviors such as breathing and heartbeat.

Melatonin – A hormone involved in regulating daily sleep-awake cycle. Nature's sleeping pill.

Myelin – Coats and insulates the neuron, increasing speed and efficiency in communication between neurons, making thinking quicker.

Neurons – The brain cells that send and receive signals to and from the brain and nervous system. Individuals have about 100 billion neurons in the brain. They consist of a cell body, dendrites, and an axon.

Neuroscience – Neuroscience is the study of the brain and the nervous system.

Neurotransmitters – Chemicals that are released from one neuron and transmit the signal to the next neuron. Neurotransmitters include: norepinephrine, serotonin, dopamine, and adrenaline.

Occipital Lobe – Located toward the back of the cerebral cortex, this area of the brain controls vision and color recognition.

Parietal Lobe – It is located above the occipital lobes and behind the frontal lobes. The parietal lobe is associated with sensory information such as touch, temperature, and pain.

PET scan – Positron emission tomography, gives a three-dimensional view of the functions occurring in the brain.

Pituitary Gland – The pituitary gland is located at the base of the hypothalamus. It produces growth hormones and other hormones in response to signals from the hypothalamus.

Plasticity – Plasticity, or neuroplasticity, is the lifelong ability of the brain to learn new information.

Pons – They are located on the brainstem and involved in arousal, sleep, and some speculate dreaming. They relay sensory information between the cerebrum and cerebellum.

Pruning – A term used to describe the elimination of dendrites and synaptic connections.

Reptilian Brain – The brain stem is the oldest and smallest region in the human brain. It evolved hundreds of millions of years ago and is more like the entire brain of present day reptiles, hence its name. It regulates breathing and heartbeat. Basic emotions of love, anger, fear, and lust are lodged in this area of the brain.

Reticular Formation – It is located in the brain stem and is associated with sleep and wake cycle.

Right Brain Hemisphere – Psychologists often associate the right hemisphere with creativity, random thought, and intuitiveness.

Serotonin – A neurotransmitter that modulates mood, emotion, sleep, and appetite. It creates a sense of calm.

Synapse – Information from one neuron flows to another neuron across a synapse. The synapse is a small gap separating neurons. This process enables neurons to communicate with each other.

Temporal Lobe – Part of the cerebrum, it is involved in hearing and memory.

Testosterone – Testosterone is a hormone produced by the testes and adrenal glands. It is required for sperm production, the development of the male reproductive organs, and the male secondary sexual characteristics, such as lowered voice and beard growth.

Thalamus – The thalamus is located at the top of the brain stem, in the middle of the brain. It receives auditory and visual sensory signals and sends selected sensory information to the cerebral cortex.

Wernicke's Area –Wernicke's area is located in the left hemisphere of the brain in the temporal lobe. It is instrumental in language understanding and comprehension.

White Matter –White matter refers to the myelin coated areas under the cerebrum's gray matter.

Bibliography

A study reveals link to obesity with dementia in old age. (2005, April). [On-line]. Retrieved October 25, 2005, from: *http://www.money-plans.net/frontend2verify–6240.html.*

Allen, R. H. (2001). *Impact teaching: Ideas and strategies for teachers to maximize student learning.* Boston: Allyn & Bacon.

Allgeier, E.R., & Albert, R. (2000). *Sexual interactions.* New York: Houghton Mifflin.

Allman, J. (1999). *Evolving brains.* New York: Scientific American Library.

Amabile, T. (1989). *Growing up creative.* New York: Crown.

Amen, D. (1999). *Change your brain, change your life: The breakthrough program for conquering anxiety, depression, obsessiveness, anger, and impulsiveness.* San Diego, CA: Three Rivers Press.

Amen, D. G. (2002). *Healing ADD: The breakthrough program that allows you to see and heal the six types of attention deficit disorder.* New York: G. P. Putnam's Sons.

Ames, C. (1999). Motivation: What teachers need to know. In A. C. Ornstein & L. S. Behar Horenstein (Eds.), *Contemporary Issues in Curriculum* (2nd ed., pp. 135–144). Boston: Allyn & Bacon.

American Psychological Association. *Just like us: Chimpanzee brains are asymmetrical in key areas and their handedness reflects it* [On–line]. Retrieved June 25, 2005, from *http://www.apa.org/releases/chimp-brains.html.*

Andersen, C. (2002). Thinking as and thinking about: Cognitive and metacognitive processes in drama. In B. Rasmussen & A. Østern (Eds.), *Playing betwixt and between: The IDEA dialogues 2001* (pp. 265–270). Oslo, NOR: Landslaget Drama i Skolen.

Andersen, C. (2004). Throwing out the baby with the bathwater?: A psychologist's view of "brain-based drama." *Drama, 11*(2), 29–30.

Anderson, J. R., Reder, L. M., & Simon, H. A. (1996). Situated learning and education. *Educational Researcher, 25*(4), 5–11.

Anderson, O., Marsh, N., & Harvey, A. (1999). *Learn with the classics: Using music to study smart at any age.* San Francisco: Lind Institute.

Apps, J. W. (1988). *Higher education in a learning society.* San Francisco: Jossey-Bass.

Armstrong, T. (1999). *7 kinds of smart: Identifying and developing your multiple intelligences.* New York: Plume.

Armstrong, T. (2000). Multiple intelligences in the classroom. Alexandria, VA: Association for Supervision and Curriculum Development.

Attwood, T. (1997). Asperger's syndrome: A guide for parents and professionals. London: Jessica Kingsley Publishers.

Atwell, N. (1990). *In the middle: Writing, reading, and learning with adolescents.* Portsmouth, NH: Heinemann.

Ayres, J. (1996). *Sensory integration and the child.* Los Angeles, CA: WPS Publishing.

Bailey, B. A. (1994). *There's gotta be a better way: Discipline that works!.* Oviedo, FL: Loving Guidance.

Bailey, B. A. (2000). *Easy to love, difficult to discipline.* New York: Perennial Currents. *I love you rituals.* New York: Perennial Currents.

Bailey, B. A. (2001). *Conscious discipline: 7 basic skills for brain smart classroom management.* Oviedo, FL: Loving Guidance.

Baird, A. A., et al. (1999). Functional magnetic resonance imaging of facial affect recognition in children and adolescents. *Journal of the American Academy of Child and Adolescent Psychiatry, 38*(2), 195–199.

Baker, Colin. (1993). *Foundations of bilingual education and bilingualism.* Clevedon, ENG: Multilingual Matters.

Bandura, A. (1994). Self-efficacy. In V.S. Ramachaudran (Ed.), *Encyclopedia of human behavior* (Vol. 4, pp. 71–81). New York: Academic Press.

Barlow, D.H., & Durand, V.M. (2005). *Essentials of abnormal psychology* (5th ed.). New York: Wadsworth.

Bar-On, R. (1997). *EQ-I: Bar-on emotional quotient inventory.* Toronto, ON: Multi-health Systems.

Barron, B. (2000). Problem solving in video-based microworlds: Collaborative and individual outcomes of high-achieving sixth-grade students. *Journal of Educational Psychology, 92*(2), 391–398.

Barry, L. M., & Messer, J. J. (2003). A practical application of self-management for students diagnosed with attention-deficit/hyperactivity disorder [Electronic Version]. *Journal of Positive Behavior Interventions, 5*(4), 238–248. Retrieved January 17, 2005, from EBSCOhost Academic Search Premier Database.

Baverstock, A. C., & Finlay, F. (2003). Who manages the care of students with attention deficit hyperactivity disorder (ADHD) in higher education? [Electronic Version]. *Child: Care, Health, & Development, 29*(3), 163–166. Retrieved January 17, 2005, from EBSCOhost Academic Search Premier Database.

Bebko, J. M. (1998). Learning, language, memory, and reading: The role of language automatization and its impact on complex cognitive activities. *Journal of Deaf Studies and Deaf Education, 3*(1), 4–14.

Beck, A.T., Rush, A.J., Shaw, B.F., & Emery, G. (1979). *Cognitive therapy of depression.* New York: Guildford Press.

Bereiter, C., & Scardamalia, M. (1993). *Surpassing ourselves: An inquiry into the nature and implications of expertise.* Chicago: Open Court.

Berenbaum, S. A. (2000). Psychological outcome in congenital adrenal hyperplasia. In B. Stabler & B. B. Bercu (Eds.), *Therapeutic outcome of endocrine disorders* (pp. 186–199). New York: Springer-Verlag.

Bergen, D. (2002). The role of pretend play in children's cognitive development [Electronic Version]. *Early Childhood Research & Practice, 4*(1). Retrieved June 25, 2005, from *http://ecrp.uiuc.edu/v4n1/bergen.html.*

Bergen, D. (2003). *Play's role in brain development.* Olney, MD: Association for Childhood Education International.

Bergen, D., & Coscia, J. (2001). *Brain research and childhood education: Implications for educators.* Olney, MD: Association for Childhood Education International.

Berne, R.M., & Levy, M.N. (Eds.). (1998). *Physiology* (4th ed.). St. Louis, MO.: Mosby.

Bialystok, E. (Ed.). (1991). *Language processing in bilingual children.* Cambridge, ENG: Cambridge University Press.

Biklen, D., & Cardinal, D. (Eds.). (1997). *Contested Words, Contested Science: Unraveling the Facilitated Communication Controversy.* New York: Teachers College Press.

Bloom, F. E., Beal, M. F., & Kupfer, D. J. (2003). *The Dana guide to brain health.* New York: Free Press.

Boesch, C., & Boesch-Achermann, H. (2002). *The chimpanzees of the Tai Forest: Behavioral ecology and evolution.* Cambridge, UK: Oxford University Press.

Bondy, A., & Frost, L. (2001). *A Picture's Worth: PECS and Other Visual Communication Strategies in Autism.* Bethesda, MA: Woodbine House.

Boozer, M., & Rouse, C. (2001). Intraschool variation in class size: Patterns and implications. *Journal of Urban Economics, 50*(1), 163–189.

Borba, M. (2002). *Building moral intelligence: The seven essential virtues that teach kids to do the right thing.* San Francisco: Jossey-Bass.

Bourtchouladze, R. (2002). *Memories are made of this.* London: Columbia University Press.

Bransford, J.D., & Schwartz, D.L. (1999). Rethinking transfer: a simple proposal with multiple implications. *Review of Research in Education, 24,* 61–100.

Bremner, J. D. (2005). *Does stress damage the brain?: Understanding trauma-related disorders from a neurological perspective.* New York: W. W. Norton & Co.

Brendtro, L. Brokenleg, M., & VanBockern, S. (2002). *Reclaiming youth at risk.* Bloomington, IN: National Educational Service.

Brendtro, L., & Shahbazian, M. (2004). *Troubled children and youth: Turning problems into opportunity.* Champaign, IL: Research Press.

Brewer, C. B., & Campbell, D. G. (1991). *Rhythms of learning.* Tucson, AZ: Zephyr Press.

Brockman, J. (2003). A bozo of a baboon: A talk with Robert Sapolsky. [On-line]. Retrieved June 24, 2005, from *http://www.edge.org/ 3rd_culture/sapolsky03/sapolsky_index.html.*

Brody, B. A., Kinney, H. C., Kloman, A. S., & Gilles, F. H. (1987). Sequence of central nervous system myelination in human infancy. *Journal of Neuropathology and Experimental Neurology, 46,* 283–301.

Brooks, J. G., & Brooks, M. G. (1999). *In search of understanding: The case for constructivist classrooms.* Alexandria, VA: Association for Supervision and Curriculum Development.

Brooks, R. (1994). Children at risk: Fostering resilience and hope. *American Journal of Orthopsychiatry, 64,* 266–278.

Brothers, L. (1990). The neural basis of primate social communication. *Motivation & Emotion, 14,* 81–91.

Brothers, L. (1997). *Friday's footprint: How society shapes the human mind.* New York: Oxford University Press.

Brothers, L. (2002). Neurophysiology in a new domain. In J. Cacioppo, et al. (Eds.), *Foundations of Social Neuroscience* (pp. 367–385). Cambridge, MA: MIT Press.

Burke, M. J., & Curcio, F. R. (2000). *Learning mathematics for a new century: Yearbook.* Reston, VA: National Council of Teachers of Mathematics.

Burns, D. D. (1980). *Feeling good: The new mood therapy.* New York: Avon.

Burton, J., Horowitz, R., & Abeles, H. (1999). Learning in and through the arts: Curriculum implications. In E. Fiske (Ed.), *Champions of change: The impact of the arts on learning.* [On-line]. Retrieved June 19, 2005, from *http://www.artsedge.kennedy-center.org/champions/.*

Byrne, R. W., & Whiten, A. (Eds.). (1988). *Machiavellian intelligence: Social expertise and the evolution of intellect in monkeys, apes and humans.* Cambridge: Oxford University Press.

Byrnes, J.P. (2001). *Minds, brains and learning: Understanding the psychological and educational relevance of neuroscientific research.* New York: The Guilford Press.

Cabeza, R. (2001). Cognitive neuroscience of aging: Contributions of functional neuroimaging. *Scandinavian Journal of Psychology, 42,* 277–286.

Cacioppo, J., et al. (Eds.). (2002). *Foundations of Social Neuroscience.* Cambridge, MA: MIT Press.

Caine, G., & Caine, R. (2001). *The brain, education and the competitive edge.* Lanham, MD: Scarecrow Press.

Caine, R., & Caine, G. (1994). *Making connections: Teaching and the human brain.* Menlo Park, CA: Addison Wesley Longman.

Caine, R., & Caine, G. (1997). *Education on the edge of possibility.* Alexandria, VA: Association for Supervision and Curriculum Development.

Caine, R., Caine, G., McClinitic, C., & Klimek, K. (2005). *The 12 brain mind learning principles inaction: The field book to "Making Connections: Teaching and the Human Brain."* Thousand Oaks, CA: Corwin Press.

Calvin, W. (1996). *How brains think: Evolving intelligence, then and now.* London: Weidenfeld & Nicolson.

Carbone, E. (2001). Arranging the classroom with an eye (and ear) to students with ADHD [Electronic Version]. *Teaching Exceptional Children, 34*(2), 72–81. Retrieved October 17, 2004, from EBSCOhost Academic Search Premier Database.

Cardinal, R. N., & Everitt, B. J. (2004). Neural and psychological mechanisms underlying appetitive learning: Links to drug addiction. *Current Opinion in Neurobioogy, 14,* 156–162.

Carter, R. (1998). *Mapping the mind.* Berkeley, CA: University of California Press.

Caulfield, J., Kidd, S., & Kocher, T. (2000). Brain-based instruction in action. *Educational Leadership, 58*(3), 62–65.

Childhood Bilingualism: Current Status and Future Directions. [On-line Report]. (2005). Retrieved July 2, 2005, from *http://www.nichd.nih.gov/crmc/cdb/Childhood-Bilingualism_2005.pdf.*

Clark, D. A., Beck, A. T., & Alford, B. A. (1999). *Scientific foundations of cognitive theory* and therapy of depression. New York: John Wiley & Sons, Inc.

Clarke, H. F., Dalley, J. W., Crofts, H. S., Robbins, T. W., & Roberts, A. C. (2004). Cognitive inflexibility after prefrontal serotonin depletion. *Science, 304*(5672), 878–880.

Claxton, G. (1997). *Hare brain, tortoise mind: How intelligence increases when you think less.* New York: Ecco Press.

Clement, J. (1983). A conceptual model discussed by Galileo and used intuitively by physics students. In D. Gentner & A. Stevens, (Eds.), *Mental models* (pp. 325–340). Hillsdale, NJ: Laurence Erlbaum Associates, Inc.

Corina, D. P. (1998). Studies of neural processing in deaf signers: Toward a neurocognitive model of language processing in the deaf. *Journal of Deaf Studies and Deaf Education, 3*(1), 35–48.

Cornet, C. (2003). *Creating meaning through literature and the arts.* Upper Saddle River, NJ: Merrill Prentice Hall.

Corsini, R. *J. (1999). The dictionary of psychology.* Philadelphia: Taylor & Francis.

Cowan, N. (2001). The magical number 4 in short-term memory: A reconsideration of mental storage capacity. *Behavior Brain Science, 24,* 87–185.

Craik, F. I. M., & Salthouse, T. A. (Eds.). (2000). *The handbook of aging and cognition.* Hillsdale, NJ: Lawrence Erlbaum Associates, Inc.

Cummins, J. (1986). Empowering minority students: A framework for intervention. *Harvard Educational Review, 56,* 18–36.

Cummins, J. (1987). Bilingualism, language proficiency, and metalinguistic developments. In P. Homel, M. Paliz, & D. Aaronson (Eds.), *Childhood bilingualism: Aspects of linguistic, cognitive, and social development.* Hillsdale, NJ: Lawrence Erlbaum Associates, Inc.

Cuoco, A. A., & Curico, F. R. (2001). *The roles of representation in school mathematics: Yearbook.* Reston, VA: National Council of Teachers of Mathematics.

Damasio, A. R. (1994). *Descartes' error: Emotion, reason and the human brain.* New York: Avon Books.

Damasio, A. R. (1999). *The feeling of what happens: Body and emotion in the making of consciousness.* New York: Harcourt.

Damasio, A. R. (2003). *Looking for Spinoza: Joy, sorrow, and the feeling brain.* New York: Harcourt.

D'Arcangelo, M. (2000). How does the brain develop?: A conversation with Steven Peterson *Educational Leadership, 58*(3), 68–71.

D'Arcangelo, M. (2000). The scientist in the crib: A conversation with Andrew Meltzoff. *Educational Leadership, 58(3),* 8–13.

Davatzikos, C., & Resnick, S. M. (1998). Sex differences in anatomic measures of inter-hemispheric connectivity: Correlations with cognition in women but not men. *Cerebral Cortex, 8,* 635–640.

Dave, A. S., & Margoliash, D. (2000). Song replay during sleep and computational rules for sensorimotor vocal learning. *Science, 290*(5492), 812–816.

Deci, E., Vallerand, E. R., Pelletier, L. G., & Ryan, R. M. (1991). Motivation and education: The self-determination perspective. *Educational Psychologist, 26*(3–4), 325–346.

Delfos, M.F. (2004). *Children and behavioural problems: Anxiety, aggression, depression ADHD – A biopsychological model with guidelines for diagnostics and treatment.* London: Jessica Kingsley Publishers.

Dennison, P., & Dennison, G. (1986). *Brain gym.* Ventura, CA: Edukinesthetics.

DePorter, B., Reardon, M., & Singer-Nourie, S. (1999). *Quantum teaching: Orchestrating student success.* Boston: Allyn & Bacon.

Diamond, A., & Goldman-Rakic, P. S. (1989). Comparison of human infant and rhesus monkeys of Piaget's AB task: Evidence for dependence on dorsolateral prefrontal cortex. *Experimental Brain Research, 74,* 24–40.

Diamond, M. (1967). Extensive cortical depth measurements and neuron size increases in the cortex of environmentally enriched rats. *Journal of Comparative Neurology, 131,* 357–364.

Diamond, M. (1988). *Enriching heredity: The impact of the environment on the anatomy of the brain.* New York: The Free Press.

Diamond, M., & Hopson, J. (1998). *Magic trees of the mind: Nurturing your child.* New York: Penguin.

Druckman, D., & Sweets, J. A. (1988). *Enhancing human performance: Issues, theories, and techniques.* Washington, DC: National Academy Press.

Durkin, K. (1995). *Developmental social psychology: From infancy to old age.* Oxford, UK: Blackwell Publishers.

Ekman P., Levenson, R.W., & Friesen, W. V. (1983). Autonomic nervous system activity distinguishes among emotions. *Science, 221*(4616), 1208–1210.

Eliot, L. (2000). *What's going on in there? How the brain and mind develop in the first five years of life.* New York: Bantam.

Erlauer, L. (2003). *The brain-compatible classroom: using what we know about learning to improve teaching.* Alexandria, VA: Association for Supervision and Curriculum Development.

Esman, M. J. (1987). Ethnic politics and economic power. *Comparative Politics, 19,* 295 417.

Fairburn, C.G., & Harrison, P.J. (2003). Eating disorders. *The Lancet, 361,* 407–416.

Feingold, A. (1996). Cognitive gender differences: Where are they and why are they there?. *Learning & Individual Differences, 8,* 25–32.

Feinstein, S. (2004). *Secrets of the teenage brain: Research-based strategies for reaching and teaching today's adolescents.* San Diego, CA: The Brain Store.

Ferguson, E. D. (1996). Motivation. In R. J. Corsini & A. J. Auerbach (Eds.), *Concise encyclopedia of psychology* (pp. 578–580). New York: John Wiley & Sons, Inc.

Fischer, K. W., & Rose, S. P. (1998). Growth cycles of brain and mind. *Educational Leadership, 56*(3), 56–60.

Fiske, E. (Ed.). (1999). *Champions of change: The impact of the arts on learning.* [On-line]. Retrieved June 19, 2005, from *http://www.artsedge.kennedy-center.org/champions/*.

Flippen Group. (2003). *Capturing kids' hearts.* College Station, TX: The Flippen Group.

Ford, M. (1992). *Motivating humans.* Newbury Park, CA: Sage Publications.

Fountas, I., & Pinnell, G. (2001). *Guiding readers and writers (Grades 3–6): Teaching comprehension, genre, and content literacy.* Portsmouth, NH: Heinemann.

Frank, M. G., Issa, N. P., & Stryker, M. P. (2001). Sleep enhances plasticity in the developing visual cortex. *Neuron, 30*(1), 275–287.

Freeman, H. D., Cantalupo, C., & Hopkins, W. D. (2004). Asymmetries in the hippocampus and amygdala of chimpanzees (Pah troglodytes), *Behavioral Neuroscience, 118*(6), 1460–1465.

Frith, C. & Frith, U. (1999) Interacting minds-biological basis. *Science, 286,* 1692–1695.

Funk, A. (1992, November 8). Art integral part of learning. *The Topeka Capital-Journal*, p. C2.

Fuster, J. M. (2003). *Cortex and mind: Unifying cognition.* New York: Oxford University Press.

Gardiner, M. (1996). Learning improved by arts training. *Nature, 381*(580), 284.

Gardner, A. (2004). Fast food linked to obesity, insulin problems. *HealthDayNews* [On-line]. Retrieved October 25, 2005, from: *http://www.healthfinder. gov/news/ newsstory.asp?docID=523168.*

Gardner, H. (1991). *The unschooled mind: How children think and how schools should teach.* New York: Basic Books.

Gardner, H. (1993). *Frames of mind: The theory of multiple intelligences.* New York: Basic Books.

Gardner, H. (2000). *Intelligence reframed: Multiple intelligences for the 21st century.* New York: Basic Books.

Garrick-Duhaney, L. M. (2003). A practical approach to managing the behaviors of students with ADD. [Electronic Version]. *Intervention in School & Clinic, 38*(5). Retrieved January 17, 2005, from EBSCOhost Academic Search Premier Database.

Gazzaniga, M. S., Ivry, R. B., & Mangun, G. R. (1998). *Cognitive neuroscience: Biology of the mind.* New York: W. W. Norton & Co.

Gee, J. P. (2003). *What video games have to teach us about learning and literacy.* New York: Palgrave Macmillan.

Genesee, F. (1981). A comparison of early and late second language learning. *Modern Language Review, 12*, 115–128.

Genesee, F. (1987). *Learning through two languages: Studies of immersion and bilingual education.* Cambridge, MA: Newbury House.

Genesee, F. (2001). Portrait of the bilingual child. In: V. Cook (Ed.) *Portraits of the second language user.* Clevedon, ENG: Multilingual Matters.

Giedd, J. N., et al. (1999). Development of the human corpus callosum during childhood and adolescence: A longitudinal MRI study. *Progress in Neuro-Psychopharmacology & Biological Psychiatry, 23*(4), 571–588.

Goodall, J. (1986). *Chimpanzees of Gombe.* Cambridge, MA: The Belknap Press.

Goodall, J. (2000). *In the shadow of man* (Rev. ed.). New York: Houghton Mifflin.

Goodenow, C. (1992). Strengthening the links between educational psychology and the study of social contexts. *Educational Psychologist, 27*(2), 177–196.

Goodlad, J. I. (1984). *A place called school: Prospects for the future.* New York: McGraw Hill.

Gendlin, E. T. (1982). *Focusing.* New York: Bantam.

Ghaith, G. (2002). The relationship between cooperative learning, perception of social support, and academic achievement. *System, 30*(3), 263–273.

Gillies, R., & Ashman, A. (1998). Behavior and interactions of children in cooperative groups in lower and middle elementary grades. *Journal of Educational Psychology, 90*(4), 746–757.

Goldberg, E. (2002). *The executive brain: Frontal lobes and the civilized mind.* New York: Oxford University Press.

Goldberg, M. (2004). The Test Mess. *Phi Delta Kappan, 85*(3), 361–366.

Goleman, D. (1995). *Emotional intelligence: Why it can matter more than IQ.* New York: Bantam.

Goleman, D. (1998). Working with emotional intelligence. New York: Bantam.

Goleman, D. (2002). *Primal Leadership: Realizing the power of emotional intelligence.* Boston: Harvard Business School Publishing.

Gopnik, A., Meltsoff, A. N., & Kuhl, P. (1999). The scientist in the crib: Minds, brains, and how children learn. New York: William Morrow.

Gore, A. (1996). The metaphor of distributed intelligence. *Science, 272*, 177–180.

Grandin, T. (1996). *Thinking in pictures: And other reports from my life with autism.* New York: Random House.

Greene, R. (2001). *The explosive child: A new approach for understanding and parenting easily frustrated, chronically inflexible children.* New York: HarperCollins Publishers.

Gutstein, S., & Rachelle, S. (2002). *Relationship development intervention with children, adolescents and adults.* London: Jessica Kingsley Publishers.

Hanson, A. (2001). *Visual writing.* New York: Learning Express.

Hanson, A. (2002). *Write brain write.* San Diego, CA: The Brain Store.

Haskell, R.E. (2001). *Transfer of learning: Cognition, instruction, and reasoning.* London, Eng.: Academic Press, Inc.

Harlow, H. F. (1965). Sexual behavior in the rhesus monkey. In F. A. Beach (Ed.), *Sex and behavior* (pp.234–265). New York: John Wiley & Sons, Inc.

Hart, L. A. (1999). *Human brain and human learning.* Covington, WA: Books for Educators.

Harvey, S., & Goudvis, A. (2000). *Strategies that work: Teaching comprehension to enhance understanding.* Markham, ON: Stenhouse Publishers.

Hawkins, J. (2004). *On Intelligence.* New York: Henry Holt.

Hayes, S.C., & Smith, S. (2005). *Get out of your mind and into your life: The new acceptance and commitment therapy guide.* Oakland, CA: New Harbinger Publications.

Healy, J. (1987). *Your child's growing mind.* Garden City, NY: Doubleday.

Heffner, M., & Eifert, G.H. (2004). *The anorexia workbook: How to accept yourself, heal suffering, and reclaim your life.* Oakland, CA: New Harbinger Publications.

Heidenhain, G. (2003). *Learning beyond boundaries: Fundamental experiences using accelerated learning.* Colorado Springs, CO: An International Alliance for Learning Publication.

Helmuth, L. (2001). ADDICTION: Beyond the pleasure principle. *Science, 294,* 983–984.

Hodgdon, L. (1995) *Visual strategies for improving communication: Practical supports for school & home.* Troy, MI: Quirk Roberts Publishing.

Hoerr, T. (2003). Distributed intelligence and why schools need to foster it. *Independent School, 63*(1), 76–83.

Holloway, J. H. (2000). How does the brain learn science? *Educational Leadership, 58*(3), 85–86.

Howard, P. J. (2000). *The owner's manual for the brain.* Austin, TX: Bard Press.

Huang, S. C., Tsai, S. J., & Chang, J. C. (2004). Fluoxetine-induced memory impairment in four family members. *Journal of Psychiatric Medicine, 34*(2), 197–200.

Hughes, D. (2003). *Behavioral neurogenetics: A complementary strategy to understanding neuropsychiatric disorders* [Electronic Version]. Retrieved June 24, 2005, from *http://neuropsychiatryreviews.com/apr03/npr_apr03_neurogenetics.html.*

Huttenlocher, P. R. (1990). Morphometric study of human cerebral cortex development. *Neuropsychologia, 28,* 517–527.

Izard, C. E. (1971). *The face of emotion.* New York: Appleton-Century-Crofts.

Jacobs, B., Schall, M., & Scheibel, A. B. (1993). A quantitative dendritic analysis of Wernieke's area in humans. II. Gender, hemispheric, and environmental factors. *Journal of Comparative Neurology, 327,* 97–111.

Jamieson, J. R. (1995). Interactions between mothers and children who are deaf. *Journal of Early Intervention, 19*(2), 108–117.

Janzen, J. E. (1996). *Understanding the nature of autism: A practical guide.* San Antonio, TX: Therapy Skill Builders.

Jensen, E. (2000). Learning smarter: The new science of teaching and training. San Diego, CA: The Brain Store.

Jensen, E. (2001). *Arts with the brain in mind.* Alexandria, VA: Association for Supervision and Curriculum Development.

Jensen, E. (2003). *Tools for engagement: Managing emotional states for learner success.* San Diego, CA: The Brain Store.

Jensen, E. (2005). *Teaching with the brain in mind* (2nd ed.). Alexandria, VA: Association for Supervision and Curriculum Development.

Johnson, D., & Johnson, R. (1999). Learning together and alone: Cooperative, competitive and individualistic learning. Boston: Allyn & Bacon.

Johnson, D., Maruyama, G., Johnson, R., Nelson, D., & Skon, L. (1981). Effects of cooperative, competitive, and individualistic goal structures on achievement: A meta-analysis. *Psychological Bulletin, 89*(1), 47–62.

Johnson, S. (2004). Antonio Damasio's theory of thinking faster and faster. *Discover, 25*(5), 44–49.

Johnson-Laird, P. (1983). *Mental models.* Cambridge, MA: Harvard University Press.

Johnston, V. (1999). *Why we feel: The science of human emotions.* Cambridge, UK: Perseus.

Katchadourian, H. A. (1990). The biological aspects of human sexuality. Austin, TX: Holt, Rinehart, and Winston, Inc.

Kauchak, D. P., & Eggen, P. D. (1998). *Learning and teaching: Research-based methods.* Boston: Allyn & Bacon.

Kaufeldt, M. (1999). *Begin with the brain: Orchestrating the learner-centered classroom.* San Diego, CA: The Brain Store.

Khilnani, S., Field, T., Hernandez-Reif, M., & Schanberg, S. (2003). Massage therapy improves mood and behavior of students with Attention-Deficit/Hyperactivity Disorder [Electronic Version]. *Adolescence, 38*(152). Retrieved January 17, 2005, from EBSCOhost Academic Search Premier Database.

Kilander, L., Nyman, H., Boberg, M., & Lithell, H. (1997). *Cognitive function, vascular risk factors and education: A cross-sectional study based on a cohort of 70-year-old men. Internal Medicine, 242*(4): 313–321.

Kim, J., & Diamond, D. (2002). The stressed hippocampus, synaptic plasticity and lost memories. *Nature Reviews Neuroscience, 3*(6), 453–462.

Kimura D. (2002) Sex hormones influence human cognitive pattern. *Neuroendocrinology Letters, 23*(4), 67–77.

Kinoshita, J. (1997). Nourishing thoughts: The surprising role of " Neurotrophins" in memory [Electronic Version]. *Brainwork: The Neuroscience Newsletter, 7*(1). Retrieved June 25, 2005, from *http://www.dana.org/articles/bwn_0297.cf #contents.*

Klosko, J. S., & Sanderson, W. C. (1999). *Cognitive-behavioral treatment of depression.* New York: Aronson.

Kluth, P. (2003). *You're going to love this kid: Teaching students with autism in the inclusive classroom.* Baltimore, MD: Paul H. Brookes Publishing Co.

Knowles, M. (1980). *The modern practice of adult education.* (Rev. ed.). Chicago: Follet Co.

Kotulak, R. (1996). *Inside the brain: Revolutionary discoveries of how the mind works.* Kansas City, MO: Andrews McMeel Publishing.

Kovalik, S. J., & Olsen, K. D. (2002). *Exceeding expectations: A user's guide to implementing brain research in the classroom* (2nd ed.). Covington, WA: Books for Educators.

Kranowicz, C. S. (1998). *The out-of-sync child: Recognizing and coping with sensory integration dysfunction.* New York: Berkley Publishing Group.

Lambert, L., et al. (2002). *The constructivist leader* (2nd ed.). New York: Teachers College Press.

Lambert, W. E., & Taylor, D. M. (1990). *Coping with cultural and racial diversity in urban America.* New York: Praeger.

Lambert, W. E., & Tucker, G. R. (1972). *Bilingual education of children: The St. Lambert experience.* Rowley, MA: Newbury House.

Laumann, E. O., et al. (2000). The organization of sexuality: Sexual practices in the United States. Chicago: The University of Chicago Press.

Lazaer, D. (2004). *Higher order thinking the multiple intelligence way.* Chicago: Zephyr Press.

LeDoux, J. (1996). *The emotional brain: The mysterious underpinnings of emotional life.* New York: Simon and Schuster.

LeDoux, J. (2002). *Synaptic self* (1st ed.). Toronto, ON: Viking-Penguin Books.

Leary, M. R., & Downs, D. L. (Eds.). (1995). *Efficacy, agency, and self-esteem.* New York: Plenium Press.

Lerner, R., & Benson, P. (Eds.). (2003). *Developmental assets and asset-building communities: Implications for research, policy,* and practice. Minneapolis, MN: Search Institute.

Lipsey, M., & Wilson, D. (1993). The efficacy of psychological, educational and behavioral treatment. *American Psychologist, 48*(12), 1181–1209.

Lock, R. H., Church, K., Gottschalk, C. M., & Leddy, J. (2003). Enhance social and friendship skills. [Electronic Version]. *Intervention in School & Clinic, 38*(5). Retrieved January 17, 2005, from EBSCO-host Academic Search Premier Database.

Lonsdorf, E. (2004).Sex differences in learning in chimpanzees, *Nature, 428,* 715.

Lopes, P. N., Brackett, M. A., Nezlek, J., Schutz, A., Sellin, I., & Salovey, P. (in press). Emotional intelligence and social interaction. *Personality and Social Psychology Bulletin.*

Lou, Y., Abrami, P., Spence, J., Paulsen, C., Chambers, B., & d'Apollonio, S. (1996). Within-class grouping: A meta-analysis. *Review of Educational Research, 66*(4), 423–458.

Lupien, S. J., & Lepage, M. (2001). Stress, memory, and the hippocampus: Can't live with it, can't live without it. *Behavioural Brain Research, 127*(1–2):137–158.

Lurie, K. (2005). ADHD brain scan [Online]. Retrieved June 25, 2005, from *http://www.sciencentral.com/articles/view.php3?language=english&type=& article_id=218392460.*

MacDonald, A. (2003). Imaging studies bring ADHD into sharper focus [Electronic Version]. *Brainwork: The Neuroscience Newsletter, 13*(2). Retrieved June 25, 2005, from, *http://www.dana.org/pdf/periodicals/brainwork_0403.pdf.*

Maddux, J. (1999). Expectancies and the social-cognitive perspective: Basic principles, processes, and variables. In I. Kirsch (Ed.), *How expectancies shape experience* (pp. 17–39). Washington, DC: American Psychological Association.

Mann, V. A., Sasanuma, S., Sakuma, N., & Masaki S. (1990). Sex differences in cognitive abilities: A cross-cultural perspective. *Neuropsychologia, 28,* 1063–1077.

Marieb, E.N. (1995). *Human anatomy and physiology* (3rd ed.). Redwood City, CA.:

The Benjamin Cummings Publishing Company, Inc.

Marschark, M., Lang, H. G., & Albertini, J. A. (2002). *Educating Deaf Students: From research to practice.* New York: Oxford University Press .

Marshall, M. L. (2001). *Discipline without stress.* Los Alamitos, CA: Piper Press.

Marton, F. & Saljo, R. (1976). On qualitative differences in learning-II: Outcome as a function of the learner's conception of the task. *British Journal of Educational Psychology, 46,* 115–127.

Marzano, R.J. (2001). *Designing a new taxonomy of educational objectives.* Thousand Oaks, CA: Corwin Press.

Marzano, R. J. (2003). *Classroom management that works: Research-based strategies for* Development.

Marzano, R. J., Pickering, D. J., & Pollock, J. E. (2001). *Classroom instruction that works.* Alexandra, VA: Association for Supervision and Curriculum Development.

Matsuzawa, T. (2001). Reproductive memory processes in chimpanzees: Homologous approaches to research on human working memory. *Primate Origins of Human Cognition and Behavior.* Tokyo: Springer-Verlag.

Mayberry, R. I., & Eichen, E. B. (1991). The long-lasting advantage of learning sign language in childhood: Another look at the critical period for language acquisition. *Journal of Memory and Language, 30*(4), 486–512.

Mayer, J.D., Caruso, D., & Salovey, P. (1997). The Multifactor Emotional Intelligence Scale: Emotional intelligence a key to success. Simsbuy, CT: Charles J. Wolfe Associates, LLC Publisher.

Mayer, J. D., Salovey, P., Caruso, D. R., & Sigarenios, G. (2001). Emotional intelligence as a standard intelligence. *Emotion, 1,* 232–242.

Mayer, J. D., & Salovey, P. (1997). What is emotional intelligence? In P. Salovey & D. Sluyter (Eds.), *Emotional development and emotional intelligence: Educational implications* (pp. 3–31). New York: Basic Books.

Mayer, J. D., Salovey, P., & Caruso, D. R. (2002). Mayer-Salovey-Caruso Emotional

Intelligence Test. Toronto, ON: Multi-Health Systems, Inc.

McClannahan, L. E., & Krantz, P. J. (1998). *Activity schedules for children with autism: Teaching independent behavior.* Bethesda, MD: Woodbine House.

McEwen, B., Lasley, E. N., & Lasley, E. (2002). *The end of stress as we know it.* Washington, DC: National Academies Press.

Mendez-Sanchez, N., Ponciano-Rodrigoez, G., Chavez-Tapia, N., & Uribe, M. (2005). *Effects of leptin on biliary lipids: Potential consequences for gallstone formation and therapy in obesity.* Curr Drug Targets Immune Endocr Metab Disord, 5(2), 203–8.

Michael, E., Keller, T., Carpenter, P., & Just, M. (2001). fMRI investigation of sentence comprehension by eye and by ear: Modality fingerprints on cognitive processes. *Human Brain Mapping 13*(4), 239–252.

Miller, P. (2002). Another look at the STM capacity of prelingually deafened individuals and its relation to reading comprehension. *American Annals of the Deaf, 147*(5), 56–69.

Molteni, R., Wu, A., Vaynman, S., Ying, Z., Barnard, R. J., & Gomez-Pinilla, F. (2004). Exercise reverses the harmful effects of consumption of a high-fat diet on synaptic and behavioral plasticity associated to the action of brain-derived neurotrophic factor. *Neuroscience, 123*(2), 429–440.

Moore, B., & Caldwell, H. (1993). Drama and drawing for narrative writing in primary grades. *Journal of Educational Research, 8*(2), 100–110.

Mukhopadhyay, T. R. (2000). *Beyond the silence: My life, the world and autism.* London: The National Autism Society.

Myles, B. (2001). *Asperger syndrome and adolescence: Practical solutions for school success.* Shawnee Mission, KS: Autism Asperger Publishing Company.

Nakamura, K. (1993). A theory of cerebral learning regulated by the reward system. *Biological Cybernetics, 68*(6), 491–498.

National Reading Panel. (2000). *Teaching Children to Read* [On-line]. Retrieved Oct. 24, 2005, from: *http://www.nationalreadingpanel.org/Publications/publications.htm.*

Nelson, C. A., & Carver, L. (1998). The effects of stress and trauma on brain and memory: A view from developmental cognitive neuroscience. *Development and Psychopathology, 10*(4), 793–809.

Nemoto, S., & Finkel, T. (2004). Ageing and the mystery at Arles. *Nature, 429, 149–152.*

Nestler, E. J., & Malenka, R. C. (2004). The addicted brain. *Scientific American, 290*(3), 78–85.

Niehoff, D. (1999). *The biology of violence: How understanding the brain, behavior, and environment can break the vicious circle of aggression.* New York: The Free Press.

Nolan, K. A., & Blass, J.P. (1992). Preventing cognitive decline. *Clinics in Geriatric Medicine, 8*(1), 19–34.

Novak, J. D. (1998). *Learning, creating, and using knowledge.* Hillsdale, NJ: Lawrence Erlbaum Associates, Inc.

Novak, J. D., & Gowin, D. B. (1984). *Learning how to learn.* New York: University Press.

O'Neil, R., Welsh, M., Parke, R. D., Wang, S., & Strand, C. (1997). A longitudinal assessment of the academic correlates of early peer acceptance and rejection. *Journal of Clinical Child Psychology, 26*(3), 290–303.

Paddison, S. (1998). *The hidden power of the heart: Discovering an unlimited source of intelligence.* Boulder Creek, CA: Planetary Publications.

Padgett, D., Sheridan, J., Dorne, J., Berntson, G.., Candelora, J., & Glaser, R. (1998). Social stress and the reactivation of latent herpes simplex virus type 1. *Proceedings of the National Academy of Sciences, 95*(12), 7231–7235.

Panksepp, J. (1998). Attention deficit hyperactivity disorders, psychostimulants, and intolerance of childhood playfulness: A tragedy in the making? *Current Directions in Psychological Science, 7*(3), 91–98.

Papalos, D., & Papalos, J. (2002). *The bipolar child: The definitive and reassuring guide to childhood's most misunderstood disorder* (2nd ed.). New York: Broadway Books.

Paradis, M. (2004). *A neurolinguistic theory of bilingualism.* Philadelphia: John Benjamins.

Parr, A. (2001). Cognitive and physiological markers of emotional awareness in chimpanzees (Pan troglodytes), *Animal Cognition, 4,* 223–229.

Pearson, S. (2000). *Tools for citizenship and life: Using the ITI lifelong guidelines and lifeskills in your classroom.* Kent, WA: Susan Kovalik & Associates.

Pellegrini, A., & Bjorklund, D. F. (1996). The place of recess in school: Issues in the role of recess in children's education and development. *Journal of Research in Childhood Education, 11*(1), 5–13.

Perachio, A. A. (1978). Hypothalamic regulation of behavioral and hormonal aspects of aggression and sexual performance. In D. C. Chivers, & J. Herbert (Eds.), *Recent advances in primatology* (Vol. 1, pp. 549–566).

Perkins, D.N., & Salomon, G. (1992). Transfer of learning. In Husen, T., & Postlethwaite, T.N. (Eds.), *International Encyclopedia of Education* (2nd ed.). Oxford, ENG: Pergamon Press. Retrieved also Oct. 24, 2005, from: *http://learnweb.harvard.edu/alps/thinking/docs/traencyn.htm.*

Pert, C. (1997). *Molecules of emotion.* New York: Scribner.

Peterson, C., Maier, S., & Seligman, M. (1993). *Learned helplessness.* New York: Oxford University Press.

Phelps, E., et al. (2002). Performance on indirect measures of race evaluation predicts Amygdala activation. In J. Cacioppo, et. al. (Eds.), *Foundations of social neuroscience,* (pp. 615–627). Cambridge, MA: MIT Press.

Phillips, P. E. M., Stuber, G. D., Heien, M. L. A. V., Wightman, R. M., & Carell, R. M. (2003). Subsecond dopamine release promotes cocaine seeking. *Nature, 422,* 614–618.

Piaget, J. (1976). *To understand is to invent: The future of education.* New York: Penguin.

Piaget, J. & Inhelder, B. (1969). *The pyschology of the child.* New York: Basic Books.

Pinker, S. (1997). *How the mind works.* New York: W. W. Norton, Inc.

Pinker, S. (2002). *The blank slate: The modern denial of human nature.* New York: Viking.

Polanyi, M. (1958). *Personal knowledge: Towards a post–critical philosophy.* London: Routledge and Kegan Paul.

Popham, J. (2001). *The truth about testing: An educator's call to action.* Alexandria, VA: Association for Supervision and Curriculum Development.

Popham, J. (2002). *Classroom assessment: What teachers need to know* (3rd ed). Boston: Allyn & Bacon.

Preston, S. D., & deWaal, F. B. M. (2002). Empathy: Its ultimate and proximate bases. *Behavioral and Brain Sciences, 25*(1), 1–71.

Preuschoft, S., & vanHooff, J. A. R. A. M. (1995). Homologizing primate facial displays: A critical review of methods. *Folia Primatologica, 65,* 121–137.

Prietula, M. J., & Simon, H. A. (1989). The Experts in your midst. *Harvard Business Review, 1,* 120.

Prior, M., Smart, D., Sanson, A., & Oberklaid, F. (1993). Sex differences in psychological adjustment from infancy to 8 years. *Journal of the American Academy of Child and Adolescent Psychiatry, 32,* 281–304.

Project Zero. (2000). The arts and academic improvement: What the evidence shows [On-line]. Retrieved June 24, 2005, from *http://www.pz.harvard.edu/Research/Reap/REAPExecSum.htm.*

Public Broadcasting Station. (2002) *Frontline: Interviews inside the teenage brain [On-line]. Retrieved July 6, 2005, from* http://www.pbs.org/wgbh/pages/frontline/shows/teenbrain/.

Ratey, J. J. (2001). *A user's guide to the brain: Perception, attention and the four theaters of the brain. New York: Vintage Books.*

Reid, R. (1999). Attention deficit hyperactivity disorder: Effective methods for the classroom [Electronic Version]. *Focus on Exceptional Children, 32*(4). Retrieved January 17, 2005, from EBSCOhost Academic Search Premier Database.

Restak, R. (1995). *Brainscapes.* New York: Hyperion.

Restak, R. (2003). *The new brain.* New York: Rodale.

Rhodes, L. (1996). *Readers and writers with a difference.* Portsmouth, NH: Heinemann.

Richards, R. G. (2001). *The source for learning and memory*. East Moline, IL: Lingui-Systems.

Rogers, D. A. (1998). Computer-assisted learning versus a lecture and feedback seminar for teaching a basic surgical technical skill. *American Journal of Surgery, 175*(6), 508–510.

Rogers, K. (1986). Do the gifted think differently? *Journal for the Education of the Gifted, 100*, 17–39.

Rogers, K. (2002). *Re-forming gifted education*. Scottsdale, AZ: Great Potential Press.

Ronis, D. (2000). *Brain-compatible assessments*. Glenview, IL: Skylight Professional Development.

Root-Bernstein, R., & Root-Bernstein, M. (1999). *Sparks of genius*. New York: Houghton Mifflin.

Rothenberg, J., McDermott, P., & Martin, G. (1998). Changes in pedagogy: A qualitative result of teaching heterogeneous classes. *Teaching and Teacher Education, 14*(6), 633–642.

Rothschild, B. (2000). *The body remembers: The psychophysiology of trauma and trauma treatment*. New York: W. W. Norton & Co.

Ryan, R. M., Connell, J. P., & Deci, E. L. (1985). A motivational analysis of self determination and self-regulation in education. In C. Ames & R. Ames (Eds.), *Research on motivation in education: The classroom milieu* (Vol. 2, pp. 13–51). New York: Academic Press, Inc.

Sackett, G. P. (1966). Monkeys reared in isolation with pictures as visual input: Evidence for an innate releasing mechanism, *Science, 154*(3755), 1468+1471–1473.

Salend, S. J., Elhoweris, H., & Van Garderen, D. (2003). Educational interventions for students with ADD [Electronic Version]. *Intervention in School & Clinic, 38*(5). Retrieved January 17, 2005, from EBSCOhost Academic Search Premier Database.

Salend, S. J., & Rohena, E. (2003). Students with attention deficit disorders: An overview [Electronic Version]. *Intervention in School & Clinic, 38*(5). Retrieved January 17, 2005, from EBSCOhost Academic Search Premier Database.

Salomon, G., & Perkins, D. N. (1988). Individual and social aspects of learning. In P. D. Pearson & A. Iran-Nejad (Eds.), *Review of Research in Education, 23*, 1–24.

Salomon, G., Brown, J. S., & Pea, R. (1996). *Distributed cognitions*. Cambridge, UK: Cambridge University Press.

Salovey, P. & Mayer, J. D. (1990). Emotional intelligence. *Imagination, Cognition, and Personality, 9*, 185–211.

Schick, B., de Villiers, J., de Villiers, P., & Hoffmeister, B. (2002). Theory of mind: Language and cognition in deaf children [On-line]. Retrieved August 20, 2004, from *http://www.asha.org/about/publications/leader-online/archives/2002/q4/f021203.htm*.

Schewe, P. F., & Stein, B. (February 10, 2005). Chain reactions in neuron firing might be used to store information [Electronic Version]. *The American Institute of Physics Bulletin of Physics News, 719*. Retrieved June 29, 2005, from *http://physics.about.com/od/biophysics/a/MemoryAvalanche_p.htm*.

Schunk, D. H. (2004) *Learning theories: An educational perspective* (4th ed.). Boston: Pearson.

Schutte, N. S., et al. (1998). Development and validation of a measure of emotional intelligence. *Personality and Individual Differences, 25*, 167–177.

Schwartz, J. M., & Begley, S. (2003). *The mind and the brain: Neuroplasticity and the power of mental force.* New York: Regan Books.

Schwiebert, V. L., Sealander, K. A., & Dennison, J. L. (2002). Strategies for counselors working with high school students with attention-deficit/hyperactivity disorder [Electronic Version]. *Journal of Counseling & Development, 80*(1). Retrieved January 17, 2005, from EBSCOhost Academic Search Premier Database.

Science A Go Go. (2001). *Stress and aggression reinforce each other* [Electronic Version]. Retrieved July 2, 2005, from *http://www.scienceagogo.com/news/20040903231503data_trunc_sys.shtml*.

Senge, P. M. (1990). *The fifth discipline: The art and practice of the learning organization*. New York: Doubleday.

Sergiovanni, T. J. J. (1996). *Moral leadership: Getting to the heart of school improvement*. New York: John Wiley & Sons, Inc.

Sexuality Information and Education Council of the United States. (2004). *Guidelines for comprehensive sexuality education: Kindergarten through 12th grade* (3rd ed.) [Online Report]. Retrieved July 2, 2005, from *http://www.siecus.org/pubs/guidelines/guidelines.pdf*.

Shank, P. (2004, September 7). Can they do it in the real world? Designing for transfer of learning. *The Learning Developers' Journal*. [On–line]. Retrieved Oct. 24, 2005, from *http://www.learningpeaks.com/pshank_Transfer.pdf*.

Shaywitz, B., et al. (2000). The neurobiology of reading and reading disability (dyslexia). In M. Kamil, P. Mosenthal, P. Pearson, & R. Barr (Eds.), *Handbook of reading research (Vol. III, pp. 229–249). Hillsdale, NJ: Lawrence Erlbaum Associates, Inc.*

Shonkoff, J. P. & Phillips, D. A. (Eds.). (2000). *From neurons to neighborhoods*. Washington, DC: National Academies Press.

Shore, S. (2001). *Beyond the wall: Personal experiences with autism and Asperger syndrome*. Shawnee Mission, KS: Autism Asperger Publishing Company.

Siegel, D. (1999). *The developing mind: Toward a neurobiology of interpersonal experience*. New York: Guilford Press.

Siegel, J. M. (2001). The REM sleep-memory consolidation hypothesis. *Science, 294*(5544), 1058–1063.

Silverman, L.K. (1993). The gifted individual. In L.K. Silverman (Ed.). *Counseling the gifted and talented* (pp. 3–28). Denver, CO: Love Publishing.

Simos, P. G., et al. (2001). Mapping of receptive language cortex in bilingual volunteers by using magnetic source imaging. *Journal of Neurosurgery, 95*, 76–81.

Siviy, S. M. (1998). Neurobiological substrates of play behavior: Glimpses into the structure and function of mammalian playfulness. In M. Bekoff & J. Byers (Eds.), *Animal play: Evolutionary, comparative, and ecological perspectives*. New York: Cambridge University Press.

Slavkin, M. (2002). Brain science in the classroom. *Principal Leadership, 2*(8), 21–23.

Smilkstein, R. (2003). *We're born to learn: Using the brain's natural learning process to create today's curriculum*. Thousand Oaks, CA: Corwin Press.

Smith, D. D. (2003). *Introduction to special education: Teaching in an age of opportunity* (5th ed.). Boston: Pearson.

Smith, F. (1990). *To think. New York: Teachers College Press*.

Sousa, D. (2001). *How the brain learns (2nd ed.). Thousand Oaks, CA: Corwin Press*.

Sousa, D. (2004). *How the brain learns to read*. Thousand Oaks, CA: Corwin Press.

Squire, L. R., & Kandel, E. R. (2000). *Memory: From mind to molecules*. New York: W. H. Freeman.

Squire, L. R. & Zola, S. M. (1996). Structure and function of declarative and nondeclarative memory systems. *Proceedings of the National Academy of Sciences*, 93: 13515–13522.

Stengle, J. (2004, December 4) *Obesity is rising sharply among U.S. preschoolers*. Associated Press, n. pag.

Stiggins, R. (2002). Assessment crisis: The absence of assessment for learning. *Phi Delta Kappan, 83*(10), 758–765.

Stilwell, B., Galvin, M., Kopta, S. M., & Kopta, S. *Right vs. wrong: Raising a child with a conscience*. Bloomington, IN: Indiana University Press.

Strauch, B. (2004). *The primal teen: What the new discoveries about the teenage brain tell us about our kids*. New York: Bantam Doubleday.

Summers, C. H., et al. (2004). Dynamics and mechanics of social rank reversal. *Journal of Comparative Physiology. A, Neuroethology, Sensory, Neural, and Behavioral Physiology, 191*: 241–252.

Suomi, S. (1999). Attachment in rhesus monkeys. In J. Cassidy & P. Shaver (Eds.), *Handbook of attachment* (pp. 181–197). New York, NY: Guildford Press.

Surowiecki, J. (2004). *The wisdom of crowds*. New York: Bantam Doubleday.

Swain, M., & Lapkin, S. (1982). *Evaluating bilingual education: A case study.* Clevedon, ENG: Multilingual Matters.

Sylwester, R. (1995). *A celebration of neurons.* Alexandria, VA: Association for Supervision and Curriculum Development.

Sylwester, R. (1998). Art for the brain's sake. *Educational Leadership, 56*(3), 31–35.

Temple, E., et al. (2003). Neural deficits in children with dyslexia ameliorated by behavioral remediation: Evidence from functional MRI. *Proceedings of the National Academy of Sciences, 100*(5), 2860–2865.

Terrazas, A., & McNaughton, B. (2000) Brain growth and the cognitive map. *Proceedings of the National Academy of Sciences, 97*(9), 4414–4416.

Thatcher, R.W., Lyon, G.R., Rumsby, G., & Krasnegor, K. (Eds.). (1996). *Developmental neuroimaging: Mapping the development of brain and behavior.* San Diego, CA: Academic Press, Inc.

Tileston, D.W. (2000). *What every teacher should know about motivation.* Thousand Oaks, CA: Corwin Press.

Tobin, M., Nelson, J., & Castellanos, F. (1999). Development of the human corpus callosum during childhood and adolescence: A longitudinal MRI study. *Progress in Neuro-Psychopharmacology & Biological Psychiatry, 23,* 557–588.

Tomlinson, C. (1996). Differentiating instruction in mixed ability classrooms. Alexandria, VA: Association for Supervision and Curriculum Development.

Tompkins, G. (2005). *Literacy for the 21st-Century: A Balanced Approach.* Upper Saddle River, NJ: Prentice Hall.

Toye, S. (2001). *Study shows obesity bad for the mind, too* [On-line]. Retrieved June 24, 2005, from *http:// www.sciencedaily.com /releases/ 2001/05/010529071515.htm.*

U. S. Office of Special Education Programs. (2003). Identifying and treating attention deficit hyperactivity disorder: A resource for school and home [Electronic Version]. Retrieved June 24, 2005, from *http:// www.ed.gov/teachers/needs/speced/adhd/adh d–resource–pt1.doc.*

Vail, P. B. (1996). *Learning as a way of being.* San Francisco, CA: Jossey-Bass.

Vaughn, S., & Linan-Thompson, S. (2004). *Research-based methods of reading instruction grades K-3.* Alexandria, VA: Association for Supervision and Curriculum Development.

Wagner, U., Gais, S., Haider, H., Verleger, R., & Born, J. (2004). Sleep inspires insight. *Nature, 427*(6972), 352–355.

Walberg, H. (1999) Productive teaching. In H. C. Waxman & H. Walberg (Eds.), *New directions for teaching practice and research* (pp. 75–104). Berkeley, CA: McCutchen Publishing Corp.

Walker, M. P., Brakefield, T., Morgan, A., Hobson, J. A., & Stickgold, R. (2002). Practice with sleep makes perfect: Sleep-dependent motor skill learning. *Neuron, 35*(1), 205–211.

Walsh, D. (2004). *Why do they act that way?: A survival guide to the adolescent brain for you and your teen.* New York: Free Press.

Walsh, P. (2000). A hands-on approach to understanding the brain. *Educational Leadership, 58*(3), 76–78.

Wang, G.J., et al. (2001). Brain dopamine and obesity. *Lancet, 357*(9253), 354–357.

Wang, M. C., Haertel, G. D., & Walberg, H. J. (1993). Toward a knowledge base for learning. *Review of Educational Research, 63*(3), 249–294.

Weber, E. (1998). Marks of brain-based assessment: A practical checklist. *National Association of Secondary School Principals Bulletin, 82*(598), 63–72.

Wentzel, K. R., & Wigfield, A. (1998). Academic and social motivational influences on students' academic performance. *Educational Psychology Review, 10*(2), 155–175.

West, R. L. (1996). An application of prefrontal cortex function theory to cognitive aging. *Psychological Bulletin, 120,* 272–292.

Whitehead, A. N., Griffin, D. R., & Sherburne, D. W. (1978). *Process and reality: An essay in cosmology.* New York: Free Press.

Wilkinson, I., & Fung, I. (2002). Small-group composition and peer effects. *International Journal of Educational Research, 37*(5), 483–504.

Willey, L. H. (1999). *Pretending to be normal: Living with Asperger's syndrome.* London: Jessica Kingsley Publishers.

Williams, D. (2003). *Exposure anxiety–the invisible cage: An exploration of self-protection responses in the autism spectrum and beyond.* London: Jessica Kingsley Publishers.

Wilson, M. A., & McNaughton, B. L. (1994). Reactivation of hippocampal ensemble memories during sleep. *Science, 265*(5172), 676–679.

Wlodkowski, R. (1985). *Enhancing adult motivation to learn.* San Francisco: Jossey–Bass.

Wolfberg, P. J. (1999). *Play and imagination in children with autism.* New York: Teachers College Press.

Wolfe, P. (2001). *Brain matters: Translating research into classroom practice.* Alexandria, VA: Association for Supervision and Curriculum Development.

Wolfe, P., & Nevills, P. (2004). *Building the reading brain, PreK-3.* Thousand Oaks, CA: Corwin Press.

Wood, D. (1991). Communication and cognition: How the communication styles of hearing adults may hinder-rather than help-deaf learners. *American Annals of the Deaf, 136*(3), 247–251.

Wurtman, J. (1988). *Managing your mind and mood through food.* New York: Harper Collins.

Young, J. E., Beck, A. T., & Weinberger, A. (1993). Depression. In D. H. Barlow (Ed.), *Clinical handbook of psychological disorders: A step-by-step treatment manual* (2nd ed). New York: Guildford Press.

Zentall, S. S. (1983). Learning environments: A review of physical and temporal factors. *Exceptional Education Quarterly, 4,* 90–115.

Zimmer, R. (2003) A new twist in the educational tracking debate. *Economics of Education Review, 22*(3), 307–315.

Zull, J. E. (2002). *The art of changing the brain: Enriching teaching by exploring the biology of learning.* Herndon, VA: Stylus.

HTTP On-line Sources

ADHD. *http://www.adhd.com/index.jsp.* Retrieved July 6, 2005.

The Amen Clinics. *http://www.brainplace.com.* Retrieved June 25, 2005.

American Dietetic Association. *http: //www. eatright.org/Public.* Retrieved June 25, 2005.

Americans for the Arts. *http://ww3.- artsusa.org.* Retrieved June 25, 2005.

Born to Explore! The Other Side of ADD. *http://www.borntoexplore.org/index.html.* Retrieved June 25, 2005.

BrainConnection. *http://www.brainconnec- tion.com.* Retrieved June 25, 2005.

BrainStore. *http://www.brainstore.com/brain- store.cfm?pin=1.* Retrieved June 25, 2005.

BrainWonders. *http://www.zerotothree.org/brain- wonders/index.html.* Retrieved July 2, 2005.

Center for Applied Special Technology. *http://www.cast.org.* Retrieved June 25, 2005.

The ChildTrauma Academy. *http://www.child- trauma.org.* Retrieved June 25, 2005.

CollegeBoard *http://www.collegeboard.com/ splash.* Retrieved June 25, 2005.

The DANA Foundation. *http://www.dana.org.* Retrieved June 25, 2005.

Drug Rehabilitation. *http:// www.usnodrugs.com.* Retrieved June 25, 2005.

EduScapes. *http://www.eduscapes.com.* Retrieved June 25, 2005.

Gay, Lesbian, Straight Education Network. http://www.glsen.org/cgi-bin/iowa/ home.html. Retrieved July 2, 2005.

The Henry J. Kaiser Family Foundation. *http://www.kff.org.* Retrieved June 25, 2005.

Intersex Society of North America. *http:// www. isna.org.* Retrieved July 2, 2005.

Learning Disabilities. *http://www.ldonline.org.* Retrieved June 25, 2005.

Learning Enrichment. *www.learningenrich- ment.org.* Retrieved July 6, 2005.

LifeSounds. *http://www. musicandlearning. com.* Retrieved June 25, 2005.

National Council of Teachers of Mathematics. *http://nctm.org.* Retrieved June 25, 2005.

New Horizons for Learning. http:// www.newhorizons.org/index.html.Retrieved June 25, 2005.

Neuroscience for Kids. *http://faculty. washington.edu/chudler/neurok.html.* Retrieved June 25, 2005.

The Office for Studies in Moral Development and Education. *http://tigger.uic. edu/~lnucci/MoralEd/office.html.* Retrieved June 25, 2005.

Reclaiming Youth Network. *http://www. reclaiming.com.* Retrieved June 25, 2005.

Sexuality Information and Education Council of the United States. *http:// www.siecus.org.* Retrieved October 25, 2005.

Science A Go Go. *http:// www.scienceagogo.com.* Retrieved June 25, 2005.

Science Direct. *http://www.sciencedirect.com.* Retrieved July 2, 2005.

Starr Commonwealth. *http:// www. starr.org/site/PageServer.* Retrieved June 25, 2005.

U.S. Department of Education. *http:// www.ed.gov/index.jhtml.* Retrieved July 6, 2005.

U.S. National Institutes of Health: National Institute on Aging. *http://www.nia.nih.gov.* Retrieved June 25, 2005.

U.S. National Institutes of Health: National Institute on Drug Abuse.*http: //www. nida.nih.gov.* Retrieved June 25, 2005.

Wisconsin Assistive Technology Initiative. *http://www.wati.org.* Retrieved June 25, 2005.

About the Contributors

Linda G. Allen, M.Ed., is President and CEO, Apple Tree Consulting, Inc., LaGrange, KY and Strategies Consultant with the Exceptional Children Services at Ohio Valley Educational Cooperative, Shelbyville, KY. She is the coauthor of Karp, Karen, Brown, Todd, Allen, Linda G. (1998). *Feisty Females: Inspiring Girls to Think Mathematically* and contributing author of *Assessment for Third Grade Textbook.*

Richard H. Allen, Ph.D., is a world renowned facilitator, teacher, and author and holds a Ph.D. in educational psychology from Arizona State University. He is currently president of Impact Learning, Inc. and author of *Impact Teaching: Ideas and Strategies to Maximize Student Learning* and *Train Smart: Perfect Trainings Every Time.*

Christopher Andersen is Assistant Professor in the School of Teaching and Learning at Ohio State University. His research and teaching focus on the translation of psychological theory into classroom practice.

Sharon E. Andrews, Ed.D., is Chairperson of the Education Department at Augustana College in Sioux Falls, South Dakota; her areas of interest include reading and writing in the content area classroom.

Thomas Armstrong, Ph.D., is an award-winning author and speaker with over thirty years of teaching experience from the primary through the doctoral level, and over one million copies of his books in print on issues related to learning and human development. He is the author of eleven books including *Multiple Intelligences in the Classroom, In Their Own Way, Awakening Your Child's Natural Genius, 7 Kinds of Smart, The Myth of the A.D.D. Child, ADD/ADHD Alternatives in the Classroom,* and *Awakening Genius in the Classroom.*

Kevin D. Arnold, Ph.D., ABPP, is the Director of The Center for Cognitive & Behavioral Therapy of Greater Columbus, and serves as a clinical faculty member at The Ohio State University Department of Psychiatry. He is the author of many scholarly and practice-oriented works, recently publishing the Integrated Functional Behavior Analysis Protocol assessment manual. He has also authored chapters on self-help for adolescents to manage test anxiety and improve academic study skills.

Becky A. Bailey, Ph.D., is an award-winning author, renowned teacher, and internationally recognized expert in childhood education and developmental psychology. She is the originator of the Conscious Discipline program, and founder and co-owner of Loving Guidance, Inc.

Sandy Baumann, M.S., is Program Manager at the Center for Lifelong Learning, Henry Ford Community College, in Dearborn Heights, Michigan. As a biochemist with eighteen years experience in health promotion, she is the author of *Feed Your Brain for Learning Feed Your Bones Naturally* and *Feed Your Brain for Memory.*

Linda S. Behar-Horenstein, Ph.D., is Professor of Educational Leadership, Policy, and Foundations at the University of Florida, Gainesville. She has published four books and over forty book chapters and refereed articles. She is on the Editorial Board of the *Journal of Professional Studies* in Canada and *World Studies in Education* in Australia. Dr. Behar-Horenstein is a member of the Professors of Curriculum, a national group of distinguished professors elected for their contributions to research and teaching in curriculum studies.

Doris Bergen, Ph.D., is Professor of Educational Psychology at Miami University in Oxford, Ohio. She has published six books, including three on play development and two on infant/toddler assessment and curriculum. Her most recent book is *Brain Research and Childhood Education: Implications for Educators* (coauthored with Juliet Coscia). In 2000, she received the NAECTE/Allyn-Bacon award as Outstanding Early Childhood Teacher Educator and was also recognized as a Miami University Distinguished Scholar.

Charlotte A. Boettiger is Assistant Research Scientist at the Ernest Gallo Clinic and Research Center, a part of the University of California, San Francisco Department of Neurology devoted to the study of drug and alcohol addiction. Her research focuses on investigating executive control and decision-making processes that may be impaired in the context of addiction. Dr. Boettiger was awarded the Hugh O Connor Memorial Fellowship by the Wheeler Center for the Neurobiology of Addiction in 2002.

Larry K. Brendtro, Ph.D., is the founder and president of Reclaiming Youth International, a non-profit research and training institute. He is the former president of Starr Commonwealth, Albion, Michigan, and continues to serve as dean of Starr Commonwealth's International Research Council. Dr. Brendtro has forty years experience as an educator and psychologist, specializing in troubled children and youth, and has taught at the University of Michigan, the University of Illinois, The Ohio State University, and Augustana College. He co-edits the journal *Reclaiming Children and Youth* and is the author of ten books on troubled youth.

Chris Brewer-Boyd, M.A., FAMI, teaches educators about the integration of music into education and brain-based learning methods through university programs and as a consultant. She is fellow in the Bonny Method of Guided Imagery and Music, a psychotherapeutic method of using music, and is certified in the MARI© mandala art assessment. Chris has written extensively on the use of music in education and about medical applications of vibroacoustic music. She is coauthor of *Rhythms of Learning* and author of *Soundtracks for Learning.*

Evie J. Brouwer, M.A., is Assistant Professor of Education at Augustana College, Sioux Falls, SD. She has worked with at-risk youth for seven years. She has presented at various conferences particularly on the subject of reading comprehension strategies. Brouwer is experienced in educating all levels of learners from kindergarten through adults.

Trez Buckland, M.A., has his Masters in Counseling and is currently the Site Coordinator at the School of Nursing at the University of Washington, Seattle, WA. He is the 2001 recipient of the Washington State Recognition Award for National Alliance for the Mentally Ill.

Martha S. Burns, Ph.D., CCC-SLP, has been a practicing speech language pathologist in the Chicago area for thirty-five years. She serves on the Faculty of Northwestern University, department of communication sciences and disorders, and on the medical staff of Evanston-Northwestern Hospital, both in Evanston, Illinois. Dr. Burns has received honors from Northwestern University, Evanston Hospital Corporation, the American Speech Language Hearing Foundation and St. Xavier University. Doody's Rating Service selected her book on Right Hemisphere Dysfunction published through Aspen Press as one of the best health sciences books of 1997. In addition to that book, Dr. Burns is the author of a book on aphasia and the test *Burns Brief Inventory of Communication and Cognition* published by The Psychological Corporation.

Geoffrey Caine, LL.M., is the Executive Director of the Caine Learning Institute. He has published extensively. His work includes *Making Connections: Teaching and the Human Brain, Education on the Edge of Possibility, Unleashing the Power of Perceptual Change: The Promise of Brain Based Learning, Mindshifts, The ReEnchantment of Learning, The Brain and the Competitive Edge,* and *The 12 Brain/Mind Learning Principles in Action.*

Adam M. Campbell, Ph.D., recently completed his doctoral work at USF on stress, memory, and antidepressant actions on the brain. He is in the Department of Psychology, University of South Florida, Tampa, Florida and Medical Research Service, Veterans Hospital, Tampa, FL.

Mary A. Carskadon, Ph.D., is Professor of Psychiatry and Human Behavior at Brown Medical School and Director of Chronobiology and Sleep Research at E.P. Bradley Hospital. She has studied sleep and circadian rhythms in children and adolescents and is editor of *Adolescent Sleep Patterns: Biological, Social, and Psychological Influences* she is recipient of the National Sleep Foundation Lifetime Achievement Award.

Susan Catapano, Ed.D., is an Assistant Professor of Early Childhood Education at the University of Missouri-St. Louis. She is the former owner and operator of two state licensed, nationally accredited early care and education programs that served 400 children and their families in St. Louis City and County. She is a principle investigator on a US Department of Education Teacher Quality Enhancement Grant ($3.2 million) that supports new teachers and student teachers learning to teach in urban settings.

Joan Caulfield, Ph.D., is the president of The Brain Incorporated and is a former teacher, principal, associate superintendent, and professor. She is the co-facilitator of the Brain Compatible Learning Network sponsored by the

Association for Supervision and Curriculum Development. She is co-publisher of the *Brain Compatible Learning Networker* newsletter and the author of numerous articles and books.

Tammy Chung, Ph.D., is Assistant Professor of Psychiatry at University of Pittsburgh, Pennsylvania. She conducts research on the assessment, diagnosis, and course of substance-related problems in adolescents.

Susan Clayton is a private consultant, former teacher, teacher counselor, and staff developer. Research interests: planning and teaching for understanding, the role of conversation in the learning process, and teacher study groups.

John J. Clementson, Ph.D., is Professor and Chair of Education at Gustavus Adolphus College in St. Peter, Minnesota. His expertise is with the middle-school learner.

Suzanne Corkin, Ph.D., is Professor of Behavioral Neuroscience in the Department of Brain and Cognitive Sciences at the Massachusetts Institute of Technology. Her research focuses on human memory systems and memory in aging. She has written extensively on these topics.

Kimberly Cornia, M.A. (MFT), graduated from the marriage and family therapy (MFT) program at Chapman University in August, 2005. She also worked as a therapist trainee in the Chapman University Community Clinic as part of her graduate studies.

Laura Crawford, M.A., is the Community Education Coordinator for HOME-FRONT, a collaboration of more than fifty agencies throughout the Kansas City metropolitan area that work together to provide resources to support and encourage the positive development of children, parents, and families. In addition, Laura is a trained ACT Facilitator.

Craig A. Davis, M.Ed., is a doctoral student in the Department of Educational Leadership, Policy, and Foundations, of the University of Florida's College of Education. His research interests include qualitative theory and methodology, educational sociology, and curriculum studies.

Mark D'Esposito is Professor of Neuroscience and Psychology, and Director of the Henry H. Wheeler, Jr. Brain Imaging Center at the Helen Wills Neuroscience Institute at the University of California, Berkeley. His research spans the disciplines of neurology, psychology, and neuroscience specifically focusing on investigating the role of prefrontal cortex in working memory and executive control processes. Dr. D'Esposito was awarded the Norman Geschwind Prize in Behavioral Neurology from the American Academy of Neurology in 1999 and is currently the Editor-In-Chief of the *Journal of Cognitive Neuroscience.*

Gloria Dey, Ph.D., is an Associate Professor in the Education Department at Washburn University in Topeka, Kansas. Her writing and speaking interests include learning disabilities, multicultural education, and the Comer School Development Program.

David M. Diamond, Ph.D., is a Professor in the Departments of Psychology and Pharmacology at the University of South Florida and is a Research Biologist in the Medical Research Service Division of the Tampa Veterans Hospital. He has been studying the neurobiology of stress and memory for the past 25 years.

Charlene K. Douglass, D.A.S.L., is affiliated with the Hillbrook School, Los Gatos, California. Her research interests include learning styles, child growth and development, and technology in education. She is the recipient of the ALSC Frederic G. Melcher Scholarship and Beta Phi Mu Award.

Georg H. Eifert, Ph.D., is Professor and Chair of the Department of Psychology at Chapman University in Orange, CA. He was ranked in the top thirty of Researchers in Behavior Analysis and Therapy in the 1990s and has authored over 100 publications on psychological causes and treatments of anxiety and other emotional disorders. He is a clinical fellow of the Behavior Therapy and Research Society, a member of numerous national and international psychological associations, and serves on several editorial boards of leading clinical psychology journals. He also is a licensed clinical psychologist. He is the author of *The Anorexia Workbook, Acceptance and Commitment Therapy for Anxiety Disorders,* and *ACT on Life, Not on Anger.*

John Elfers is a sex educator and marriage family therapist specializing in sexuality education and HIV/STD prevention with adolescents. He has written curricula for peer educators and is a trainer for teachers and persons living with HIV.

Lise Eliot, Ph.D., is Assistant Professor of Neuroscience at Rosalind Franklin University of Medicine and Science/the Chicago Medical School. She is author of *What's Going On in There? How the Brain and Mind Develop in the First Five Years of Life* and a forthcoming book on sex differences in children's brains and learning styles. She also serves as Neuroscience Consultant for the Erikson Institute in Chicago.

Sue Elliott is a teacher, teacher counselor, and staff developer. Research interests include: planning and teaching for understanding, the role of conversation in the learning process, and teacher study groups.

Laura Erlauer is an author, national consultant, and school principal at Brookfield Elementary School in Brookfield, Wisconsin. She is the author of *The Brain-Compatible Classroom: Using What We Know About Learning to Improve Teaching*, and several professional articles on the topic.

Jennifer Feinstein, J.D., received her law degree at George Mason University in Fairfax, Va. She is currently an attorney with Lewis Brisbois Bisgaard & Smith, LLP in New York.

Sheryl Feinstein, Ed.D., is an Associate Professor at Augustana College in Sioux Falls, SD. She is the author of the book, *Secrets of the Teenage Brain.* Her research interests include secondary education, middle school after-school programs, and at-risk adolescents. She presents nationally and internationally on the Adolescent Brain.

Susan Gibbons, M.A., has a bachelor's degree in psychology and a master's degree in Health Services Administration. She is currently pursuing a doctoral degree in Adult Education. She is the author of, *"I Can Sign My ABC's"* and has had a lifetime interest in animal studies.

Jill Gierach, M.S.E., ATP, is a special education teacher with over eighteen years of classroom experience. She currently is a regional consultant for seventy-five school districts in the area of assistive technology. She has been with the wisconsin assistive technology initiative (WATI) since its inception and holds national certification as an assistive technology practitioner (ATP) from RESNA (rehabilitation engineering and assistive technology society of north america).

Daisy Grewal, M.S., is a doctoral candidate in social psychology at Yale University. Her master's thesis investigated the relationship between emotional intelligence and creativity. Her other research interests currently include gender and emotion.

David Halstead, M.Ed., is a career educator with extensive classroom and counseling experience at the secondary and post secondary levels plus national and international (Caribbean, West Africa and Asia) student services administrative experience. He currently develops and delivers professional development programs for educators based on those applications of neuroscience that have application in the areas of teaching, learning, and classroom management. His publications include *Putting the Brain into the Classroom - 39 Brain Facts and 231 Teaching Strategies* and *Career Focus.*

Anne M. Hanson, M.A., is a National Board Certified Teacher in Early Adolescence/English Language Arts. She has lectured and written extensively on writing and the brain and is the author of *Write Brain Write* and *Visual Writing* as well as *Thin Veils* a young adult novel dealing with anorexia. Anne, whose honors include Fulbright Memorial Fund Scholar, Scottsdale Middle School Teacher of the Year, and Arizona Teacher of the Year finalist is currently working on her doctoral degree in Educational Leadership.

Mariale M. Hardiman is the principal of Roland Park Elementary/Middle School in Baltimore City. During her more than 30 years with the Baltimore City Public School System, Dr. Hardiman has served as a school administrator, staff developer, and teacher. Under her leadership, Roland Park Elementary/Middle School received numerous awards for continuous student achievement gains as well as its designation as a Blue Ribbon School of Excellence. Dr. Hardiman also serves as adjunct instructor at The Johns Hopkins University in Baltimore, MD. Her book, *Connecting Brain Research with Effective Teaching: The Brain Targeted Teaching Model* and article, "Connecting Brain Research with Dimensions of Learning" have generated widespread interest from educators worldwide.

Gail Heidenhain is an expert in Accelerated Learning and she has facilitated in the training of thousands of teachers. She serves as President of Delphin, Inc. and President of International Alliance for Learning.

Thomas R. Hoerr, Ph.D., is the head of the New City School in St. Louis, MO. The faculty has been implementing the theory of multiple intelligences (MI) since 1988. Hoerr has written more than forty articles and one book (*Becoming A Multiple Intelligences School*, ASCD Press, 2000) about how MI can be used in schools. His new book, written for school leaders, *Leadership That Respects the Art of Teaching* will be published in fall 2005.

Jack Huhtala, M.A., is an educational consultant (www.CoachingTheBrain.com) and Adjunct Professor of Education at Pacific University, Forest Grove, Oregon. He has published on Group Investigation and facilitating classroom inquiry discussion.

Carol A. Isaac is a Ph.D. candidate in the Department of Educational Leadership at the University of Florida.

Lisa M. Jackson, Ph.D., is the Agency Accountability Specialists at the Arizona Schools for the Deaf and the Blind, Tucson, Arizona. She specializes in assessment of students who are visually impaired and students who are deaf and hard of hearing. Her dissertation was titled *"The Effects of Testing Adaptations on Students' Standardized Test Scores for Students with Visual Impairments in Arizona"*

Wayne B. Jennings, Ph.D., is the Director of The Institute for Learning and Teaching and is a former teacher, principal, superintendent, and professor. He is the co-facilitator of the Brain Compatible Learning Network sponsored by the Association for Supervision and Curriculum Development. He is co-publisher of the *Brain Compatible Learning Networker* newsletter and the author of numerous articles and books.

Eric Jensen is one of the leaders in educational neuroscience. He has taught at three universities and authored twenty-six books on the brain and learning. He is a longtime member of the Society for Neuroscience and conducts research and staff development worldwide.

Susan J. Jones, M.A., is an Independent Education Consultant. Adjunct faculty member: Aurora University IL, Central Michigan University, Chapman University CA; Flagler College, FL. Regional Director and '02–'03 President of Florida Association for Supervision and Curriculum, former member Board of Directors of ASCD. She is the author of numerous books including *Blueprint for Student Success: A Guide to Research-Based Teaching Practice K-12* and *Backstage Pass for Trainers, Facilitators and Public Speakers.*

Spencer Kagan, Ph.D., is a former clinical psychologist and Professor of Pschology and Education, University of California. Kagan and co-workers created over 200 structures — simple instructional strategies. His books, *Cooperative Learning, Multiple Intelligences, Win-Win Discipline,* and *Silly Sports and Goofy Games* have been translated into many languages and are used worldwide in teacher education programs.

Martha Kaufeldt, M.A., is a full time trainer and consultant with an extensive background in brain compatible teaching and learning theory. She was a K-12 classroom teacher for over 20 years. She is the author of *Begin with the Brain: Orchestrating the Learner-Centered Classroom* and *Teachers, Change Your Bait! Brain Compatible Differentiated Instruction.*

Duke R. Kelly is president of Calculated Success, Inc., a staff development, training, and research company specializing in making instruction congruent with how the brain learns. Duke travels worldwide coaching and observing classrooms of all types.

Doreen Kimura, Ph.D., is Visiting Professor at Simon Fraser University, Burnaby, British Columbia, Canada. She has written extensively on biological influences on cognition, including individual differences. She is a Fellow of the Royal Society of Canada, and has received honorary degrees from Simon Fraser and Queen's universities. She has also received the Distinguished Scientist award from the Canadian Psychological Association, and in 2005 received the Hebb award for distinguished contributions from the canadian society for brain, behavior and cognitive sciences (CSBBCS). Her most recent book, *Sex and Cognition* has been translated into several languages.

Michael B. Knable, D.O., is Executive Director of the Stanley Medical Research Institute. He is also an Assistant Clinical Professor of Psychiatry at George Washington University and an Adjunct Professor of Psychiatry at the Uniformed Services University of the Health Sciences.

Susan J. Kovalik, classroom teacher and curriculum innovator for over thirty-five years, has spent the past twenty-three years developing a model for curriculum and instruction based on brain research. She developed the (integrated thematic instruction) ITI Model. In 1998, Susan was nominated a NASA Woman of the Year. She is the author of a number of books, her new newest book is *Exceeding Expectations: A User's Guide to Implementing Brain Research in the Classroom.*

James E. Longhurst, Ed.D., is vice president of Clinical and Psychological Services at Starr Commonwealth of Albion, Michigan, where he has been involved in various professional and leadership roles for over thirty years. He helped develop Starr's No Disposable Kids® Program, which focuses on creating positive school climates. He is a lead facilitator of the Institute for the Healing of Racism, a national trainer in Life Space Crisis Intervention, and an adjunct professor in psychology at Albion College. He is a licensed psychologist and a member of the American Psychological Association.

Jean Blaydes Madigan is an internationally known educational consultant for Action Based Learning in Dallas, Texas. She has thirty years teaching experience in classroom and physical education. She is the author of *Thinking on Your Feet* and co-creator of the Action Based Learning Lab. She has won numerous awards including one of six National Physical Educators of the Year and most recently the PE4LIFE National Advocacy Award.

Karen Mahan, M.A., is an Assistant Professor of Communication Disorders at Augustana College in Sioux Falls, South Dakota. Her research interests include the study of joint attention in children who have autism, and the effects of early joint attention on language development. She has presented on functional skills curriculum at CSUN and at local and state conferences.

Michael E. Martinez, Ph.D., is an Associate Professor of Education at the University of California, Irvine. His research centers on the nature of intelligence as a learnable ability, and on the cognitive, linguistic, semiotic, and biological foundations of intelligence.

Laurie Materna, Ph.D., RN is a nursing professor at Milwaukee Area Technical College. Her interest in adult learning has led to the development of a wide variety of brain-compatible teaching methodologies that she offers to students as well as faculty though workshops and seminars. She is currently writing a resource book, *Jump Start Your Brain: Creative Learning Strategies for Adults.* After examining the impact between nutrition and learning, Dr. Materna developed a nutritional snack alternative, Brain Fuel Energy Snack.

Allison Maxwell is a senior high school science teacher and curriculum mentor. She is a Professional Development Specialist in emotional intelligence and research-driven teaching and learning. She is a trainer associated with Mind Matters.

Judith Lynne McConnell, Ed.D., is a Professor of Education at Washburn University, Topeka, Kansas. Dr. McConnell is a previous preschool and elementary school teacher. She has spoken at more than a hundred conference presentations, published a book, *Teaching Renewal: Professional Issues, Personal Choices,* and has numerous article and chapter publications. Dr. McConnell is a faculty member of People to People International and led delegations of early childhood professionals to the Peoples Republic of China, Cuba, The Czech Republic, Russia, and Spain. During the past two years she has co-directed the *Oxford Round Table,* Manchester Campus, Oxford, England.

Cristal L. McGill, Ph.D., is an Adjunct Professor of Curriculum and Instruction at Arizona State University. Tempe Arizona. At the University and during *Educational Professional Development Seminars* she is known for delivering powerful, upbeat, interactive, and creative experiences for teachers, and youth.

Kathleen A. Mulligan, Ph.D., is in the Department of Biological Structure at the University of Washington in Seattle, WA. She has worked in neuroscience research in visual system and is the coauthor of over a dozen research publications. Currently, she teaches gross anatomy and neuroscience to health professionals at UW, and co-teaches in an online certificate program called "brain research in education." She is the proud recipient of the students' "Teacher of the Year" award three times.

Carole Naasz, M.A., taught in the public school setting in South Dakota for three years before moving into a Minnesota juvenile corrections classroom five years ago. Ms. Naasz has a Bachelors Degree in Social Sciences from Dakota Wesleyan University and a Masters Degree in Education Administration from South Dakota State University.

LeAnn Nickelsen, M.Ed., delivers presentations nationally on brain research topics, reading strategies, and vocabulary strategies, all based on the latest research. She is the author of the following teacher resource books published by Scholastic, Inc.: *Quick Activities to Build a Very Voluminous Vocabulary Teaching Elaboration & Word Choice Comprehension-Building Activities for Reading in Social Studies & Science* Four book Mini-Comprehension Reading series: *Inferences & Cause/Effect; Sequencing & Context Clues; Point of View & Fact/Opinion, Main Idea & Summarizing* (2004), and *Memorizing Strategies & Other Brain-Based Activities.*

Lori Niles, M.A., is completing her doctoral work in Educational Foundations and Leadership at George Fox University. She is an adjunct instructor at George Fox University. She has written a number of teacher resource and curriculum books including *Touching Hearts, Changing Lives: Becoming a Treasured Teacher* coauthored with Jody Capehart, and *The Warm and Wonderful Church Nursery,* coauthored with Kim Sikes.

Karen D. Olsen, Ed.D., worked for the California State Department of Education for twelve years. She was one of the original founders of the California Institute of School Improvement. She is the author of the definitive mentor book, *California Mentor Teacher.* She has been author and co-author of numerous books on the integrated technology Instruction (ITI) model.

Lyelle L. Palmer, B.M., M.M., Ph.D., is Professor Emeritus of Special Education (Learning Disabilities) at Winona State University, Minnesota. He is co-founder of the SMART early brain stimulation program and research scientist at the Minnesota Learning Resource Center in Minneapolis. He is editor of the *Journal of Accelerated Learning and Teaching* (www.ialearn.org) and is coauthor *of Bright Brain: Neuro-stimulators in Early Childhood.*

Collin R. Park, Ph.D., is a research Assistant Professor in the Department of Psychology at the University of South Florida and is a Research Biologist in the Medical Research Service Division of the Tampa Veterans Hospital.

Katherine D. Perez, Ed.D., is a Professor of Education at Saint Mary's College in Moraga, California. She is an international consultant on brain-based teaching and differentiating instruction; has published several articles and was awarded a Rotary International Fellowship Award.

Raleigh Philp is an Adjunct Professor of Education at Pepperdine University in Los Angeles, CA. He has studied neuroscience applications to education and is the author of a new book on primary neuroscience for secondary teachers. He received the Presidential Award for Teaching Science and the Outstanding Biology Teacher for California.

Rae Pica is a children's physical activity specialist and founder of Moving & Learning. She is the author of fourteen books, including the text *Experiences in Movement,* the *Moving & Learning Series,* and *Your Active Child.* Rae is nationally known for her workshops and keynotes and has shared her expertise with such groups as the *Sesame Street* Research Department, the Head Start Bureau,

Centers for Disease Control, and numerous state health departments throughout the country.

Olivier Piguet, Ph.D., is a postdoctoral fellow in the Department of Brain and Cognitive Sciences at the Massachusetts Institute of Technology, currently supported by a National Health & Medical Research Council Neil Hamilton Fairley fellowship (222909). His research interests include normal and pathological cognitive aging in very old individuals. His particular interest is memory and executive functions.

Lynette Poolman has completed Certification through the University of Florida's Carnegie Foundations Starting Points initiative on Brain Development. Since 1999 Lynette has worked for The Family Conservancy as the Director of HOMEFRONT. Her commitment to children and families has driven the HOMEFRONT partnership to identify initiatives and collaborations that enhance and support parents in their most important role; "raising children." Lynette is a National Trainer for the ACT Against Violence Program and has received a Presidential Commendation from the American Psychological Association for her dedication to violence prevention and young children.

Linda H. Rammler, M.Ed., Ph.D., is an educational consultant in private practice with Rammler & Wood, Consultants, LLC. She is a nationally renowned presenter on autism spectrum disorders and behavioral/emotional challenges focusing on brain research, positive behavior supports, and inclusion.

Linda Reimond, M.S., has been the director of the Lawrence Arts Center Arts-Based Preschool, in Lawrence, Kansas, since it began in 1985. She has taught kindergarten and preschool. She has been a presenter at early childhood conferences at the state, regional, and national levels. Linda has been an adjunct instructor at Washburn University. In January 2004, Linda received the Mayor's Award for Excellence in Teaching and in November 2004 received the Phoenix Award from the Lawrence Arts Commission for Arts Educator.

Regina G. Richards, M.A., an educational therapist in Riverside California, is Founder and Director of Richards Educational Therapy Center & former Director of Big Springs School, agencies that provide multidisciplinary evaluations and treatment programs for students with language learning disabilities. She has authored a variety of journal articles and books on reading, dyslexia, dysgraphia, and visual development. She is currently President of her local Inland Empire Branch of the International Dyslexia Association and presents workshops and keynotes at school districts and conferences nationally. She is President of RET Center Press.

Diane Ronis, Ph.D., is Associate Professor of Education at Southern Connecticut State University. She has written extensively on instruction and assessment and is the author of *Clustering Standards in Integrated Units Critical Thinking in Math Problem-based Learning for Math & Science: Integrating Inquiry & the Internet, Brain-compatible Assessments* and *Brain-compatible Mathematics* She has presented at numerous conferences and workshops throughout the country.

Tracy L. Rupp, M.S., is a graduate student in experimental psychology at Brown University.

Peter Salovey, Ph.D., The Chris Argyris Professor of Psychology, Peter Salovey was appointed Dean of Yale College in 2004. Dr. Salovey is also Professor of Management and Professor of Epidemiology and Public Health. He directs the Health, Emotion and Behavior Laboratory and is deputy director of the Yale Center for Interdisciplinary Research on AIDS. With John D. Mayer, he developed a broad framework, coined "emotional intelligence," to describe how people understand, manage, and use their emotions. Salovey has published more than 200 articles and chapters, and he has authored, coauthored, or edited thirteen books including *Peer Counseling: Skills and Perspectives; Reasoning, Inference, and Judgment in Clinical Psychology; The Psychology of Jealousy and Envy; Psychology; The Remembered Self: Emotion and Memory in Personality; Peer Counseling: Skills, Ethics, and Perspectives; Emotional Development and Emotional Intelligence; At Play in the Fields of Consciousness; mayer-salovey-caruso emotional intelligence Test (MSCEIT): User's Manual; The Wisdom in Feeling: Psychological Processes in Emotional Intelligence; Key Readings in the Social Psychology of Health,* and *The Emotionally Intelligent Manager.*

Linda Weisbaum Seltzer, Ph.D., of Seltzer Educational and Behavioral Consultants has presented nationally on the current brain research and its implications to school climate, learning, and behavior. She has been the supervisor and principal of alternative education programs and Lee School in the public schools in Springfield, Illinois.

Rita Smilkstein, Ph.D., is Professor Emerita (English), North Seattle Community College, and teaches at Western Washington University's Woodring College of Education, Seattle Urban Campus. She has received a number of teaching awards, including two Excellence Awards from the National Institute for Staff and Organizational Development. A frequent speaker nationally and internationally, her publications include textbooks for constructivist teaching of study skills and grammar as well as articles on how to apply the brain's natural learning process to curriculum development and instructional methods across the disciplines. Her book, *We're Born to Learn: Using the Brain's Natural Learning Process to Create Today's Curriculum* won the Delta Kappa Gamma Society International's Educator's Award for 2004.

Dwayne Smith, Ph.D., has over twenty years of professional experience in higher education. He is currently an assistant vice-president for academic affairs at Avila University. Some of his awards include, Who's Who in America, Who's Who in American Education, The ACCESS Award from the Introspect Organization, and a Truman State University Alumnus of the Year Award.

Rick Smith is an international education consultant and national presenter, focusing on classroom management, brain compatible ways to motivate students, and strategies for mentor teachers. He has taught students in San Rafael, CA for over fifteen years (with a primary focus on students at-risk), and been a Mentor and Mentor Coordinator for many years. He has trained American Peace Corps Volunteer Teachers in Ghana, West Africa. He was awarded the Golden Bell Award for Outstanding Teaching, Marin County California, 1999 and is the author of *Conscious Classroom Management: Unlocking the Secrets of Great Teaching.*

Monica Soukup, Ed.D., is Assistant Professor of Education at Augustana College in Sioux Falls, South Dakota. She teaches courses in Deaf Education at Augustana College and has presented on topics related to effective communication strategies with deaf students, learning disabilities and deaf students, and creating environments that address all needs of deaf children.

David A. Sousa is an international educational consultant and the author of five books and numerous articles on the applications of brain research to educational practice. A former science teacher, school superintendent, and adjunct professor, he has been interviewed on the NBC *Today* show and received awards and an honorary degree for his contributions to education.

Marilee Sprenger is a professional development consultant and adjunct professor at Aurora University. She began her teaching career in 1971 and has taught primary, middle, high school, and college students. She speaks at state and national conferences as well as internationally. As a member of the American Academy of Neurology and the Cognitive Neuroscience Society, she remains current on brain research. She has written several books on brain-based teaching and memory including: *Learning and Memory – The Brain in Action, Becoming a Wiz at Brain-based Teaching,* and *Differentiation through Learning Styles and Memory.*

Donna Starr is Director of Starr Educational Services and an adjunct faculty member at Seattle Pacific University, Seattle. She was a classroom teacher in grades Kindergarten through eight and taught Reading Recovery and Math Intervention for thirty-six years. She is the author of *Current Brain Research and its Implications for Classroom Instruction.*

Thomas M. Stephens is Professor Emeritus, College of Education, the Ohio State University. He has written extensively on various applications of behavior modification and was an early advocate of direct instruction of social behavior in schools. He has authored twelve textbooks and over hundred journal articles. He is currently the Executive Director of the School Study Council of Ohio.

Jean Seville Suffield spent almost all of her career in education on the South Shore of Montréal, the home of the early immersion model. Jean holds a Master Certification Diploma in brain-based learning through the Jensen Learning Corporation. She is a senior faculty member of The William Glasser Institute and the founder of Choice-Makers, an international training and consulting service. Jean has authored several books for classroom use and is the recipient of the Lieutenant Governor Medal for Academic Excellence.

Cathie Summerford, M.S., is the author of *Action-Packed Classrooms;* she also authored *PE-4-ME: Teaching Lifelong Health and Fitness* and is completing her third book *Obesity's Impact on the BodyBrain: A Guidebook for Parents, Teachers and All-Concerned.* As an Educational Consultant and President of Fit 4 Learning, Cathie has been recognized as a California Teacher of the Year, (NASPE) Southwest National Teacher of the Year, and california school boards association (CSBA) Golden Bell award-winning author. On top of it, she is an IRONMAN Triathlon finisher!

Susan Tapert, Ph.D., is Assistant Professor of Psychiatry at University of California, San Diego. She directs the Substance Abuse Mental Illness program at the

VA San Diego Healthcare System, and her research focuses on the relationships between brain functioning and substance use in adolescents and young adults.

Marcia L. Tate, Ph.D., is an Educational Consultant and CEO of *Developing Minds Inc.* She is the author of the bestseller, *Worksheets Don't Grow Dendrites: 20 Instructional Strategies that Engage the Brain* and two subsequent books, *Sit & Get Won't Grow Dendrites: 20 Professional Learning Strategies that Engage the Adult Brain* and *Reading and Language Arts Worksheets Don't Grow Dendrites: 20 Literacy Strategies that Engage the Brain.* She was a former classroom teacher, reading specialist, language arts coordinator and the Georgia 2002 Staff Developer of the Year.

Donna Walker Tileston, Ed.D., has served education as a leader in teaching, administration, research, writing, software development, and national consulting for the past thirty years. Her administrative responsibilities have included curriculum development, management, technology, finance, grants management, public relations, and drug abuse prevention programs. For the past twenty years Dr. Tileston has been actively involved in brain research and the factors that inhibit learning or increase the brain's ability to put information into long-term memory. Dr. Tileston's research has been published through Corwin Press under the titles: *Strategies for Teaching Differently* and *Ten Best Teaching Practices: How Brain Research, Learning Styles and Standards Define Teaching Competencies* which has been on Corwin's Best Seller List since its first year of print.

E. Fuller Torrey, M.D., is Associate Director for Laboratory Research, Stanley Medical Research Institute, Bethesda, Maryland. He is also the President of the Treatment Advocacy Center (www.psychlaws.org), a Professor of Psychiatry at the Uniformed Services University of the Health Sciences, and the author or coauthor of nineteen books.

Dianna Townsend is a doctoral candidate in Educational Leadership at the University of California, Irvine. Her research interests include vocabulary development and the relationship between language and intelligence.

Laurie Wenger, Ed.D., is a Professor of Education at Augustana College in Sioux Falls, SD, serves as a trainer/speaker for Reclaiming Youth International and also directs the gifted program for an area school district.

Doris Señor Woltman, Ed.S. is the Superintendent at the Arizona Schools for the Deaf and the Blind, Tucson, Arizona. Ms. Woltman has worked in the field of visual impairment and blindness since 1980. Her specialties include community-based instruction and mental health issues for individuals with sensory impairment. Ms. Woltman is a Member of the Governor's Council for the Blind and Visually Impaired and a Commissioner for the Arizona Council for the Deaf and Hard of Hearing.

James C. Woodson, Ph.D., is an Assistant Professor in the Department of Psychology at the University of Tampa, Tampa, Florida.

James E. Zull, Ph.D., is Professor of Biology at Case Western Reserve University in Cleveland Ohio. He is a biochemist with over 100 publications. He has received many grants in support of his biochemistry research, including a Research Career Development Award from the National Institutes of Health. He is the Founding Director of the Center for Learning and Teaching (UCITE) at Case Western Reserve, and the author of the first book on the connection between the biology of learning and teaching written by a scientist: *The Art of Changing the Brain; Enriching Teaching by Exploring the Biology of Learning.*

INDEX